THE PERENNIAL GARDENER

Perennials: How to Select, Grow & Enjoy
(with Pamela Harper)

The Perennial Gardener

FREDERICK McGOURTY

THE PERENNIAL
Gardener

Houghton Mifflin Company

BOSTON

1989

To Mary Ann

Copyright © 1989 by Frederick McGourty

ALL RIGHTS RESERVED

For information about permission to reproduce selections from this book, write to Permissions, Houghton Mifflin Company, 2 Park Street, Boston, Massachusetts 02108.

Library of Congress Cataloging-in-Publication Data

McGourty, Fred.
The perennial gardener / Frederick McGourty.
p. cm.
Includes index.
ISBN 0-395-45373-9
1. Perennials — Connecticut — Norfolk. 2. Garden borders — Connecticut — Norfolk. 3. Hillside Gardens (Norfolk, Conn.)
4. Perennials. 5. Garden borders. I. Title.
SB434.M38 1989
635.9'32'09746 — dc19   88-29397
CIP

Printed in the United States of America

J 10 9 8 7 6 5 4 3 2 1

Portions of this book have appeared in *American Horticulturist, Avant Gardener, Flower & Garden, Green Scene* (Pennsylvania Horticultural Society), and *Plants & Gardens*. Unless otherwise noted, photographs appear courtesy of the author. Garden plans originally drawn by Kathleen Tonan, Hillside Gardens.

Contents

· PART I ·

*BORDERS,
AND BEYOND*

· I ·

Siting the Blimp

MY CLIENT, Mrs. Plum, had a dreamy, faraway look in her eyes. Glistening birches and large old pines extended right down to the lake, several hundred yards from the house. Across the lake to the east was a view of the mountains.

"I think the perennial border ought to go right here in front of the lake. That way we can come down and see it at sunrise and pick incarvilleas for the breakfast table. A gardener needs to have vision, don't you think, Mr. Mc-Gourty?"

I swatted a mosquito as my feet sank deeper in the mud. A loon could be heard in the distance. Consultations sometimes begin like this.

Mrs. Plum had been traveling again. Best to let her talk a bit.

"Oh, I don't mean anything grand. Only a fair-sized border, perhaps a hundred feet long and twenty deep. I do have to take care of it myself. This is just a summer place, not our main residence."

"How did you get the idea for the border, Mrs. Plum?"

"We were in England a few weeks ago and visited Little Wimper. They have the most marvelous border there, designed by Sackville-Repton, I think, and it would be great fun to recreate it here. You will include crinums, won't you?"

Sometimes I feel like an air traffic controller in charge of landing blimps on checkerboards.

Fashions are never half-hearted in America. We jump in with zest, whether it is dieting or finding the perfect ice cream. However, during the current fascination with perennials a lot of gardeners may be unwittingly digging graves for their enthusiasm while choosing locations for their borders. And not a few of the borders may end up abandoned, their owners turned away from gardening.

Probably half of my work as a garden designer has to do with correcting existing flaws of border placement, shape, and size — and trying to salvage the dream.

BACK TO BASICS

Three fundamental aspects of border design — site, shape, and size — have at least as great an effect on the ease of garden maintenance as does the actual selection of plants, which seems to get everybody's attention these days, including Mrs. Plum's. I've known people who seem to have all the accredited low-maintenance perennials in the world but still have high-maintenance gardens because they ignored design. True, the real aim of a garden is beauty, not low maintenance, but if we can attain a measure of beauty without spending all of our spare moments on weeding, pinching, staking, deadheading, spraying, encouraging, restraining, dividing, and conquering, we might have time to enjoy the garden more. Good design helps. Let's look at a few ways to head off trouble before it begins.

Viki Ferreniea

A summer medley in a mixed border. *Coreopsis verticillata* 'Golden Showers', pale yellow *Coreopsis* 'Moonbeam', *Veronica* 'Icicle', and red begonias form part of the scene.

The word *border* has come to mean different things to gardeners over the years, including flower beds, but it might help to look at the origin of the word. A border, in its strictest sense, is an edge. In the landscape this refers to a planting strip at the edge of a lawn or other homogeneous area. Beyond is a sharply different area — a wall, a fence, a building, or another structure, or shrubs and trees, perhaps a hedge, that separates the landscape. A border can also be a planting strip along a walk or driveway, or in the area between driveway and house. Visually, this strip or border, planted with appropriate perennials, annuals, and perhaps shrubs, binds the different elements in the landscape by serving as the transition zone and gives a sense of unity. A border, then, is meant to do more than just grow pretty flowers conveniently.

Borders are part of a larger scheme, the garden. The classic garden was an enclosed space protected from the outside world, a sanctuary from its clatter, frustrations, and woe. But it was also much more. It was perceived as paradise, the original paradise. Indeed, the Old Persian word *pairidaeza* means an enclosure, and the Greek word *paradeisos* means a garden.

Viki Ferrenica

Formal borders in spring at Nemours
in Wilmington, Delaware.

The rise of interest in gardening has focused attention on new plants, especially perennials but also annuals, shrubs, and even trees. There are lots of reasons for this rise, most of them wholesome, or at least benign. Clearly, some of this enthusiasm is also due to the trendiness of the times, keeping up with the Joneses and getting one up on the Browns. A deeper stimulus is perhaps our growing sensitivity toward the landscape, both natural and manmade, and our larger surroundings. We feel a malaise because we haven't done very well by them and are unsure whether they can be corrected now. Positivism has died, a victim of its own excess. And so we turn inward again, toward sanctuaries, toward personal paradises where we can lounge in deck chairs and read Voltaire when we aren't plucking organically grown Granny Smiths.

But even in paradise there are practical problems eventually — apart, of course, from setting up spray schedules for the fruit trees. Most new and enthusiastic gardeners face the question of making the greatest visual use of garden space while growing a fairly wide variety of plants. This latter aspect is important, because unlike the French, who are content to plant a line of red salvia to the horizon and call it a garden, Americans are collectors. Some are even pack rats, though not as markedly as the English, whose cottage gardens with one plant of this, one of that, strike us as delightfully quaint but claustrophobic. England is also home to island beds in the lawn, which sometimes provide the best cultural conditions for plants, but their placement must be carefully conceived in cold climates lest winter cause them to resemble backyard scars that look like giant kidney beans.

At the risk of alienating my friends who are engaged in the seemingly free lunch of meadow gardening, I have to say that carefully streamlined, controlled borders are probably the best way for most eastern gardeners to have both unity and diversity over a long season. Based on our experience with twenty or so borders at Hillside, my wife and I believe that they are also the most salubrious way to grow and display a wide variety of plants in relation to their surroundings.

The main border at Hillside, which I have steered, pushed, and shoved for twenty-five years, is sixty feet long and now requires fifteen to twenty hours of care each year. I say "now" because at two points it required more time. One of these was in the early stages, before perennials had filled in properly and when weeds thought the open spaces were theirs for the taking. The other was after I neglected the border entirely one summer, which caused a geometric progression of weeds that took years to cap. Borders need *regular* attention, not vast amounts of it, unless they have been neglected. We have spent about one quarter of the time exacted by border chores here on dividing perennials.

The main border has given the owners of this house a century of pleasure. It also softens a masonry wall that has been falling down ever since I can remember, one part aiming toward Montreal, the other to Miami, someday to tumble completely and make disks out of nearby globe thistles. The border even deflects our eyes from three late-middle-aged Colorado spruces, which have suffered from lower-branch-drop syndrome and from spruce gall aphids, which cause the branchlet tips to swell, droop, and brown until they resemble pine cones. There is trouble in paradise, but fortunately paradise covers a lot of sins.

The main border, whose appropriate placement was the decision of a previous owner, begins just twenty-two feet from a small back porch, the most heavily used entrance to the house. Proximity to the house has been a tremendous stimulus for maintenance, for no one can pass a gasping impatiens more than three times on a hot summer day without giving it a drink. It is a stimulus to weed control, too. As we sit on the porch at the end of the day contemplating spiritual refreshment, the encroaching eupatorium is spotted, usually by Mary Ann, who gently says, "By the time you pull that Joe-Pye weed, your gin-and-tonic will be ready." There is no escape from this until the sun is well over the yardarm, but it is the most effective weed-control device I know.

Our main border is broader at the far end than at the close end, where our prime vantage point is. This makes the border seem smaller, creating the illusion that it is closer to the house and more intimate than would be the case if the far end were narrower. The lawn is substantial, and though we recognize the value of vistas and are careful not to intrude on them, they can be intimidating if borders taper in the distance and make the property seem larger than it already is.

In contrast, if we had a small property and wanted to create the illusion of size, the first step would be to make a border narrower at the far end (and have a few large-leaved plants in the foreground). To enhance the effect of size in small gardens all the more, we could make formal twin borders, both tapered accordingly. In fact, formal borders with their ninety-degree angles (or illusions of such angles) and strong sense of symmetry are usually most effective in small gardens, matching with the surrounding architectural features as one piece of a jigsaw puzzle fits with its proper companions.

Before committing any plan to paper a gardener should understand that most borders have some prime vantage point, some spot from which they are seen most often. Perhaps the section of the border that will be seen the most should be angled or curved outward to give the fullest impact. Certainly you should give the choice of plants for that section extra attention, for high visibility during the entire growing season makes it unwise to give priority to plants with a brief

The main border at Hillside in July. From front: silver mound (*Artemisia schmidtiana*), feverfew (*Chrysanthemum parthenium*), *Heliopsis helianthoides* 'Gold Greenheart', *Astilbe* 'Fire', *Lilium regale*, black snakeroot (*Cimicifuga racemosa*), *Phlox* 'Sir John Falstaff'.

Left: Regal lily (*Lilium regale*) with black snakeroot (*Cimicifuga racemosa*) and *Phlox* 'Sir John Falstaff', in the main border at Hillside in July.
Right: A perennial border can soften a stone wall, which in turn serves as a frame.

bloom period or undistinguished foliage. These may be sound perennials that are stunning for a couple of weeks at a certain time of year, but let them provide the element of surprise in less conspicuous positions in the garden, away from the front of the stage.

There is no rule that all of the elements of a border must be equally visible at one time. In fact, borders seen straight on, from a vantage point extending from the center, are often the least successful. If you can see everything as well from a distance, why bother to go closer?

BORDER PLACEMENT

Most of our borders are arranged along stone walls, with which the glaciers and previous generations of industrious Yankee farmers endowed us. In winter these dry walls, our contemporary enclosure, provide a starkly rectangular scene until buffered by snow. We have come to terms with them then, as long as we can harness them during other seasons. They serve as frames for the borders, which in turn soften the walls. Time has weathered the granite gently, and interesting patterns of lichens and moss abound. Lady ferns and not-so-lady ferns form clumps at the base of the walls, and along with thousands of crevices contribute to overconfidence in chipmunks. Most of all, the walls give a sense of unity to the borders.

We can see one end of the main border from our kitchen, which is the most frequented room in the house. When drying dishes gets tedious, a quick glance to check the status of the campanulas or heliopsis helps, though once in a while we scorch a pot on the stove when the astilbes are in bloom.

The border faces south, and about two thirds of it receives six hours or more of sunlight each day, which means that in theory we can grow about 60 percent of the commonly available hardy perennials there, the sun lovers. The remainder of the area, lightly shaded for most of the day, is capable of growing such perennials, but they will have fewer flowers and need more staking. So that leaves us about 40 percent of the perennials, the shade lovers, to choose from.

A distant portion of the main border, about one fifth of the total, has sluggish drainage. The early spring rains in particular form puddles that are slow to dry out, despite the fact that we raised the planting areas a few inches higher than the surrounding lawn. A number of plants died in this section of the border in the early years. Here our choice of perennials is greatly circumscribed, less than 25 percent. (Appropriate ones are discussed beginning on page 28.) We would prefer more latitude, but not enough to install drainage tile, which gets costly.

When we have a choice of siting a new border in a well-drained or a poorly drained location, we opt for the former.

Some of our borders are situated north to south, others east to west, still others northeast to southwest. Occasionally I read a flat statement from a desk horticulturist that borders should be placed on an east-west axis to get the greatest amount of sun, and that they are meant to be viewed from the south. We haven't noticed here that it makes a major difference in growth or flowering. Trees in the background affecting the light patterns are a more important consideration. So are the lay of the land, natural or manmade backdrops, and exposures. Above all, a border should look natural on the site, not imposed on it.

A significant southern exposure, with no trees blocking the light, means that growth will start earlier in spring. This is an advantage for bulbs, but not necessarily for herbaceous perennials, whose precocious growth can be nipped by a cold spell. On south-facing slopes plants are likely to suffer more from winterkill, especially in late winter. These sites heat up quickly on a sunny February or March day, then refreeze at night; the alternating pattern forces roots to break with the soil and dry out. A light covering of evergreen boughs, salt hay, or even pine needles is desirable on such sites in winter, for it cushions the wide swing in temperatures. We apply the cover about December 1, when the ground freezes here in Connecticut, and remove it when the big Dutch crocus bloom in spring.

West- and south-facing sites are likely to dry out more quickly in summer than north- and east-facing ones. The former require more watering unless trees filter the afternoon sun, which is twice as intense as morning sun. In these hot spots it is wiser to concentrate on long-blooming perennials, for the unrelenting sun can curtail flowering and bleach blossom color on the rank-and-file, three-week-blooming sorts. Of course, drought-tolerant plants should get the nod here, notably the artemisias, sedums, lamb's-ears, yarrows, coreopsis, and kin. Western exposures are also often windy, arguing against the use of weak-necked delphiniums and other plants that need splints to stand erect.

On balance, we would rather have an eastern exposure for a border, because it allows the widest choice of plants, satisfying the light requirements of both sun and shade lovers. However, you can have a fine border regardless of exposure, including a northern one, where shade dwellers are logical candidates in most instances. The attentive gardener learns to work with the available site.

Gardeners are usually urged not to place borders within the root zones of trees, especially the drip-line area, that imaginary line from the ends of the branches to the ground, where the most active root growth is said to occur.

(Indeed, roots often extend much farther than the drip line.) Sound advice in theory, to be sure! However, when I hear it given in the Northeast I suspect that the giver grew up in a cornfield and is out of touch with real gardens. Trees are everywhere, and often the best sites aesthetically for borders experience some sort of root competition and light blockage from them. However, even here the gardener has some choice, and the more you can keep borders away from the roots of established trees, especially maples and ashes, the better it is for the growth of border plants. Finally, there are places where borders simply don't belong, but which would be delightful for informal spring woodland gardens.

DEPTH AND LENGTH

Few of our borders are more than six or seven feet deep (front to back). In addition, most have a two- or three-foot-wide catwalk in the back, which provides easy access for weeding so we don't always have to step into the borders, compacting the soil with our feet. This is important because a loose, airy soil encourages root growth, with eventual benefits up top. Without fail, the tallest, lushest weeds in deep borders are in the most remote areas, the areas we say we will attack tomorrow. The greatest single aid to low maintenance in a perennial border, and probably the most widely ignored by designers who have never had to maintain a garden, is easy access. Incidentally, the catwalk behind the border is not noticeable during the growing season if you choose back-of-the-border plants for appropriate height. Only you and the cat, on its way to check out the chipmunk population behind the scene, will ever know.

Occasionally a deeper border, or part of a border, is called for, especially if the vantage point is from a higher elevation. In this case, consider placing a few flat fieldstones or flagstones in the border to provide discreet puddle jumpers for access for weeding. A key point is to be sure that your eye is not deflected from the plants to the stones.

Finally, if you have considerable height for the vantage point, as from the second story or a lofty deck, think of a *trompe l'oeil* border — actually two borders set one in front of the other, with a three-foot-wide path separating them. The path can be turf, as in the *trompe l'oeil* border we see from our bedroom, or for lowest maintenance gray trap rock or pine-bark minichips. The path, of course, should not be visible from the vantage point, and the plants in the far border should be taller than those in the near border. The far border is also a useful harbor for plants that are showy for a week or two, then nondescript for the rest of the year — though too many of these can sink a garden.

Length of a border is more important than depth for impact, for it brings economy of display. You can have a planting of summer phlox six feet deep, but visually, much of it is lost space unless you have a higher vantage point. For effect, it is better to think in terms of an informal rectangle or drift, with the widest part exposed to the viewer.

The optimum border length varies according to site, and the more years I create borders, the less I think in terms of strict ratios that determine border length and depth or that restrict plant height in relation to border length and depth; these are for design bureaucrats chained to a desk. True, a border sixty feet long by two feet deep might strike most people as out of proportion, but this depends on the surroundings; it might be the only logical way to treat a dead area between a walk and a wall. In our hearts we might really like to curve the walk out to vary the planting space and make the element of surprise possible, or at least to sustain our interest.

Concerning plant height, its ratio to border depth is more important if the

A perennial border in the making. The fieldstone path in the rear facilitates weeding and will not be noticed when plants are growing in summer. For low maintenance, borders should not be wider than six or seven feet.

vantage point is close in. We probably wouldn't want to plant a five-foot-tall aster in a two-foot-deep border. However, many borders are meant to be seen primarily from the distance, and good-sized units of larger, taller plants with bold foliage and heavy-textured flowers are the practical course, even if some physical aspect of the site constricts the border dimensions. Such borders can be sumptuous close up, too, but the large units that make them successful from the distance may be so heavy in texture as to make a gardener passing nearby feel as bloated as a Roman patrician at the end of the banquet season.

HIDING MISS JEKYLL

The site usually suggests the best length for a border. It might be just fifteen or twenty feet by the back door. For some, fifty feet is right. American gardeners who have been reading too many English gardening books, or too many Amer-

Borders and boulders in the lawn in August, Hillside. On the right is *Astilbe chinensis* var. *pumila,* the best astilbe for a ground cover.

ican gardening books based on English ones, frequently have the notion that a real perennial border should be about two hundred feet long by fourteen feet deep. Those were in fact the dimensions of the main border of Gertrude Jekyll (1843–1932), whose grand color schemes couldn't be done in much less space. Miss Jekyll, grandmother of the herbaceous border as Americans (and some English people) conceive the term, had her heyday at the height of the British Empire, when there was plenty of loose change around for the right people to have the right gardens. Gardeners, some very good ones, could be hired for a modest sum to care for such places.

Miss Jekyll's books have become gardening classics, reprinted in England and here, most recently in the past few years. They contain much wisdom, refinement, and charm. Her comments on color uses, honed by her early years as a painter, are important to all who garden seriously. Bits and pieces of her writing still have validity, but the frame has long been broken.

This is the second Jekyll revival in America. We have forgotten that she had considerable influence here earlier this century, and in the 1920s many a garden on Long Island or in the Philadelphia or Boston suburbs had its spiritual sources in her writings. My mother was saddled with one of these. I have a trace of a childhood memory of it, but other things in my life seemed more interesting at the time, such as yanking the tail of our pony, Toby, when I saw my sister feeding him sugar.

My main recollection of the garden is of the 1950s, years after it had been put asunder in favor of a new, green, all-season garden designed by a landscape architect who left a little planting strip for marigolds and ageratum. In drought summers we could always pick out the lines of the old borders, heavily manured in their heyday but still green, around the lawn. Good old Toby had left his mark.

Virtually all the Jekyll gardens died in England, as the Jekyll-inspired ones did here. The Depression extinguished some, the Second World War others. But mainly the culprit was time: those highly complicated borders, as labor-intensive as any gardens anywhere, could not survive the test. They were mirrors of their age, or one part of it.

Though I have occasionally designed some very large borders, I wonder what longer-term sense they make for most situations in our country. Money does not seem to be a limiting factor. The greatest problem is the shortage of skilled gardeners to care for these potential Hindenburgs. We Americans also have many interests, indeed many obsessions, and gardening is but one of them. What is the point of trying to recreate the grand gardens of yesterday? Let us settle for paradise and make it our own.

· 2 ·

The Dennis Hill
Borders

BORDERS ARE ALL the more successful in our minds if there is something personal about them. We may have special associations with certain plants. Perhaps you have a big, floppy peony with a name no one remembers, given to you as a little offset years ago by Aunt Effie, or a phlox you rescued from an abandoned garden, or a chrysanthemum you bought at a nursery in Virginia when you were on vacation a decade ago.

Sometimes the personal aspect is just the way you look at a border. There may be a vantage point no one else is aware of, from which the border looks totally different from anywhere else. Or it could be that you yourself planned certain plant combinations that worked out better than you dared hope, and you savor them on a summer evening as much as some gardeners do the ripening of the first tomato. Gardening can be intensely personal, and it is often the better for it.

Nearly all of our borders at Hillside have one or more of these qualities, but the one that comes most readily to mind is Dennis Hill #2, so christened because it is near an access road that leads to an adjacent state park called Dennis Hill. It blends visually with another border in back, separated by a grass walk three and one-half feet wide. The latter is called Dennis Hill #1, and behind it are a fieldstone path to facilitate weeding, a strip of pachysandra by a stone wall, and a Cornelian-cherry (*Cornus mas*) whose twigs bear a bundle of small yellow flowers in March, two or three weeks before forsythia blooms. The grass walk provides access for weeding, too, and for getting a close view of plants in the back border. Neither border is more than five feet wide, but as an aesthetic unit they give the appearance of depth. The borders are about thirty feet long.

HIDDEN PLEASURE

Dennis Hill #2 is my secret delight, and from May until October there is hardly a morning that I don't look out on it from my bedroom window as I am rising. But it is hardly a border for eternity. I have reshaped it mentally fifty times over the years, and physically several times as plants come and go or my tastes change. Right now it is the most beautiful thing in the world to me. Some people do pushups or aerobic exercises in the morning, or read cereal packages while practicing yoga. I just stare at Dennis Hill #2 and think of a hundred faraway things or nothing. It is my regimen, and I start the day refreshed and detached, at least until the phone jangles or Mary Ann reminds me that today it is my turn to take the garbage to the dump. Well, I guess Walter Mitty suffered indignities, too.

The growing conditions are not ideal, though better than in some of our borders. At least there is good drainage through the year, which is not to be taken for granted in many parts of our garden. The far or south end of Dennis Hill #2, about 15 percent, is shaded. The remainder receives morning and midday sun, with shade after two P.M. Several large, dark green Norway spruces are off to the west, and what they giveth in afternoon shade with their arched boughs and weeping branchlets, they taketh in root space. The Creator must have been thinking of other things when he put roots on the somber Norways, for they are equipped with far more than their fair share. These roots, questing as if they were Vikings, take moisture and nutrients from the Dennis Hill borders and are periodically restrained by spade when the time comes to lift and divide groups of perennials. This is a piecemeal process, because not all groups of plants get divided in the same year, and a few, such as the butterfly weed and peony, have never been divided. As you might expect, extra watering and fertilizing are necessary for the plants to perform up to par, but we do not overdo it. One good watering a week in summer and two broadcastings of 10-10-10 fertilizer a year are usually sufficient. The area has a year-round mulch of shredded tree leaves.

At either end of the border are groups of lamb's-ears (*Stachys byzantina*), but not the common sort esteemed by flower arrangers from Maine to Georgia for their bloom stalks, which are interesting mainly when seen close up. One group consists of 'Silver Carpet', a much more even grower for border purposes than the typical kind. It is a nonflowering or almost nonflowering lamb's-ear, so there are no unsightly old flower stems to cut back after bloom. You must occasionally remove leaves that have prematurely turned brown, but not nearly as often as with common lamb's-ears. 'Silver Carpet' is one of the finest perennials for defining the front of a border, as its soft, light foliage complements everything nearby, including grass.

At the front of the far or south end of Dennis Hill #2 is a grouping of the uncommon large-leaved lamb's-ears, whose name is in nomenclatural limbo at the moment because its traditional appellation in Europe, *Stachys byzantina,* has been appropriated by taxonomists in this country for the smaller, well-known sort. By any name this is a fine plant, with foliage two or three times as large as common lamb's-ears. It serves well for frontal positions in distant parts of large borders, where the common lamb's-ears would be lost. I have seen the large-leaved kind as far north as Montreal, where it thrives in that city's fascinating botanical garden, and I suspect it is as adaptable as the common kind. This should be a popular plant someday, because not many silverlings are adaptable over a wide range of American climates.

The repeating silvery foliage of lamb's-ears (*Stachys byzantina*) helps to define the edge of a border in Bobbi Clark's garden. Lamb's-ears is the quintessential frontal plant, making it very clear where the border begins.

Next to the grouping of 'Silver Carpet' lamb's-ears is another good frontal, a larger-than-usual catmint called *Nepeta* 'Blue Wonder'. It can easily attain fifteen inches, and after the first wave of blue flowers in June we cut plants back by two thirds to insure a compact growth habit and repeat bloom later in the season. We selected this as a frontal instead of the lower-growing *N.* × *faassenii* or *N. mussinii* because we needed some height in front of the background plants. These are butterfly weed (*Asclepias tuberosa*), sea-holly (*Eryngium planum*), and a hybrid yarrow, all of which grow nearly three feet tall.

NO TIME FOR BEREAVEMENT

Some gardeners take losses personally and become fiercely determined to succeed in growing a plant they have failed with previously. Not me. I normally escort a draped wheelbarrow to the compost pile and toss the deceased on it with equanimity, sometimes almost with relief, in the knowledge that there are plenty of other good perennials to grow. I almost always have a shortage of garden space, and almost never a shortage of plants to fill it.

But butterfly weed got to me. Over the years I had killed it three or four times, which is not surprising in view of the heavy soil and questionable drainage in some of our borders, but still practically every gardener I knew considered it an easy plant. Even the late Hal Bruce, one of the finest native-plant gardeners, debunked the principal claim to difficulty made for it — that established plants were hard to move successfully because of their large taproots. What made me even more irritated was that I could not blame my last loss on anyone but myself. After finally getting several plants well established, I inadvertently weeded them out one May, forgetting that butterfly weed is one of the last perennials to send up new growth in spring.

The orange flowers of butterfly weed are a good accompaniment for the many yellow-flowered perennials that begin to open in early summer, especially yarrows, such as *Achillea* 'Moonshine', 'Coronation Gold', or *A. taygetea*. There are rather few orange-flowered perennials, a fact that I do not lament, because the color, especially the marigold sort of orange, is frequently difficult to incorporate in a border; but some orange can be nice to have around for relief from muted tints in larger gardens. In practice, even gardeners who dislike orange are often well disposed to butterfly weed, because the individual flowers are small and the intensity of the hue is soft. It is the hue of the citrus fruit in Florida before the processors add the artificial color that consumers, except for some malcontent gardeners, are supposed to esteem.

The yarrow that accompanies butterfly weed in Dennis Hill #2 has sandstone-colored flowers, with a touch of apricot when they start to open in June. It is an *Achillea millefolium* hybrid, since named 'Hope', that was given to us by a friend in Germany several years ago, and to our surprise the bloom continues until October. A softness is contributed to the combination by the sea-holly (*Eryngium planum*), whose spherical blue flowers look as though they started to use globe thistle as a role model but thought better of it. There are showier sea-hollies, but this one serves its purpose, which is to blend.

In the rear of the border at this point is a drift of a white-flowered bulb from Lebanon, *Allium zebdanense,* which was given to us by a fellow alliumphile, landscape architect James Fanning. As a rule, we don't like to use bulbs in borders, because their foliage usually takes its time in withering and is at its worst in June, when such areas are coming into their own. However, this allium, which grows about one foot tall, blooms in late April and May, then quickly disappears. It takes the wispy leaves with it, and surrounding perennials fill in from the flanks to hide the blank space. The clumps increase well here, but not to the point of weediness, which might be a problem in mild climates.

Nearby are some plants of a bearded iris, an old-timer with white-and-violet flowers identified for us by a veteran gardener as 'Wabash'. It is a good robust grower, apparently the most widely sold iris of its kind earlier this century. 'Wabash' came with our garden, so it gets by on nostalgia, which doesn't happen often with bearded iris here. Borers make it necessary for us to give an undue amount of attention to the beardeds, and by and large we have settled on other kinds of iris for our garden, though some flower colors found in bearded iris are beautiful and perhaps unique in perennialdom. Oh, that the blooms were not so fleeting!

Some feet away from 'Wabash' are a few plants of *Iris pallida* 'Aureo-variegata', whose gray-green leaves are striped with soft yellow. The flowers, small by the standards of bearded iris, are an everyday purple, forgettable if acceptable. This cultivar is grown primarily for its foliage, which is attractive every week of the growing season, a claim that cannot be made by the beardeds. When Mary Ann and I have to choose between a perennial that has good flowers and poor foliage and one with good foliage and poor flowers, we almost invariably choose the latter. Our reason is that excellent foliage perennials are in a minority compared with excellent flowering perennials. There is never a problem finding a blooming stud to fill in as needed. I do not wish to give the impression, however, that I am a foliage snob, like a friend of mine who goes around clipping the flower buds off her fancy-leaved pelargoniums because they mar the display.

Right next to the yellow-variegated iris, with the butterfly weed off to one

The foliage of *Iris pallida* 'Aureo-variegata' always draws the eye in one of the Dennis Hill borders at Hillside. Lavender flowers in June are of fleeting beauty.

side, are a few plants of *Coreopsis* 'Moonbeam', a perennial outstanding for its pale yellow flowers, which bloom from July to frost. This grows about fifteen inches tall and has narrow, almost needlelike leaves. Abundant flowers also mean abundant deadheads, so to make plants look neater toward the end of the season we shear them back halfway in the latter part of August. This is less time-consuming than removing the spent blossoms individually, which we do only when we treat *Coreopsis* 'Moonbeam' as a tub plant, in which role it excels, even when the companions are orange marigolds. In a week or two a wave of new coreopsis flowers appears that will carry through the season.

The origin of *Coreopsis* 'Moonbeam' is a mystery. We were given our initial plant under that name by Dr. Nicholas Nickou, a very fine gardener, who in turn obtained it from the late Edward Alexander, a one-time taxonomist at the New York Botanical Garden. Alexander was secretive about its origins. Apparently it existed marginally in the nursery trade, but without a name and without recognition for its potential in the garden. My friend Pamela Harper, a photographer and author, and I have suspected that it may be a cross of *C. verticillata* and *C. rosea* f. *leucantha*, but others have suggested *C. tripteris* and *C. major* as the second (third) parents. How, where, and by whom it was developed may never be known. After we realized the good traits of 'Moonbeam', we propagated it and were instrumental in distributing it to the nursery trade under that name. Within a few years it even won an award from an international horticultural group based in Germany.

Apart from the pleasure we have derived from popularizing a little-known plant with good qualities is the awareness that a number of first-rate perennials, already present in the plant collectors' underground, are waiting for recognition. These are not just clones in familiar, overworked genera that add to horticultural clutter, but distinct species and forms that can give us a much wider range of enjoyment in the garden. Some of these plants will never make it to the garden center or mail-order catalogue but may be available here and there from small nurseries. Good gardeners usually become good sleuths.

CRANESBILLS AND OTHERS

Some of the harshest colors in the perennial world are to be found among the cranesbills, and gardeners must choose these plants with care so they don't become garden busters. I have long mused that the name bloody cranesbill (*Geranium sanguineum*), as used in common parlance, has really more to do with the British slang expression than with the true color of blood, which is not ugly except in the context of hospital or battlefield. The flowers of bloody cranesbill are actually magenta, the most reviled word in the lexicon of some gardeners. *Geranium sanguineum* has some excellent cultural qualities, though. It is a survivor, adaptable, rugged, and robust, without being a weed. Fortunately, there is a white-flowered form, *Geranium sanguineum* 'Album', which goes with virtually everything, and it has lots of good garden uses.

In Dennis Hill #2 the white cranesbill makes a topnotch front-of-the-border grouping on the south side of *Nepeta* 'Blue Wonder'. The small, finely cut leaves, borne on wiry stems about eighteen inches tall, are attractive through the season, serving also as a good background for the flowers, which begin to open in mid-June and continue for five or six weeks. We shear the plants back halfway after bloom, and they make interlocking webs of refined green foliage for the remainder of the season. This white cranesbill performs best in the sun here, but friends in the South tell us it really benefits from shade there.

Beyond the cranesbill, also in the front of Dennis Hill #2, are several plants of *Penstemon* 'Prairie Fire'. They grow to about eighteen inches, also forming loose mounds, and are attractive for four or five weeks in early summer. Many penstemons do not thrive here over the long term, so we have concentrated our efforts on several rugged sorts, including this one and *Penstemon digitalis*, of which the white-flowered form is especially handsome.

To cool the 'Prairie Fire' we place next to it a blending annual, which most years is one of the dusty-millers, *Senecio cineraria* 'Silverdust', because the foliage combines well with almost anything. Other years we may use white sweet-alyssum or Chinese forget-me-not (*Cynoglossum* 'Firmament'). These plants serve as a color transition to another frontal, betony (*Stachys officinalis*), an unsung but useful herb with two-foot spikes of pinky purple flowers in July and early August. I might mention here that taller plants, especially if they are spiky in bloom and more or less low-mounded in growth habit the rest of the season, are good change-of-pace frontals from evenly low sorts, which become a bit too ordered if you use many.

The height of frontal groups is also suggested by the plants behind them. With betony the backdrop is a pristine white daisy from the Caucasus, *Chrysanthemum corymbosum*, which grows three feet tall, has neat, clean-cut foliage, and flowers in late June and July, overlapping on the early end with pink peony 'Mons. Jules Elie'. The flowers of *C. corymbosum* suggest a feverfew (*C. parthenium*) that has been on a high-nutrition diet, but it is a much tidier and longer-lived plant. *C. corymbosum* has been overlooked during the perennials boom, no doubt because most gardeners thinking of white daisies turn automatically to Shastas. You are not likely to find plants of *C. corymbosum* at the local garden center, but we grew ours easily from seeds ordered some years ago from the American Horticultural Society seed list.

Beyond betony is a group of *Anemone* × *hybrida* 'Prince Henry', which at fifteen inches is probably the lowest-growing Japanese anemone of note. It has deep pink flowers in late August or September and seems better adapted here than many Japanese anemones, whose longevity in the cooler parts of the Northeast is not legendary.

Yellow flax (*Linum flavum*) is on the wane before *Anemone* 'Prince Henry' comes into flower, which is important because its flowers are bright as a goldfinch, and the combination would not be easy on the eye. We do not have a great deal of yellow in Dennis Hill #2, but an occasional patch of it gives depth. The flax grows to about fifteen inches in height and blooms nearly six weeks. Along with *Inula ensifolia*, it strikes me as being one of the best yellow-flowered frontals for small perennial borders in the sun, provided drainage is good — a necessity for nearly all of the plants I have mentioned.

Stokesia (*S. laevis* 'Blue Danube') grows next to the yellow flax, blooming in late July and August on somewhat lax fifteen-inch stems. Its lavender-blue flowers consort well with yellow flax on one side and the last frontal in the border, the large-leaved lamb's-ears, on the other. Directly behind the lamb's-ears is the white balloon flower (*Platycodon grandiflorus* 'Albus'), which blooms well on three-foot stalks in partial shade in August, just after white foxglove (*Digitalis purpurea* 'Alba'), which is planted behind, ends its flowering period. Having a plant with some height in front of the foxgloves is important, because we cut the latter back to rosette stage right after flowering to encourage another year of bloom. We usually refrain from cutting a stalk or two, because we like always to have some seedlings of the white foxglove coming along.

White foxglove is one of the most hauntingly beautiful plants in our garden, and we take pains to remove the common pink sort when seedlings of it bloom. It too is a pretty enough plant, but for our purposes the white foxglove is more important, and it will breed true only if the pink one is not around. White foxglove, which blooms here in June and July on five-foot stems, is exquisite in light shade and toward dusk. We will always associate the plant with Beth Chatto, England's premier nurserywoman, who gave us our original seeds.

There is some overlap in June with the flowering of white foxglove and *Geranium* × *magnificum*, which has wonderfully rich violet flowers and rounded, deeply cleft leaves. Seeds do not develop on this cranesbill, but plants are easily divided in early spring or late summer. They grow nearly two feet tall and benefit from a hard shearing after flowering, so they will have a good mounded habit during the remainder of the season. This is also true for *G. platypetalum* and other lanky cranesbills with flowers in the lavender range, including 'Johnson's Blue'. Otherwise, because of their sprawling nature, they can all detract from the border as the season progresses. Also, the more sun these particular geraniums receive, the better their bloom and growth habit will be.

You do not need exact balance in such a border, but you can give a sense of unity by repeating several groupings. Earlier I mentioned the two lamb's-ears we use as frontals at either end of Dennis Hill #2. *Iris pallida* 'Aureo-variegata' toward the beginning of the border, halfway back, is matched on the far end by *I. p.* 'Variegata', which is similar but has white stripes instead of pale yellow ones along sage-green leaves. Neither cultivar is overly vigorous, but each holds its own and yields a few divisions periodically.

Finally, and in the same manner, we have roughly balanced plantings of *Artemisia ludoviciana* 'Silver King' and 'Silver Queen' in sunken tubs with drainage holes. These are very useful foliage plants in a good height range (two to three feet) for midborder placement, but they also have far-questing roots that make them octopi of the border unless contained. In light sandy soil these

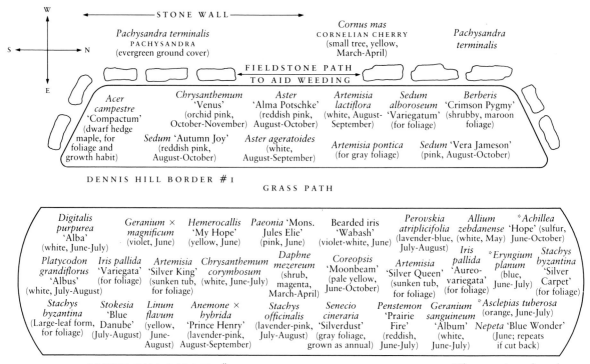

W — S — N — E

STONE WALL

Pachysandra terminalis
PACHYSANDRA
(evergreen ground cover)

Cornus mas
CORNELIAN CHERRY
(small tree, yellow,
March-April)

*Pachysandra
terminalis*

FIELDSTONE PATH
TO AID WEEDING

*Acer
campestre*
'Compactum'
(dwarf hedge
maple, for
foliage and
growth habit)

Chrysanthemum
'Venus'
(orchid pink,
October-November)

Aster
'Alma Potschke'
(reddish pink,
August-October)

*Artemisia
lactiflora*
(white, August-
September)

*Sedum
alboroseum*
'Variegatum'
(for foliage)

Berberis
'Crimson Pygmy'
(shrubby, maroon
foliage)

Sedum 'Autumn Joy'
(reddish pink,
August-October)

Aster ageratoides
(white,
August-September)

Artemisia pontica
(for gray foliage)

Sedum 'Vera Jameson'
(pink, August-October)

DENNIS HILL BORDER #1

GRASS PATH

*Digitalis
purpurea*
'Alba'
(white, June-July)

*Geranium ×
magnificum*
(violet, June)

Hemerocallis
'My Hope'
(yellow, June)

Paeonia 'Mons.
Jules Elie'
(pink, June)

Bearded iris
'Wabash'
(violet-white, June)

*Perovskia
atriplicifolia*
(lavender-blue,
July-August)

*Allium
zebdanense*
(white, May)

Achillea
'Hope' (sulfur,
June-October)

*Platycodon
grandiflorus*
'Albus'
(white, July-August)

Iris pallida
'Variegata'
(for foliage)

Artemisia
'Silver King'
(sunken tub,
for foliage)

*Chrysanthemum
corymbosum*
(white, June-July)

*Daphne
mezereum*
(shrub,
magenta,
March-April)

Coreopsis
'Moonbeam'
(pale yellow,
June-October)

Artemisia
'Silver Queen'
(sunken tub,
for foliage)

*Iris
pallida*
'Aureo-
variegata'
(for foliage)

*Eryngium
planum*
(blue,
June-July)

*Stachys
byzantina*
'Silver
Carpet'
(for foliage)

*Stachys
byzantina*
(Large-leaf form,
for foliage)

Stokesia
'Blue
Danube'
(July-August)

*Linum
flavum*
(yellow,
June-
August)

*Anemone ×
hybrida*
'Prince Henry'
(lavender-pink,
August-September)

*Stachys
officinalis*
(lavender-pink,
July-August)

*Senecio
cineraria*
'Silverdust'
(gray foliage,
grown as annual)

Penstemon
'Prairie
Fire'
(reddish,
June-July)

*Geranium
sanguineum*
'Album'
(white,
June-July)

Asclepias tuberosa
(orange, June-July)

Nepeta 'Blue Wonder'
(June; repeats
if cut back)

DENNIS HILL BORDER #2   LAWN   HOUSE ——▶   *Plants are interplanted

artemisias, especially 'Silver King', are aggressive and need yearly division if they are not straitjacketed. 'Silver King' has deeply cut, almost skeletal leaves during a good portion of the growing season, and 'Silver Queen' has wider leaves that are largely smooth-edged as summer progresses. Because the latter cultivar has more leaf surface, it is more conspicuous from a distance. Like lamb's-ears, neither has flowers that show as well in the garden as in table arrangements. All three are among the best perennials for dried flower designs.

DENNIS HILL #1

This is a shallower and simpler border than Dennis Hill #2. It has more root competition from the Norway spruces, so plants must be watered and fertilized with greater frequency. The mortality toll over the years has been highest among perennials with great or distinctly even moisture requirements, including astilbes, delphiniums, and trollius. It is basically a sun border, but with afternoon shade from the spruces.

The Dennis Hill borders, with planted steps in the foreground.

Since Dennis Hill #1 serves as a background for Dennis Hill #2, the majority of plants are taller and in larger groupings. The peak of bloom comes in September, when Dennis Hill #2, at its zenith in late June and July, is on the wane. It is important always to have something to look forward to in the garden, and the one-two effect of different peaks has a certain synergy. Although each border can stand on its own, the combination of the two is greater than the sum of their parts.

There are six major groups in Dennis Hill #1, along with several minor ones. Let us concentrate on the former. Toward the far (south) end are about ten plants of *Sedum* 'Autumn Joy', whose flower and seed-stage color is a much deeper red here than in similar groups in other parts of the garden. The reason is dryness. We initially wondered if another clone had made its way into the garden by mistake, but rooted cuttings from this group had lighter coloring just like the others when we grew them in more evenly moist soils. It is easy to understand how bogus cultivars get named when growers ignore cultural factors in a plant's appearance.

Sedum 'Autumn Joy', which grows about eighteen inches tall, has a long period of effectiveness and complements a late, single-flowered, orchid-pink chrysanthemum named 'Venus' next to it. I admired this chrysanthemum for years before learning its name, for I saw it thriving here and there in older neighborhoods of nearby mill towns, where it was obviously a survivor from better days. It always came into bloom about mid-October and some years lasted until Thanksgiving. What a boon for cut flowers late in the season in cold climates! Winter survival is so great a problem with many of the newer chrysanthemums that lots of gardeners have stopped thinking of them as hardy perennials; but that was obviously not a question with this old-timer.

Finally, one autumn in the garden of a friend who was a casual gardener I noticed a seminaturalized planting of 'Venus'. It was about three and one-half feet tall, and the group must have been twelve feet across, spreading by stolons until restrained from time to time by the lawn mower when my friend thought of mowing the periphery. The plants were neat, erect, fragrant in bloom, and bug-free.

If 'Venus' was such a good plant, why had it disappeared from the nursery trade? It was one of the widely sold chrysanthemums of its day, which was the period between the two world wars. 'Venus' was in fact one of the early selections of Korean chrysanthemums, a much-heralded strain derived from the iron-clad *C. zawadskii* crossed with the florist's chrysanthemum, *C. × morifolium*. The original and principal breeder was Alex Cummings, who then owned Bristol Nurseries in Bristol, Connecticut. Cummings was responsible for the development of some fine perennials, including *Gypsophila* 'Bristol Fairy', but his strongest interest was the chrysanthemum.

'Venus' was but one of a number of selections named for the planets in Cummings's Korean series, and not the showiest. As breeding continued, it became clear that earlier blooming chrysanthemums with larger, double, or fancier flowers were wanted, by both homeowners and nurseries. In the North a nursery can't sell many perennials after mid-October, when 'Venus' comes into its own. Cummings and other breeders obliged, and the new chrysanthemums superseded the original Koreans. It was a pity, because much of the innate hardiness and a good deal of the grace of the later blooming mums were discarded along the way. I have always thought of it as the cocker spaniel breeding process, in which cuteness, not constitution or temperament, prevails. Also, a chrysanthemum blooming in late July strikes me as being about as appropriate as a lavender cocker. I'll keep to 'Venus' and *Sedum* 'Autumn Joy' in Dennis Hill #1.

Next to *Chrysanthemum* 'Venus' in the front of the border is *Aster ageratoides*, or at least a Japanese plant given to us under that name. It came to us with a soft question mark from Harold Epstein, a veteran rock gardener who has long had a strong interest in the flora of Japan. It grows about fifteen inches tall and bears an abundance of tightly held, soft white flowers in August and September. The flowers are smaller and more delicate than those borne by the familiar, stridently colored, low-growing hybrid asters that are apt to come on in an Ethel Merman manner during those months, unless powdery mildew paralyzes them first. Fortunately, *Aster ageratoides* is more resistant to mildew, provided the plants get their fair share of moisture and air circulation in summer. They need good light but are not intended to bake under the kliegs.

A quite different aster of the Michaelmas daisy sort, named 'Alma Potschke' for a member of a leading German nursery family, grows nearby. It has deep cherry-red flowers with no trace of the purple that is so characteristic of asters. This is a distinctly unusual color for the genus, indeed closer to the knock-your-socks-off red of summer phlox 'Starfire', and a gardener can identify the plant from one hundred feet away, which cannot be said for all Michaelmas daisies. The color, which is bright but not harsh, is all the more valuable because it has few late-season counterparts. Bloom is from mid-August to early October. This aster is one of the finest new perennials of the past twenty-five years.

White mugwort (*Artemisia lactiflora*), with loose sprays of small white flowers in August and September, is a perfect companion for *Aster* 'Alma Potschke'. This is the roast beef and horseradish sauce, the yin and yang, the Rogers and Astaire. Dryish soil keeps the artemisia to about four feet in height, which is a blessing, because in rich, moist soil it can reach over six feet.

A few plants of *Sedum alboroseum* 'Variegatum', which is often sold incorrectly as a cultivar of *S. spectabile,* help set off the above combination. Plants grow about fifteen inches tall and have very pale pink flowers in open clusters in August and September, but the pleasing cream center to the foliage is what appeals to me most through the season. As with most variegated plants, it is important to remove the occasional shoots that have all-green leaves. Out of curiosity I once rooted some of these, but the resulting plants struck me as not being worth garden space, because the flowers simply weren't strong enough to carry them.

People usually have strong feelings, pro or con, about the variegated cultivars. Thank goodness we don't all feel the same about particular plants. Our gardens would be carbon copies, and they are meant to be personal. The Dennis Hill borders remind me of people and places I've seen before.

· 3 ·

Gardening on a
Quagmire

"SOME PEOPLE have wet suits, others have wet bars. We just have a wet border," Mary Ann said with a pout. It was a June afternoon, and nine inches of rain had fallen on our hillside over the preceding two days. The pine border had several rivulets meandering through, an improvement over the cascading waterfall that had occurred a few hours earlier. Little Venice, our drainage ditch on the upper side of the hill, had failed again, despite improvised sandbags of pine-bark minichips. "Why on earth did you ever put a border here, Fred?" Some questions are unanswerable, especially at the time they are asked.

Rains such as this are uncommon in the hills of northern Connecticut where we live, but they occur every several years, usually in autumn or late winter, not during the height of the growing season. When I think of these deluges, the nor'easters, the hurricane edges, ice storms, blizzards, even tornadoes, hail, and other weather-related monstrosities that afflict our area, I understand full well why this region is not known for its two-hundred-year-old specimen trees. For people in more benign climates who suffer the storm of the century, my sympathy, while sincere, is tempered. New England gets the storm of the century once or twice a decade. And we happen to garden in the Tierra del Fuego of the North.

But sooner or later the gardener comes to terms with his or her lot. Our own lot consists of clay, ledge rock, hardpan, seeps, and springs in varying degrees. Most of the classic dry-soil plants sulk and rot in a year or two unless we are careful to plant them in the relatively few areas here with impeccable drainage. Even then, if we receive our yearly average of one hundred inches of snow,

Top: The pine border, in the background of an island planting in the lawn, in late May. This border holds the eye even when plants are not in bloom. Handsome foliage is critical to the success of a perennial border.

Bottom (from front): *Hosta sieboldiana* 'Frances Williams', *Sedum* 'Autumn Joy', and *Hosta lancifolia* in the pine border at Hillside.

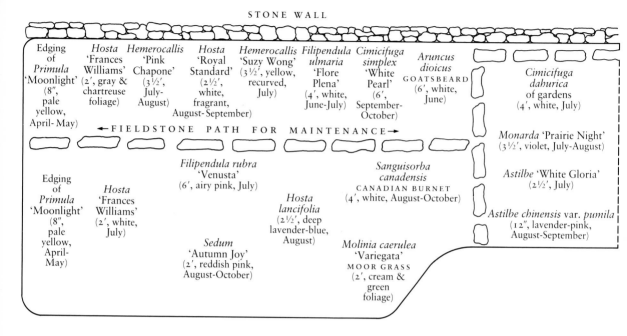

PINES   PINES

STONE WALL

Edging of *Primula* 'Moonlight' (8", pale yellow, April-May)

Hosta 'Frances Williams' (2', gray & chartreuse foliage)

Hemerocallis 'Pink Chapone' (3½', July-August)

Hosta 'Royal Standard' (2½', white, fragrant, August-September)

Hemerocallis 'Suzy Wong' (3½', yellow, recurved, July)

Filipendula ulmaria 'Flore Plena' (4', white, June-July)

Cimicifuga simplex 'White Pearl' (6', September-October)

Aruncus dioicus GOATSBEARD (6', white, June)

Cimicifuga dahurica of gardens (4', white, July)

←FIELDSTONE PATH FOR MAINTENANCE→

Monarda 'Prairie Night' (3½', violet, July-August)

Edging of *Primula* 'Moonlight' (8", pale yellow, April-May)

Hosta 'Frances Williams' (2', white, July)

Filipendula rubra 'Venusta' (6', airy pink, July)

Hosta lancifolia (2½', deep lavender-blue, August)

Sanguisorba canadensis CANADIAN BURNET (4', white, August-October)

Astilbe 'White Gloria' (2½', July)

Astilbe chinensis var. *pumila* (12", lavender-pink, August-September)

Sedum 'Autumn Joy' (2', reddish pink, August-October)

Molinia caerulea 'Variegata' MOOR GRASS (2', cream & green foliage)

which takes its time melting and forming puddles around plants in late winter, there are losses. I should also mention that a great many plants can take quite moist conditions in summer, when they are in active growth, but not in winter. The greatest cause of winter death for most perennials is in fact overly wet soil. Therefore, we have had to determine by trial and error — more error than we usually like to admit — which plants are best able to keep a few steps ahead of the compost heap.

PINE BORDER

The area about which Mary Ann asked her indelicate question is our pine border, named for several forty-year-old Austrian pines that are behind a stone wall at the rear. From late March, when frost begins to ooze from the ground, until early June the soil is saturated like a sponge. Underneath the soil is a rock ledge, or a series of ledges, that traps water. The water disappears mainly by evaporation, and a heavy spring rain can set the process back several weeks.

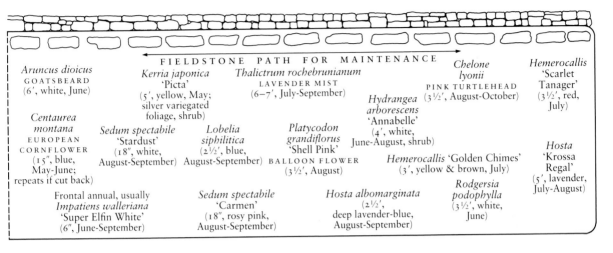

PINES   PINES

FIELDSTONE PATH FOR MAINTENANCE

Aruncus dioicus
GOATSBEARD
(6', white, June)

Kerria japonica
'Picta'
(5', yellow, May;
silver variegated
foliage, shrub)

Thalictrum rochebrunianum
LAVENDER MIST
(6–7', July-September)

*Chelone
lyonii*
PINK TURTLEHEAD
(3½', August-October)

Hemerocallis
'Scarlet
Tanager'
(3½', red,
July)

*Centaurea
montana*
EUROPEAN
CORNFLOWER
(15", blue,
May-June;
repeats if cut back)

Sedum spectabile
'Stardust'
(18", white,
August-September)

*Lobelia
siphilitica*
(2½', blue,
August-September)

*Platycodon
grandiflorus*
'Shell Pink'
BALLOON FLOWER
(3½', August)

*Hydrangea
arborescens*
'Annabelle'
(4', white,
June-August, shrub)

Hemerocallis 'Golden Chimes'
(3', yellow & brown, July)

Hosta
'Krossa
Regal'
(5', lavender,
July-August)

Frontal annual, usually
Impatiens walleriana
'Super Elfin White'
(6", June-September)

Sedum spectabile
'Carmen'
(18", rosy pink,
August-September)

Hosta albomarginata
(2½',
deep lavender-blue,
August-September)

*Rodgersia
podophylla*
(3½', white,
June)

THE AUSTRIAN PINE BORDER AT HILLSIDE

The double digging of the soil that I did years ago, as much as three feet deep, didn't help drainage one bit, and if anything created a sump into which water flows from the sides. Raising the soil level by a foot would have helped, but the dimensions of the border (fifty feet by seven feet) and its inaccessibility to soil-delivery trucks made this financially impractical. Nor was the installation of drainage tile a reasonable option, because of cost. I made my bed and had to sleep in it, but during fits of insomnia I pondered Mary Ann's question many times before she asked it.

The previous owners of our property, who had a garden, didn't seem to have a consuming interest in plants, and when we came to Hillside in 1963 the pine border consisted of several groupings of named varieties of daylilies (*Hemerocallis*). There is much to be said for these plants, to be sure, but I've always felt that borders devoted entirely to them have as much interest as a TV dinner. When all is said and done, they have the same straplike foliage, which is usually tatty by midsummer, and the flower form is pretty much the same open trumpet. It's a monoculture, copycat plants plunked here and there to fill space in hopes of attaining that great American sedative — no maintenance. It is not the kind of gardening that requires much imagination or even thought.

Still, the daylilies served a purpose, as I discovered after removing them and planting delphiniums, Shasta daisies, pinks, gaillardias, veronicas, and other plants of short life expectancy on wet sites. In the distance, the daylily flowers make an attractive statement, even an exclamation, and one is not likely to notice the dead blooms that cling to their scapes — the flower stalks — like flies to flypaper. The further away daylilies are, the better landscape subjects they become.

Among the qualities generally thought of as beneficial, one stands out in daylilies: it is virtually impossible to kill them, at least the older sorts (some of the fancy new cultivars don't have the same constitution). Most important, old-timers such as 'Hyperion' are able to thrive on soil that is very wet in late winter and spring. Interplant them with hostas, ferns, and rugged old cultivars of daffodils, the least expensive, large-growing named sorts you can get, such as 'King Alfred' and the poet's narcissus, which are usually moisture-tolerant too. Then the daylilies cease to be just plants and start to become part of a garden. The daffodils provide the spring show, and their slowly yellowing leaves, which shouldn't be cut until dead, are obscured by the daylily foliage. The daylilies themselves bloom in summer.

NEW VISTAS FOR HOSTAS AND RODGERSIAS

No part of the pine border receives full sun all day, but the northern or downhill section, which is the wettest, gets approximately six hours. We think of hostas as plants for shaded areas, and that is generally true, but many are capable of growing adequately in sun if the soil is wet. A grouping of 'Frances Williams', the large, sumptuous cultivar of *Hosta sieboldiana* with chartreuse markings on puckered, gray-green, foot-wide leaves, grows luxuriantly in the sun here. It may need one or two waterings during midsummer drought to keep the leaf margins from scorching. The nearly white flowers rise slightly above the foliage mounds in early summer and are pleasing for a sieboldiana, which usually hides its bloom among a bushel of leaves, but the foliage of this one is the real winner. About fifteen plants are in our grouping, which is conspicuous from the back porch, some 110 feet away.

Almost every year for the past dozen years the members of the American Hosta Society have voted 'Frances Williams' number one in their poll of favorites. Considering that there are upwards of six hundred hostas and that the society's members are not known for unanimity on horticultural matters, this is a remarkable distinction.

It helps to remember that most hosta species are indigenous to moist or wet areas in the wilds of Japan and China, and some are virtually bog plants, including *Hosta lancifolia*. This veteran with fairly narrow dark green leaves and, in late summer, dependably profuse deep lavender flowers on two-and-one-half-foot scapes is one of the most appropriate hostas for a wet border. Despite foliage that is on the smallish side for this genus, *H. lancifolia* is also one of the best of the older and less expensive kinds for ground-cover purposes. It is also virtually indestructible but never takes over the garden. If I were to be reincarnated as a slug in 2089, I would know exactly where to go in our garden to get a dependable meal.

We have separate groupings of three other hostas in the border, and all are satisfactory. One is *Hosta albomarginata*, with general appearance and flowers, including late summer bloom, similar to *H. lancifolia* but with a modest white margin to the leaves, which from the distance gives a light gray appearance. Medium gray is provided by *Hosta* 'Krossa Regal', a beautiful large-leaved sort with great substance that can be appreciated from across the lawn. Even in midsummer, when they appear, the five-foot scapes of lavender flowers, among the tallest in hostadom, are upstaged by the magnificent clumps of foliage. *Hosta* 'Royal Standard', with fragrant white flowers in August and large, pale green leaves, completes the scene. Many other hostas would be as appropriate.

The distant or uphill end of the pine border, which receives sun briefly at

Left: Astrantia major 'Sunningdale Variegated', *Anemone canadensis*, and *Hosta sieboldiana* 'Elegans' grow luxuriantly in a moist border at the McGourtys'.
Right: Rodgersia podophylla blooms on three-foot stalks in early summer. This astilbe relative demands moisture and shade.

midday, is given to groupings of bold-leaved plants, because they are more readily picked up by the eye than plants with thin foliage texture are. Here is *Hosta* 'Krossa Regal' and next to it, in a frontal position as well, is *Rodgersia podophylla*. The emerald green foliage, occasionally with a reddish tint, is remarkable, consisting of giant glossy wedges a foot or more long, ending in tridents. The species name is an allusion to mayapple, but no mayapple has such majesty of foliage.

At maturity, which it attains slowly, *Rodgersia podophylla* makes a three-foot-tall jagged mound, with creamy white flowers borne on stalks that rise another foot or eighteen inches above the foliage. They resemble astilbe blooms, and in fact astilbe and rodgersia are in the same botanical family, the Saxifragaceae; but the clusters in rodgersia are more rounded, suggesting a series of small pagodas banded in loose spires. They bloom at Hillside in June and early July. Plants are eventually stoloniferous, and each spring I take a few minutes to restrain them without a whisper about high maintenance.

Horticulturally, rodgersias are very good when they are good, and just plain horrid when they are terrible. They don't ask, they demand. They shout up and down for moist, deeply dug soil in the shade, though in the North they can take pondside conditions in partly sunny areas if the soil is consistently wet during the growing season. Many an American gardener, having seen them rather often in the large English gardens and thinking them versatile, is in for a rodgersia tantrum unless he or she closely heeds the cultural requirements. In our diverse but often harsh American climate, there is not the margin of choice that exists in England. But that doesn't mean you can't make a rodgersia smile, even if the first flush of foliage in spring is blackened by a late frost in some years and slugs find it as appetizing as a hosta. Some plants are worth the hassle.

SEDUM, GOATSBEARD, AND MEADOWSWEET

Sedums might be considered a curious choice for a wet border because they are succulents, with the ability to store water for use during drought. However, the tall border varieties such as the superior hybrid 'Autumn Joy', which has reddish pink flowers in fall, are equally at home in dry or wet soil. *Sedum spectabile*, about fifteen inches tall, has a much shorter bloom period and the seed heads don't have the protracted interest of those of 'Autumn Joy'; but several cultivars are better than the wild type, which has an unfortunate amount of blue in the pink flowers. Among them are 'Carmen', 'Brilliant', and 'Meteor', which run the gamut of crimson to pink.

In the pine border we grow 'Carmen' and 'Stardust', a white-flowered cultivar that starts to bloom at the end of September, nearly a month later than the others. 'Stardust' appears to be a sport of 'Meteor' and will occasionally issue a stalk bearing deep reddish pink flowers. *Sedum* 'Stardust' is nice in front of the long-blooming purple coneflower (*Echinacea purpurea*), especially 'Bright Star', whose ray flowers don't droop like those of the species from which it is derived. Another good late-season companion is false dragonhead (*Physostegia virginiana* 'Bouquet Rose'). Both the purple coneflower and false dragonhead are at home in moist soil, too.

We try to stagger the bloom in our borders so we will always have something of interest, but there are peaks. For the pine border it is the latter part of June and early July, when goatsbeard (*Aruncus dioicus*) and two stout meadowsweets, *Filipendula rubra* 'Venusta' and *Filipendula ulmaria* 'Flore Plena', are in flower. Goatsbeard luxuriates in the moist, humus-laden soil, growing six feet tall and several feet wide. The shaggy but mostly upright white plumes are, in their brief season of glory, the most conspicuous plants in our garden. They are matched only by Pacific Giant delphiniums, which grow in another, better-drained border in full sun. The two together would be striking, perhaps overpowering.

Goatsbeard is very variable in plant size, flower cluster, and bloom time, and in fact has one of the widest distributions in nature of any perennial. I have enjoyed seeing it in the wilds of Europe, along the Skyline Drive in Virginia, and on the Olympic Peninsula of Washington, and never have I witnessed a bad one. Although nurseries do not sell goatsbeard by gender, it is dioecious, as the name suggests. The staminate or male plants have showier flowers, but they wither poorly and become unsightly before their time. The clusters on pistillate or female plants, though not quite so conspicuous, age gracefully in the seed-setting stage and extend the period of interest for a few weeks. By good fortune, as several of our plants fade from bloom, others begin their display. This is important, because in most years the effective flowering period of a particular goatsbeard is only a week or ten days. To an extent we have also lengthened the bloom time by placing goatsbeard in different exposures around the property. Plants need a fair-sized border because of their shrubby dimensions, and frequently only one is called for.

A matching giant, sometimes even a foot or so taller than goatsbeard but with loose, more open growth, is Martha Washington's plume (*Filipendula rubra* 'Venusta'). The fluffy pink heads of this American original resemble cotton candy and are as large as a serving of it at a county fair. The flowers tower over

Nature mimics cotton candy: Martha Washington's plume (*Filipendula rubra* 'Venusta'). A colonizer, this plant grows six or seven feet tall and is lushest in moist soil on a sunny site. Bloom time is early to midsummer.

jagged maplelike leaves, which are attractive unless the plants are grown in too dry soil, in which case spider mites turn them a dull, rusty green. In severe infestations you should cut clumps to the ground after flowering, which brings about a flush of good foliage for the rest of the season. In most soils the roots quest for a couple of feet from center for moisture during the growing season, and we find it best to divide plants every two years in early spring or late summer to keep them in check. Like many aggressive perennials (and cities), the plants tend to die out in the middle, with growth strongest on the periphery.

A more restrained filipendula, from the Old World, is the double-flowered form *F. ulmaria* 'Flore Plena', which grows four feet tall and bears numerous small white buttons in early summer. It is so distinct from *F. rubra* that we do not hesitate to have the two nearby for contrast. Reasonably moist soil, at least up to bloom time, is essential for both if they are to look their best, which is very good indeed. Light gang staking, in which you place metal stakes with loops at the four corners of groupings and unite them with coarse green twine, may be necessary. This is especially desirable if sunlight patterns vary greatly during the course of the day. As their common names suggest — queen-of-the-prairie for *F. rubra* and queen-of-the-meadow for *F. ulmaria* — these plants will take as much sun as they can get, but in the garden they usually benefit from light afternoon shade if soil moisture is not ideal.

Two lower-growing filipendulas are excellent front-of-the-border plants in moist areas. One is *F. hexapetala* 'Flore Plena', which makes a ten-inch-high mound of finely cut emerald green leaves that can easily be confused with some of the fancy-leaved ferns we associate with Edwardian parlors. Arching above the mounds in early summer are clusters of tightly congested white flowers. *F. hexapetala* can also take drier soil than any filipendula we know of, but best performance here has been in a deep moisture-retentive loam, despite the species' upland origins in the Old World. (*F. vulgaris* is a new name.)

Filipendula palmata 'Nana', usually a foot tall when displaying its powder puffs of pink flowers but capable of growing taller if old or heavily fertilized, is the longest-blooming meadowsweet. The first flowers open here in early July, the latest in September. However, if the soil in summer is not evenly moist, the bloom period is contracted and the small maplelike foliage is often subject to mildew or spider mites. You will get the best results if you dig a few shovelsful of peat moss or compost into the soil and give the plants some afternoon shade. In other gardens we occasionally notice taller forms, halfway in height between 'Nana' and the species itself, which grows to four feet. These are probably seedlings raised from 'Nana'.

Towering even above the goatsbeards and meadowsweets in the pine border are some informal groupings of lavender mist (*Thalictrum rochebrunianum*). In partial shade and with some root competition from the Austrian pines, plants grow seven or eight feet tall, but I have seen them attain ten feet in full sun in rich moist soil. The tiny flowers, borne from July to September, are loosely arranged in large cobwebby inflorescences, giving the impression of a lavender baby's-breath on stilts. For all this, lavender mist has a delicate, almost lean appearance, with attractive foliage resembling a columbine.

You should have at least several plants of lavender mist in a grouping for a topnotch display. Lavender mist is particularly useful toward the front of a long border to break the monotony of even heights like soldiers in line. Also, because of the beauty of the open, airy foliage, it is a pity to consign these plants to the back recesses of a border, where only the flowers can be seen. Worried that perennials behind them won't be visible? Then plant something that attains height quickly in spring and blooms early, such as sweet cicely (*Myrrhis odorata*).

Lavender mist is arguably the finest tall meadow-rue, though there are other excellent ones for particular purposes. These include the showy lavender-pink or white spring-blooming *Thalictrum aquilegifolium* and the gray-leaved *T. speciosissimum*, which bears citron flowers in early summer. The latter is a superior foliage plant, able to serve as a foil to bring out the best qualities of many a lesser plant that blooms later in the season, including medium-sized Michaelmas daisies. After bloom you should prune the flowering stalks very heavily to encourage a flush of attractive new leaves.

LITTLE STEEPLES AND BIG SPIKES

Astilbes are at home in any moist border, especially a lightly shaded one. Most grow about two feet tall and have refined, sometimes quite attractive foliage. 'Peach Blossom', with pale pink flowers, and 'Irrlicht', with white ones, open the season here around mid-June, blooming for about three weeks. Shortly later come a raft of others, including several good dark reds, such as 'Fanal' and 'Spinel'. These have coppery new growth in spring, too, and persistent russet seed heads that look good against snow the following winter. Our immediate choices for the pine border are 'Bridal Veil', one of the best whites, and an odd man out, *Astilbe chinensis* var. *pumila*, which bears purplish pink steeples in August. The latter attains a foot in height and blooms well into September some years. This is also the most drought-tolerant astilbe and the one best suited for ground cover. It is stoloniferous and doesn't need division every few years, as most astilbes do.

Black snakeroots (*Cimicifuga*) thrive in and near the pine border. When grown in edge-of-the-woods conditions with lots of peat moss or compost dug into the soil for moisture retention, they are apt to be at their finest, the four- to six-foot stalks bearing elegant white or nearly white candles for weeks. Some bloom in early or midsummer, others in late summer, still others in autumn. The ones we have chosen for this border are *Cimicifuga dahurica* of gardens, with buttermilk candles held on ebony stalks in July, and *Cimicifuga simplex* 'White Pearl', which has stout bottlebrushes of pure white in later September and October, provided frost doesn't nip the buds. (The term "of gardens" indicates that the plant commonly grown under a given name may differ from the true species as found in the wild, but that taxonomists have not yet placed the former into a neat cubbyhole, so the "familiar" botanical name is retained for the sake of convenience.) In general the black snakeroots are at their best in areas with relatively cool summers, though I have seen excellent plants of 'White Pearl' in parts of the South, and indeed three species of *Cimicifuga* are native there.

Pink turtlehead (*Chelone lyonii*), with chunky flowers arranged on stout spikes, usually overlaps with *Cimicifuga simplex* and complements it nicely in long autumns. Turtlehead is not a showy plant as a rule, but a grouping of this very hardy southern native offers a warm surprise on a cool September day. Although associated in the wild with wet soils, pink turtlehead is quite adaptable in the garden, taking average border conditions for moisture very well. Provided it is not pushed to the limit, it performs here as respectably in sun as in shade. Height is three to four feet, and few pests bother it.

The pine border also has a small grouping of the variegated moor grass (*Molinia caerulea* 'Variegata'), a lovely butter-and-green clump-former that thrives in moist conditions and partial shade. This is not a rapid grower and may take two or even three years to settle in fully, which makes it unpopular with people used to quick results. By the same token, variegated moor grass will be much more stable in a border than some of the faster-growing medium-sized grasses that dote on moisture, including ribbon grass (*Phalaris arundinacea* 'Picta'), which gives instant gratification, then sudden remorse as it romps to town. This molinia is a foot tall at maturity, except for several weeks in summer when pale yellow sprays bearing tiny purplish blooms arch a foot or so above the foliage mounds.

We grow several other perennials in the pine border, including two indestructibles, the European cornflower (*Centaurea montana*) and perennial blue lobelia (*Lobelia siphilitica*). We have found blue lobelia more reliably perennial than its better-known cousin, the red cardinal flower (*Lobelia cardinalis*), especially in soils that dry out in summer. Two shrubs are also present, *Kerria japonica* 'Picta' and *Hydrangea arborescens* 'Annabelle'. Occasionally we squeeze in some annuals, mainly nicotiana, browallia, or impatiens. Each year we make a few changes, sometimes when groups run their course or when we tire of them; but it is ironic that this area, potentially the worst for perennial growth, has probably given us our most stable border.

As I write this, I am struck by the latitude of choice among perennials for borders that are wet during a fair portion of the year, and by the realization that they represent only a fraction of the total number of perennials available in nurseries. There are enough of them to make at least several borders of the kind I have just described, without repetition. An annotated list of some additional perennials that have survived wet soil conditions elsewhere in our garden for substantial periods appears below; the numbers refer to plant height at bloom time, and are followed by flower color and month of bloom in Connecticut.

Aconitum carmichaelii (fischeri), monkshood. 3½ ft., dark blue, Aug.–Oct.; best in areas with cool summers

Aconitum henryi 'Sparks Variety'. 5–6 ft., blue, July–Aug.

Ajuga pyramidalis. 8 in., blue, May; a clump-former, much better for borders than the vigorously stoloniferous *A. reptans*, which should have been named *A. gallopans*

Alchemilla mollis, lady's-mantle. 15 in., chartreuse, May–June

Anaphalis triplinervis. 15 in., white, Aug.–Oct.; caterpillars devouring leaves sometimes a problem; native pearly everlasting (*A. margaritacea*) usually too rampant for borders

Aster novae-angliae and *A. novi-belgii*, asters derived from New England and New York asters, often called Michaelmas daisies. 1–6 ft., purple, pink, blue, or white, Aug.–Oct. (*Caution: A. × frikartii* and its cultivars are not suited to wet sites)

Astrantia major, masterwort. 2 ft., white or pink, June–Aug.

Athyrium filix-femina, lady fern. 3 ft.; many ferns thrive on moist soil, some excessively so, especially ostrich, marsh, and sensitive ferns; royal fern (*Osmunda regalis*) can take it as wet as any

Brunnera macrophylla, perennial forget-me-not. 15 in., blue, May

Campanula lactiflora. 3–4 ft., usually blue, some white or pink, July–Aug.

Carex conica 'Variegata' of gardens. 12 in.; a sedge grown for its green-and-silver foliage

Coreopsis verticillata, thread-leaf coreopsis. 2 ft., yellow, July–Aug.; other species of coreopsis often rot in wet soil

Epimedium × rubrum. 12 in., red-and-white, May; also, *E. × versicolor* 'Sulphureum' and *E. × youngianum* 'Roseum'; others probably as good in occasionally wet soils

Euphorbia griffithii 'Fireglow'. 15 in., brick red, May–June; too stoloniferous for small borders

Geranium macrorrhizum. 15 in., pink or white, June

Helenium autumnale cultivars. 3–6 ft., yellow, orange, or red, Aug.–Oct.

Hibiscus moscheutos, selections and hybrids. 6–7 ft., pink, red, or white, Aug.; immense flowers out of scale in all but large borders; often best by ponds

Iris kaempferi, Japanese iris. 3–4 ft., purple, pink, or white, July; skip the lime

Iris pseudacorus, yellow flag. 4–5 ft., yellow, June; vigorous

Iris sibirica, Siberian iris. 3–4 ft., purple, blue, or white, June

Iris versicolor, blue flag. 3 ft., lavender-blue, June

Lamium maculatum. 8 in., pink or white, May–June; also 'White Nancy'

Ligularia, including 'Desdemona' and 'The Rocket'. 3½–6 ft., yellow or orange, July–Aug.

Lobelia cardinalis, cardinal flower. 3 ft., red, July–Aug.; usually longer-lived in wet soil

Lysimachia ephemerum. 3 ft., grayish-white, July–Aug.; *L. clethroides* and *L. punctata* usually too vigorous for borders, best at pondside

Lythrum, all named cultivars. 2–4 ft., shades of pink, July–Aug.; unlike the species, a beautiful weed of wet meadows and streamsides, the cultivars are well behaved

Mentha, various mints. 1½–3 ft., mainly culinary; plant in sunken tubs to keep order

Miscanthus sinensis, various cultivars. 5–7 ft., grayish-white plumes, Aug.–Oct.; perhaps the best of the taller grasses for moist borders

Monarda didyma 'Cambridge Scarlet'. 3–4 ft., red, July–Aug.; may require yearly division; *M. fistulosa* and hybrids are more adapted to drier soils

Myosotis scorpioides var. *semperflorens,* forget-me-not. 15 in., blue, May–Aug.; an ephemeral jump-about, but gives grace to many a moist spot

Peltiphyllum peltatum. 3 ft., pink, May; best at pondside because of its unending thirst

Primula, primrose, various. Choose as you will; among the better ones for frontal positions are *P. acaulis* and *P. × polyantha* selections, which usually need division every year or two; choose *P. japonica* for greater height and later bloom, but only in borders that will be moist in early summer; there are hundreds of others but mainly for informal woodland plantings

Pulmonaria saccharata 'Mrs. Moon'. 15 in., blue fading to deep pink, April–May; silver-spotted foliage excels as the season progresses if flower stalks are removed from base of plant after bloom

Pycnanthemum incanum, mountain mint. 3–4 ft.; mainly for superior gray-green foliage, best later in season; flowers white and inconspicuous, Aug.

Rheum palmatum var. *tanguticum,* ornamental rhubarb. Bold 3–4 ft. foliage masses, with stalks to 6 ft. in late spring bearing red, pink, or white flowers

Rudbeckia fulgida 'Goldsturm', perennial black-eyed Susan. 3 ft., yellow, Aug.

Rudbeckia nitida 'Goldquelle'. 3–4 ft., yellow, Aug.–Sept.; lower-growing version of the old-time golden-glow (*R. laciniata* 'Hortensia')

Sanguisorba canadensis, Canadian burnet. 4 ft., white, Aug.–Oct.; in cooler regions more dependable in flower than *Cimicifuga simplex*

Sanguisorba obtusa, Japanese burnet. 3½ ft., drooping pink clusters, July–Aug.

Senecio tanguticus. 5 ft., yellow, Aug.–Sept.; rhizomatous, best in large borders or at pondside

Tradescantia × andersoniana, spiderwort. 2 ft., purple, blue, pink, or white, June; repeats if cut to ground after first bloom; not a first-rank perennial but useful in large, wet borders

Trollius × cultorum, globeflower. 2½ ft., yellow or orange, May

Trollius ledebourii of gardens. 2½ ft., orange, June–July; this and the preceding need summer moisture if the foliage is to stay attractive; however, if you are globetrotting in July, you can cut trollius to the ground when you come home, and soon there will be another flush of growth

· 4 ·

A Spring Tonic

SEASONAL BORDERS are not everyone's cup of tea, but they have a place in fair-sized gardens, or in particular situations, or in climates where summer gardening is as enjoyable as a steam bath in Death Valley on the Fourth of July. Some of our friends, for example, are off to vacation homes at the crack of summer or are apt to travel a good deal during the suntan season. In such cases the heliopsis, liatris, rudbeckias, and dozens of other plants that bloom in the warmest months will have to suffer the silence of a single hand clap from the meter reader or the young man who races the mower across the lawn, dreaming he is at Daytona.

So why bother with a display you may never even see? By concentrating your attention on attractive plants that will be in bloom when you are at home, and arranging them in a pleasing manner, you can have an intensely striking garden that displays individuality as well as beauty. Making it personal helps it succeed, and honing in on a particular season enables you to avoid a lot of garden clutter. This is only one way to approach the design of a border, but it comes with the endorsement of the great-grandmother of perennialdom, Gertrude Jekyll.

TYPES OF SPRING GARDENS

Spring display usually involves one or more concentrations of color. The woodland garden that blooms then is an American classic. Naturalized bulbs, especially daffodils, give a splash of color to the meadow. Some gardens are given largely to flowering shrubs, most of which bloom within several weeks of one another in the cooler parts of the country. These can be spectacular, especially at rhododendron or azalea times, or even just when forsythia breaks forth.

There is also the rock garden, which looks best when plants become part of a larger scene, fitting natural rock outcroppings and undulating terrain as comfortably as fingers in a glove. The plants need not be alpines, and in fact few gardeners are fortunate enough to live in climates where true alpines thrive. It helps increase our sensitivity, too, if a little brook meanders through. The finest example of this I know is Millstream, the rock garden of Lincoln Foster and the late Timmy Foster of Falls Village, Connecticut. Linc has been the influential if unofficial laureate of American rock gardening for years, and Timmy was a fine artist.

Perhaps the greatest contribution of the Fosters' garden has been to curb the notion of many people that a rock garden must look like one of the pimply eruptions of the landscape commonly seen in the British botanic gardens — monstrous Matterhorns and mangled Mont Blancs. At best, such gardens are rude impositions on the landscape, even without ceramic mountain goats, and they say something about a certain mindset. At worst, because of their consummate ugliness, they have turned a lot of good souls away from a fascinating sector of gardening. To most English rock gardeners and still to quite a few American ones, it is virtually a seditious idea that a plant can look better if it is displayed in naturalistic surroundings with an aesthetically pleasing companion. Indeed, one of the hazards of rock gardening is looking at the individual plants too closely and being totally oblivious of the garden.

PROBLEMS OF CONCENTRATION

A border for early to midspring strikes me as a good way to display plants if your property does not lend itself to a rock garden or a woodland garden. It does mean that you need restraint if you are in residence during the warm months, because you will be tempted to include a few plants for summer color the first year, still a few more the second year, and eventually the purpose of the border can become eroded. The temptation is strongest if the border is in a very conspicuous part of the garden.

The site for such a border deserves special consideration, so you can enjoy it when it is in bloom and ignore it in good conscience, except for periodic weeding, the rest of the season. Because peak flowering will occur while the weather is still cool, it is usually best to have the border fairly close to the house and in partial view from a window that you often find yourself looking out of. If it is in total view, it doesn't issue quite the same invitation to wander outdoors for a closer look.

To keep the spring border from becoming a visual handicap in summer, be sure to include a good number of plants with handsome foliage, including silverlings, variegated sorts, and ornamental grasses. Their presence in spring actually augments the display, because paradoxically, the greatest effectiveness of color does not occur if all the plants are in bloom simultaneously. The border needs contrast if color is to be most gainfully employed. Sometimes, too, you can save spring borders from improvers in summer by intentionally incorporating just one or two conspicuous kinds of long-blooming perennials, such as *Achillea* 'Moonshine' or monardas. The judicious overplanting of bulbs in early June with cosmos or *Salvia farinacea*, treated as an annual, can also do wonders. But don't tamper a great deal, or else you will lose the border, as I once did.

Let us set up a framework for perennials, with the understanding that the main flowering in the border will take place before Oriental poppies, bearded iris, and most peonies come into bloom, though there will be occasional overlap. Also, the plants we are discussing are essentially for a sunny border, though

Viki Ferreniea

A spring woodland border with lavender-blue *Phlox divaricata*, *Corydalis lutea*, and foliage of bloodroot (*Sanguinaria canadensis*), whose flowers open at the crack of spring and have already departed.

← 50' →

Arabis aucasica 'ore Pleno' (o", white)	*Prunus glandulosa var. sinensis DWARF FLOWERING ALMOND (3½', pink)	Dicentra spectabilis 'Alba' WHITE JAPANESE BLEEDING-HEART (3½', white)	Fritillaria imperialis CROWN IMPERIAL (3½', burnt orange)	Miscanthus sinensis 'Purpurascens' ORNAMENTAL GRASS (4', autumn color)	*Chaenomeles speciosa ORANGE FLOWERING QUINCE (5', orange)
Centaurea montana OPEAN CORNFLOWER (15", blue)	Lunaria annua 'Alba' WHITE HONESTY (3', white, biennial)	Narcissus 'Binkie' (16", sulfur)	Athyrium filix-femina LADY FERN (3') • Tulipa 'Stresa' (16", red & yellow)	Endymion hispanicus 'Alba' SPANISH BLUEBELL (20", white)	Muscari botryoides GRAPE HYACINTH (6", blue)
Stachys yzantina MB'S-EARS 15", silver foliage)	Iris pumila 'Dark Spot' (10", violet)	Dicentra 'Luxuriant' (15", cherry pink)	Euphorbia epithymoides (18", yellow) • Phlox divaricata 'Fuller's White' (12", white)	Helictotrichon sempervirens BLUE OAT GRASS (2', for foliage) • Heuchera micrantha 'Palace Purple' PURPLE-LEAF CORALBELLS (15", white) interplanted with Phlox 'Millstream Laura' (4", light pink)	Doronicum caucasicum 'Magnificum' (2', yellow) • Polemonium reptans GREEK VALERIAN (12", blue)
onica prostrata 'Mrs. Holt' 4", light pink)	Thymus citriodorus 'Silver Queen' VARIEGATED THYME (6", silver-edged foliage)	Ajuga pyramidalis (8", blue)	Lathyrus vernus 'Albo-Roseus' (8", white & pink)		Iberis sempervirens 'Alexander's White' (10", white)

SHRUBS: one of each

SPRING TONIC BORDER

they will benefit from some afternoon shade in summer, as deciduous trees come into full leaf. This is an excellent condition for the growth of a wide range of perennials.

NO TOURNIQUET FOR BLEEDING-HEARTS

The principal challenge in planning a border with early bloom is finding plants of the right height for the rear rank, for most perennials have not attained their full height then. A logical first choice is an old-timer about which most gardeners are nostalgic, as were their grandparents and perhaps even *their* grandparents — the Japanese bleeding-heart (*Dicentra spectabilis*). The pink-and-white valentines dangling for a month or so from long arching stalks are among the first true perennial flowers to appear in spring, and mature plants quickly reach three to four feet in height.

Just how durable is the Japanese bleeding-heart? One spring a three-foot specimen was in full bloom in our garden on May 9. A freak snowfall of

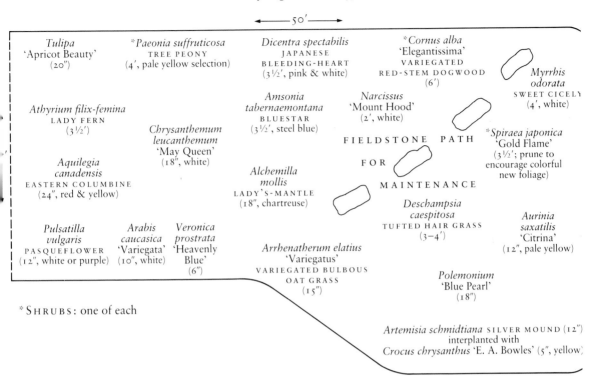

←———50'———→

Tulipa
'Apricot Beauty'
(20")

*Paeonia suffruticosa
TREE PEONY
(4', pale yellow selection)

Dicentra spectabilis
JAPANESE
BLEEDING-HEART
(3½', pink & white)

Cornus alba
'Elegantissima'
VARIEGATED
RED-STEM DOGWOOD
(6')

*Myrrhis
odorata*
SWEET CICELY
(4', white)

Athyrium filix-femina
LADY FERN
(3½')

*Chrysanthemum
leucanthemum*
'May Queen'
(18", white)

*Amsonia
tabernaemontana*
BLUESTAR
(3½', steel blue)

Narcissus
'Mount Hood'
(2', white)

FIELDSTONE   PATH

Spiraea japonica
'Gold Flame'
(3½'; prune to
encourage colorful
new foliage)

*Aquilegia
canadensis*
EASTERN COLUMBINE
(24", red & yellow)

*Alchemilla
mollis*
LADY'S-MANTLE
(18", chartreuse)

FOR

MAINTENANCE

*Deschampsia
caespitosa*
TUFTED HAIR GRASS
(3–4')

*Aurinia
saxatilis*
'Citrina'
(12", pale yellow)

*Pulsatilla
vulgaris*
PASQUEFLOWER
(12", white or purple)

*Arabis
caucasica*
'Variegata'
(10", white)

*Veronica
prostrata*
'Heavenly
Blue'
(6")

Arrhenatherum elatius
'Variegatus'
VARIEGATED BULBOUS
OAT GRASS
(15")

Polemonium
'Blue Pearl'
(18")

*SHRUBS: one of each

Artemisia schmidtiana SILVER MOUND (12")
interplanted with
Crocus chrysanthus 'E. A. Bowles' (5", yellow)

eighteen inches beat the bleeding-heart down that day. Two days later, as the snow receded, the plant was completely prostrate. I planned to remove the seemingly dead *Dicentra*, but my immediate attention had to go to trees that had been downed left and right. In another two days the bleeding-heart was upright and in full bloom again, as if there had been no storm. I never again cursed the plant for having fragile stems, which break easily when my clumsiness in the border gets in their way.

Mary Ann and I are perhaps even fonder of the white-flowered Japanese bleeding-heart (*Dicentra spectabilis* 'Alba'), which many gardeners have discovered in the past decade. A seedling strain of easy culture has become available, replacing a weakling clone that played the circuit of the horticultural underground for years. A free-seeding *Dicentra spectabilis* itself is somewhat unusual, for most plants of the common pink-and-white sort are thought to be from one clone introduced from Holland many years ago. These don't set seed much, at least in the absence of a different clone for cross-pollination.

The only landscape weakness of *Dicentra spectabilis* and its current white

Viki Ferreniea

Shaded borders in spring at the Cary Arboretum in Millbrook, New York, display doronicum, Japanese bleeding-heart (*Dicentra spectabilis*), *Hosta sieboldiana* 'Elegans' and 'Frances Williams', Japanese painted fern (*Athyrium goeringianum* 'Pictum'), and rhododendrons.

variant is that in dry summers plants are forced into early dormancy and lose their leaves, causing a somewhat awkward gap in the border. Regular watering prevents this, except in very warm climates. The problem is also lessened by growing the Japanese bleeding-heart in partial shade, which it tolerates very well. Traditional foreground perennials to hide the gap are daylilies and baby's-breath (*Gypsophila paniculata*), or hostas if the site is shady. An alternative in a sunny area is to overplant the bleeding-heart in late spring with a tall annual such as cleome or cosmos.

Although it is a lower-growing plant, *Dicentra* 'Luxuriant', a hybrid of *D. eximia* with *D. formosa,* should be mentioned here. It bears profuse if modest-sized flowers in spring, with a measure of repeat bloom the rest of the growing season, except during hot spells. Height is upwards of fifteen inches, and the refined, deeply cut foliage persists through summer. This is probably the best of the hybrids of the East and West Coast American species — and one of the longest-blooming perennials.

OTHER TALL PLANTS

The crown-imperial (*Fritillaria imperialis*), a bulb native from Turkey to the Himalayas, quickly attains a height of three to four feet in spring. The flowers are the color of new brick, although yellow and deep orange-red forms are sometimes seen. Tufts of foliage rise above a circle of pendent flowers that resemble little lilies. The stems below the flowers are bare for some distance, which, along with the foliage tufts on top, give the plant an odd appearance — a lily that has aspirations of becoming an amaryllis. The plant withers and disappears by early summer.

In 1576 the crown-imperial was introduced to Austria, where it was grown in the imperial gardens of Vienna; hence its name. In its own way the plant is stately, but it evokes the true Orient, not Austria. The crown-imperial eventually reached England and was grown in America before the Revolution.

Sweet cicely (*Myrrhis odorata*) grows rapidly to three or four feet and in midspring supports lace doilies of small white flowers above licorice-scented, fernlike foliage. Hot, searing sun and dry soil are its enemies, but it can take morning sun and afternoon shade rather well in the North. Usually the plant performs best if cut to the ground after bloom, which allows fresh new foliage to shoot up and be in respectable shape through summer (though in some drought years I have had to cut it back a second time). Extra peat moss dug into the soil at planting time helps retain moisture.

For additional height in the back of the border, turn to shrubs. You have a choice of compact-rooted sorts, whose branches will capture the eye in winter, summer-flowering sorts to lend some interest at that season, or spring bloomers, if you want to go all out. In the first instance you might choose sungold hypericum (*H. kouytchense*), with polished brown stems and quills of yellow flowers in summer; *Kerria japonica*, with green twigs in winter and orange-yellow flowers in spring; or a variegated red-twig dogwood (*Cornus alba* 'Elegantissima'). In the second instance, summer bloomers such as hills-of-snow hydrangea (*Hydrangea arborescens* 'Grandiflora'), Russian-sage (*Perovskia atriplicifolia*) with blue spikes, or bluebeard (*Caryopteris* × *clandonensis* 'Blue Mist') are logical candidates.

Spring-blooming shrubs are as common as corn in Kansas. A few good ones for our purpose are the dwarf pink flowering almond (*Prunus glandulosa* var. *sinensis*); white star magnolia (*Magnolia stellata*), with a good winter outline; and a witch-hazel relative, *Fothergilla major*, with white thimbles of flowers and good yellow-orange autumn color. The tree peony (*Paeonia suffruticosa*), which is actually shrubby, has exquisite pink, red, yellow, or white flowers. Flowering quince (*Chaenomeles speciosa*) in orange, red, pink, or white is a sound choice, as is bridal-wreath (*Spiraea prunifolia*). Do avoid forsythia in a mixed planting, because its excessively lanky growth will suck up good border space just as eggplant absorbs olive oil.

For a change of pace grow *Spiraea japonica* 'Goldflame'. This shrub has bright orange-yellow foliage which is most intense in spring. Prune the branches heavily in late winter, then again after the first flush of growth has dulled, to encourage still another flush. This will sacrifice the pink flowers, which are quite worth sacrificing. The leaves of 'Goldflame' make an excellent foil for perennials in the one- to two-foot range with yellow or orange flowers.

Taller ornamental grasses, mainly *Miscanthus* and *Calamagrostis*, are useful in spring compared with many plants; they also add interest to the border later when in bloom and when their leaves change color in autumn. *Miscanthus sinensis* 'Purpurascens', which is one of the shorter cultivars, grows to about four feet and has attractive purplish tints as cool weather approaches. Other appropriate *Miscanthus* cultivars for superior foliage are 'Variegatus' and 'Strictus', which attain close to six feet in height, and the refined, narrow-leaved 'Gracillimus', topping off at five. These all have a good winter effect, but you should cut away the old foliage before new growth starts in the succeeding spring.

Intermediate-size grasses particularly useful for midborder positions include blue oat grass (*Helictotrichon sempervirens*), the golden-leaved *Deschampsia flexuosa* 'Aurea', and variegated moor grass (*Molinia caerulea* 'Variegata'). For a bolder foliage effect in a large border, even if you dislike Adam's-needles, try one of its superb variegated cultivars, *Yucca filamentosa* 'Golden Sword.' This bears showy white flowers in summer, but the reason for including it here is the three-foot clump of winning foliage. Treat the plant as a shrub, which it technically is, and don't cut it to the ground in autumn. In front, mass orange wall-flowers (*Erysimum*), *Trollius* × *cultorum* 'Orange Globe', or even apricot pansies purchased from the garden center in earliest spring.

MIDDLE OF THE BORDER

Let's look at early flowering perennials for the middle of the border, starting with good blues. European cornflower (*Centaurea montana*) is an old standby, but prune it sharply after the first wave of flowers to keep it from becoming a derelict in growth habit and to encourage more flowering. It looks great with lamb's-ears (*Stachys byzantina*) in front as an edging plant. Jacob's-ladder (*Po-*

lemonium caeruleum), to two feet with tidy foliage in rungs and little blue saucers of bloom, is an integral part of spring, but 'Blue Pearl' comes from a better oyster. For oysters Rockefeller put chartreuse-flowered lady's-mantle (*Alchemilla mollis*) and the lemony basket-of-gold (*Aurinia saxatilis* 'Citrina') on either side. A less common but available white-flowered variant, *Polemonium caeruleum* var. *lacteum*, has lots of potential uses too.

Greek-valerian (*P. reptans*) is a lower-growing polemonium flowering two or three weeks earlier. It is very attractive with the yellow daisies of *Doronicum caucasicum* 'Magnificum' or the chrome yellow bracts of *Euphorbia epithymoides*, sometimes listed as *E. polychroma*. Greek-valerian is neither Greek nor a valerian. This plant is native to the eastern and midwestern United States, and it is too late to change the well-established common name of this false Hellene, so consider it a *feta accompli*.

The summer foliage of these polemoniums is not something you would normally want to display at the garden club flower show, and in the case of *P. reptans* it usually disappears, mildewed or not. Light shade helps a bit, but the fundamental problem of dog-day droop occurs there too. Some years I have even resorted to the fast shuffle, removing Greek-valerian and the similarly summer-tawdry doronicum from the border to an out-of-the-way nursery area after bloom and setting a few plants of *Coreopsis* 'Moonbeam' in their place. Then in autumn I exchange all of them once more. Mary Ann disapproves of this practice, calling it Victorian bedding in disguise. She would prefer to keep the combination in place, sprigging in two or three trays of *Salvia farinacea* or a dusty-miller such as *Senecio* 'Silverdust' purchased in the annuals section of a garden center in late spring. There are no arguments. Whoever is close enough to the border to do the repair work at the end of May gets his or her way.

Bluestar (*Amsonia tabernaemontana*) blooms for a couple of weeks on willowy three- to four-foot stems toward the end of the period of effectiveness for the early border. The small flowers are in modest clusters and have almost the same steel blue tint as globe thistle. Pinch the tips of new shoots in early spring for a better effect. Autumn foliage is a nice clear yellow or orange-yellow, usually better in the South and Midwest, where these plants rank higher on the perennial ladder than in the Northeast.

A more compact version of bluestar, *A. t.* var. *montana*, growing to about two feet in good soil, has more flower in relation to foliage and is more versatile for most border situations. In either case there are few pests, and plants are drought-tolerant. Amsonias are like suspenders — unexciting but dependable, and with a purpose.

A heavy-blooming selection of the oxeye daisy of the field, *Chrysanthemum leucanthemum* 'May Queen', has showy white flowers on two-foot stems for weeks, but be careful to remove the fading bloom stalks to avoid an overabundance of seedlings. In addition, plants need yearly division for restraint. 'May Queen', which is sometimes listed incorrectly as a Shasta daisy in catalogues, yields as good a cut flower as the later-blooming Shastas, though it is smaller.

Another candidate for the spring border is the white-flowered form of honesty or silver-dollar plant (*Lunaria annua*). Despite the botanical name, this member of the mustard family (Cruciferae) is a biennial, and it is capable of self-sowing in the same freewheeling way as the magenta-flowered species from which it is derived. Height is two to three feet, and the curious parchment-covered pods pose interest long after bloom has passed, indeed often till the next winter. *Lunaria annua* seems to grow equally well in sun or shade.

Opposite: Cushion spurge (*Euphorbia epithymoides*), in the foreground, and leopard's-bane (*Doronicum caucasicum*) are candidates for the spring border.
Below: European cornflower, or perennial bachelor's-button (*Centaurea montana*), an old-time stalwart of late spring, usually repeats bloom if cut back sharply after the first wave. In the background are *Achillea* 'Moonshine' (left) and lamb's-ears (*Stachys byzantina*).

Our two earliest columbines are the eastern native, *Aquilegia canadensis*, with familiar red-and-yellow flowers on one- to two-foot stalks, and a stubby white-flowered rock garden sort from Japan, *Aquilegia flabellata* 'Nana Alba', whose name is almost as long as the plant is tall, about eight inches. *Aquilegia canadensis* is at home in sun or shade, and the little runt does best in sun, though we have grown it quite passably in light shade. Each species has wispy foliage in summer and is subject to siege by the leaf miner in areas where that vile little pest abounds. They both self-sow and in time make their own informal scheme, which is frequently more attractive than ours.

One very early flowering herbaceous peony, not to be remotely confused with the big hybrid sorts that come later, deserves consideration for our border. This is the fern-leaf peony (*Paeonia tenuifolia*), which went west with the wagon trains last century and persisted in Illinois and Michigan gardens after the old farmhouses crumbled. It is not much over a foot tall and is easy to mistake for a thread-leaf coreopsis when not in bloom. The small flowers are crimson, and there is a double-flowered cultivar, 'Plena', which lasts longer in bloom. Note that the foliage disappears naturally in late summer, so don't discard the plants by mistake. Similar selections with precocious flowers and low height are listed by Klehm Nursery, Rte. 5, 197 Penny Rd., South Barrington, IL 60010.

UP FRONT

There is no shortage of good frontals for the early border. Silver mound (*Artemisia schmidtiana*) is always most striking in its spring bun stage, which is a prime reason for it to be such a well-known perennial in the cooler parts of the country, where it is best adapted. To make extra use of border space, employ it as an edging plant, setting little groups of the small, very-early-to-bloom *Crocus chrysanthus* 'E. A. Bowles' or a similar cultivar in between. By late spring the artemisia has covered the evidence of the old crocus foliage.

Another thought for displaying silver mound is to interplant it with the wonderful maroon-leaf coralbells, *Heuchera micrantha* 'Palace Purple', whose small white flowers in late summer are pleasant if unnecessary afterthoughts of nature. Keep plants of the two a couple of feet apart, because by early summer silver mound has usually become more open in growth habit, resembling a silver cloud.

After midsummer in typically rich, evenly moist border soil the foliage of *Artemisia schmidtiana*, as if recuperating from a binge, flops over, and the center of the plant becomes bald. You can repair its appearance by pruning plants down halfway, then turning your back for two weeks while new growth emerges from the base. You can sometimes kill old plants this way, but if you divide silver mound every two years or so in earliest spring, this problem may not occur. This artemisia, which is native to the mountains and coastal regions of northern Japan, is accustomed to a lean diet. Despite its wide use — and usefulness — in American perennial borders, it is most at home in the rock garden, where in meager soil the attractive mound shape can be retained through summer.

We can also turn to the rock garden for additional help for the front of the early border. Forget the wimps. The more vigorous plants there, the ones that rock garden purists usually like to rail about because of their smother-thyneighbor policies, are ideal for us. Start with A for *Arabis* and go to the very finest, *A. caucasica* 'Flore Pleno', which has white flowers that last for many weeks because they are double. *A. c.* 'Variegata', with silver-edged leaves, is also a possibility.

Continue to *Aurinia saxatilis*, the brassy basket-of-gold, but select the lemonflowered cultivar 'Citrina', which has more border uses because of its softer color. Both *Arabis* and *Aurinia* should be cut back sharply after bloom to encourage longevity and good foliage, for which neither is otherwise noted.

Pasque- or Easter flower (*Anemone pulsatilla*), perhaps best in its reddish purple color form, is for us too. The very fine, silky seed heads look as though they have undergone a permanent wave.

Complete the *A*'s with *Ajuga pyramidalis*, the safest bugle for borders because it is a clump-former, not a spreader like *A. reptans*. The good dark blue flowers complement just about anything.

There are twenty-six letters in the alphabet, and they offer a bewildering source of rock garden expatriates or deportees for us, so let us concentrate on just a few of the remaining best. The intensity of white in the flowers of perennial candytuft (*Iberis sempervirens*) makes even bridal-wreath look as though it should be tossed in the washing maching with a generous dose of bleach. Candytuft is at its best where winters are not severe. In cold climates, where winter scorching of the evergreen foliage is a problem, plants benefit from a light covering of conifer boughs or salt hay. A good reduction of shoots after flowering is beneficial. 'Alexander's White' is a sound border-size cultivar and has better growth habit than most selections. The same is true with 'Purity'. 'Autumn Snow', with repeat bloom later in the year, is also a candidate.

For years I was lukewarm toward the spring vetchling (*Lathyrus vernus*), a tidy little member of the pea genus with overwashed purple flowers. I could say nothing really good about it, but nothing really bad either. Then Beth Chatto, the English nurserywoman, introduced us to the selection 'Albo-roseus', which comes true from seed, at least if grown some distance from the species itself. It is still prim and proper, but the rosy pink lipstick marks on white flowers give this vetchling a hint of deeper passions at work. Keep the plants up front; otherwise they may be lost.

Moss pink (*Phlox subulata*) is mostly seen bearing bawdy pink flowers with grass growing up, around, and between them on eroded sun-baked slopes that should have been terraced. It is a native plant in parts of the East, but the most strident color forms, which are not all that common in the wild, were the first ones collected. They have delighted gardeners with tin eyes ever since. However, good white, lavender-blue, and clear pink selections and hybrids are available, and these are the ones to turn to for border frontals. Just be careful to keep the grass out. Try soft pink 'Millstream Laura', a hybrid, interplanted with *Heuchera micrantha* 'Palace Purple', and you will never look on moss pinks the same way again. This phlox is a vigorous grower and should be divided every year or two when used in a border.

Veronica prostrata, quite different from the tall summer-blooming speedwells with big spikes, is a solid frontal too. 'Heavenly Blue' is the standard bearer, but there is also a white-flowered cultivar ('Alba') and a pale pink ('Mrs. Holt'). The species has a hearty constitution, and plants divide well after bloom or in late summer, or you can increase them easily by cuttings.

If you want linear-leaved plants as frontals in the border, choose glaucous, reddish, or variegated kinds that stand out from lawn grasses. These include blue fescue (*Festuca ovina* 'Glauca'), bulbous oat grass (*Arrhenatherum elatius* 'Variegatum'), and Japanese blood grass (*Imperata cylindrica* 'Rubra'). The broad gray-green rubber daggers of *Iris pumila* are useful toward the border front, too. Many of the attractive bearded iris colors are available in *I. pumila* cultivars, which grow about eight inches tall and flower several weeks earlier than the big bearded sorts.

BULBS

No spring border would be complete without the pre-eminent plants of that season, bulbs; but avoid the temptation of an overload if you want a distinctive display. I have seen a few borders wrecked by bulbs over the years. There is always a price to pay for their beauty in such a setting, because you must leave the bulb foliage to wither slowly if these plants are to put on a show the next year. Also consider the gaping holes left by the ultimate demise of their leaves. Ferns (mainly the lady fern for partly sunny areas), daylilies, gypsophila, and annuals can help fill these blanks. The more bulbs you use, however, the greater the problem becomes, and eventually you may have more holes than ship in the ship.

How to minimize the damage? First, plan on keeping bulbs to a total space of not more than 15 or 20 percent of the border. Second, give a larger measure of representation to the early blooming kinds, whose foliage is usually smaller and will leave the scene earlier. Third, treat Darwin and other big tulips as annuals and discard them after bloom.

In our experience, tulips have a high mortality rate, even when they are deeply planted, heavily fed, and copiously watered at the right times. The cost of our labor to coddle them along cannot be justified when the modest cost of a dozen or two new tulip bulbs each autumn is considered. Bear in mind that a wide range of animals greatly enjoy the gustatory delight of tulips, too.

The various species tulips and near-species tulips, although not as flamboyant as the fancy hybrids, have a better track record for longevity and grace. Experiment in particular with *Tulipa tarda* and *T. kauffmanniana* selections, including 'Gaiety'. Among the larger-growing species types or primitive tulips that give the strong color impact of the fancy hybrids, try 'Shakespeare' and 'Stresa', which would put some fire engines to shame.

Daffodils, which are the most dependably perennial of the larger bulbs, are also the biggest offenders in borders, because their foliage is slowest to ripen fully. On Daffodil Hill at Brooklyn Botanic Garden the process is not totally completed until early August, a fact that always gives me pause when I site these plants in the landscape. It helps to plant daffodils far back in borders, not toward the front, where their postbloom letdown is especially noticeable. Consider also sinking them in the border in good-sized planters that you can lift after bloom and shift to the sidelines, then move back in autumn. This can involve a lot of extra work if you are particularly enthusiastic when ordering from bulb catalogues. A better solution, it seems to me, is to naturalize large numbers of daffodils around the perimeter of a property, between shrubs and anyplace where they won't be an eyesore after flowering.

· 5 ·

A Garden
of Thugs

OUR BORDERS at Hillside that are the greatest distance from the house invariably get the least attention. One of them is called the eviction border. It contains
thug plants uprooted from polite areas of the garden because of their globe-
conquering proclivities. We can expect some internecine warfare, and we take a
perverse pleasure in seeing the bullies fight it out — feisty physostegias gaining
strangleholds on lemme-at-em lysimachias, merciless monardas biting the shins
of mighty macleayas.

As a graduate student living over a Third Avenue bar in New York, I over-
heard my share of heated brawls on St. Patrick's Day evenings, but the quiet
donnybrooks in our eviction border have been more protracted and of greater
interest, if lacking in Irish tenor. On a sultry summer morning after the primulas
have been watered and the stokesias tidied in borders near the house, when the
garden becomes a bit wearying, there is always the eviction border. We can
count on a ringside seat, for visitors don't venture this way often. It is our secret
garden, and like nearly every secret garden I have seen, it is on its way to
abandonment. Out of site, out of mind.

THE WINNER IS BEE BALM

In my early years of gardening I was grateful for anything to grow. One Easter,
when I was seven, my mother gave me some pansies to plant, which I did, green
side up as I remember. They expired soon, and I took it personally. New gardeners need a sense of confidence, and when I was in my twenties, taking

another stab at gardening, I was very happy to discover bee balm (*Monarda didyma*), which in our climate is a very easy perennial to grow. I stress the phrase "in our climate" because a few years ago I met a gardener from Texas who considered bee balm "iffy," a wonderful word conceived and propagated by rock gardeners. There was a time when I considered 95 percent of the plants in our garden iffy, and we weren't even attempting to grow bluebonnet, the Lone Star State's official flower, which is not a conspicuous success in Connecticut.

Bee balm, especially the vivid cultivar 'Cambridge Scarlet', has stayed with us over the years, to the consternation of Mary Ann and gardening friends who gently inquire of her, "Hasn't he grown out of that phase yet? You poor dear. He must be very difficult to live with." Every other April Mary Ann's consternation becomes dismay, when it is her turn to divide the bee balm, which is still easy to uproot without marring in that month. Fortunately, the clumps are shallow-rooted, and a few deft incisions with the spade, almost like cuts in a deep-dish apple pie, result in ample divisions for the summer's display. We then reset these about eighteen inches apart in soil that has been replenished with a few shovelsful of compost. Otherwise, groupings tend to fade away, except at the periphery. The remaining fragments go into the garbage can, unless a new gardener in need of confidence is around that day.

In my estimation, it has been worth the extra effort we give to bee balm, which apart from summer phlox and tall delphiniums has required more of our time over the years than any other perennial. No summer has it failed us in lavish bloom, though if plants are kept too dry or grown in shade, powdery mildew may afflict the mint-scented leaves. We have a succession of brilliant, clear red flowers from mid-July until early September, and these provide nectar for our most fascinating bird of summer, the ruby-throated hummingbird. True, hummers will visit other perennials, including summer phlox, columbine, and pulmonaria, but they are most conspicuous on the bee balm.

But what about the plant consorts for bee balm? A strong color such as this, a beacon from the distance, can be dangerous in the garden because it dominates, and a little goes a long way. Sometimes the green foliage of surrounding plants is enough, or the maroon foliage of *Perilla frutescens* 'Atropurpurea', an annual that will self-sow from year to year. One approach is to group bee balm with *Phlox paniculata* 'Mt. Fuji', whose white flowers last as long as any phlox's. *Veronica* 'Sunny Border Blue', perhaps our longest flowering and most satisfactory spiky speedwell of summer, helps fix the combination.

I should mention that if you can throw maintenance cautions to the winds, one of the loveliest combinations is an interplanting of bee balm and *Artemisia ludoviciana* 'Silver King', but not in light sandy soils, where the artemisia will run amuck. As it is, both the bee balm and the artemisia will probably require lifting and resetting each year. 'Silver King', of course, is grown for its skeletal (at maturity) gray foliage, which is eminently useful for arrangements in the home; but if you want to go artemisia-wild in the garden, consider also planting white mugwort (*Artemisia lactiflora*) behind the bee balm. If the soil is good, with plenty of moisture retention, in late summer the flower clusters of this mugwort, looking like a white goldenrod, will rise a couple of feet higher than the bee balm. *Artemisia lactiflora* has green foliage similar to that of common mugwort (*A. vulgaris*) but does not have the latter's terribly weedy traits. In fact, in our clay loam it is one of the better-behaved artemisias.

Red bee balm is not every gardener's cup of tea. Mary Ann, for example, much prefers *Monarda* 'Croftway Pink', a hybrid of *M. didyma* with *M. fistulosa*. It is not nearly as aggressive, and it serves as a good base for some fine combinations. We like 'Croftway Pink' with purple coneflower (*Echinacea purpurea*), *Phlox paniculata* 'Starfire', and globe thistle (*Echinops* 'Taplow Blue'). 'Prairie Night' and 'Blue Stocking', both of which are shades of purple-violet careening toward magenta, are other monardas to try with various pink phloxes that carry a hint of purple. A few plants nearby of white false dragonhead (*Physostegia virginiana* 'Summer Snow'), a much less rampant cultivar than the species from which it is derived, can aid the marriage. If you want more body, add white coneflower (*Echinacea purpurea* 'White Lustre').

LIFE AMONG THE LYSIMACHIAS

I have always admired lysimachias more in other people's gardens than in our own, because they have victimized several plant neighborhoods here. The roots don't walk, trot, or even canter. They glide through the soil like a Vaseline-coated submarine through the sea, emerging periodically to snare navelworts, sea-lavenders, anemones, or whatever is in their way, save cement. Their motto is "Today the eviction border, tomorrow the garden." Only one species we have grown, *Lysimachia ephemerum,* a three-footer with subdued white flowers in August, is safe enough in the polite company of a border, unless you are willing to dig a trench around the others each spring. Still, they can be a pretty lot.

Gooseneck (*Lysimachia clethroides*), with three- to four-foot stalks bearing arched spikes of white flowers that the uncharitable, including Mary Ann, say resemble a veronica in drought, is the most conspicuous lysimachia in summer bloom. Masses of it are lovely in sunny areas with purple coneflower (*Echinacea purpurea*) in the background, as at the Berkshire Garden Center in Stockbridge, Massachusetts. Bear in mind that gooseneck and other lysimachias, while tolerant of average soil moisture in borders, are most luxuriant in wet soils along ponds and streams. In fact, gooseneck is one of the best plants for July-August flowers in a naturalized planting along a pond, blooming at the same time as purple loosestrife (*Lythrum salicaria*), another thug in its feral form. However, please note that the common garden cultivars of *Lythrum* are not invasive.

Purple loosestrife, whose flowers are closer to magenta-pink than purple, has belatedly been discovered by nature groups as a weed in wetlands, where it crowds out native plants along streambanks. It is an Old World species, as most of our worst-offender weeds are, and attempts to eradicate it are now as fruitless as trying to do in the dandelion and field daisy, which are also immigrants. Purple loosestrife's roots are woody, and anyone who has tried to dig the plant

Gooseneck (*Lysimachia clethroides*) belongs in a meadow or in a garden of thugs. It is a beautiful colonizer but not for the polite border. White flowers are borne on three- to four-foot stalks in midsummer.

knows that the most practical way to kill large numbers is with herbicides, which won't strike many naturalists as a sensible method of extermination in wetlands. It is also a valuable bee plant.

Some of my naturalist friends consider me especially perverse when in summer I venture miles out of my way to admire a wet meadow of purple loosestrife and then return home with a glowing report. Driving along Route 22 in eastern New York State from Brewster to Millerton in July is a greater joy for me than seeing the vast plantings of florist anemones and ranunculus north of San Diego or the fields of tulips in the Netherlands, both of which strike me as catalogue slick. A pinky purple mist of lythrum spikes to the horizon, broken occasionally with white Queen Anne's lace and sky-blue chicory, is one of the finest sights in the East. These scenes are our American Monets, and no gardener has painted finer ones.

Still, I do not esteem the *Lythrum* cultivars highly. Our garden has groupings of only two, 'Robert' and 'Morden Pink', now that we have discarded 'Happy', a semidwarf that did not bloom well for us. It is true that the flower color range is narrow, and I recall a nurseryman friend telling me that his firm tried in vain to extend this range by irradiating the seed. Also, Japanese beetles devour the leaves as voraciously as Yuppies gorge on their prey at a sushi bar. However, perhaps the main reason for my reserve toward purple loosestrife in the garden is its overabundance in the wild. For the same reason, Americans have never taken to goldenrod as a garden plant.

"Loosestrife" is a confusing name, because it also refers to one of the lysimachias, *L. punctata*, which is frequently called yellow loosestrife. A good patch is pretty in a distant, more-or-less sunny corner of the garden, but it is almost as much of a menace in neat borders as *L. clethroides*. It grows about three feet tall and has small but abundant yellow flowers in early summer. Those who like orange marigolds will probably like it as a companion, with the yellow tint continued late in summer by perennial black-eyed Susan (*Rudbeckia fulgida* 'Goldsturm'). Blue columbines may soften the combination early in the season, followed by bluebeard (*Caryopteris*) in late summer. But don't give *Lysimachia punctata* to a friend.

TOLL OF THE BELLS

False rampion (*Campanula rapunculoides*), a three-foot-tall bellflower, is the match for any thug plant. I will always have a note in my little black book about a certain gardener who, in his fascination with germinating hundreds of kinds of seeds each year without much care as to proper identification, gave me plants of this garden buster under another name, *C. sarmatica*, which is a lovely species. I think we have finally eradicated the fleshy roots of our romping rampion, but when I tread near the area where it was growing, particularly on a cool October evening during the full moon, I expect to see Count Dracula rising from the grave, trying to pull one of the roots that has pierced his heart.

I think the Korean *C. takesimana*, which has large ghostly pink-and-gray bells on three-foot stalks all summer, will be better behaved, but since I was able to make twelve healthy divisions from a one-year pot-grown plant this autumn, it will be on probation. It should be very striking in a sunny spot with blue oat grass (*Helictotrichon sempervirens*) in the foreground, but I've learned not to count my campanula combinations before the bells toll. I would hate to put a wreath on this one.

Sometimes the gardener learns to love plant devils, especially if there is no alternative. I think I could still eradicate one of the clustered bellflowers, *Campanula glomerata* 'Superba', if I set my mind to it. During June and early July the vibrant, almost electric, dark purple bells crowd around the two-and-one-half-foot stalks, extending even around the leaf axils. At that time such a thought would be heresy to everyone except Mary Ann and Kathi, our nursery manager, who have rescued a border or two from it over the years.

'Superba' is not a prim or prissy plant and deserves a no man's land at the sunny edge of the garden with lady or marsh ferns in the background to cool its passionate color. In a large, informal, sunny area it is a wonderful companion for the pale yellow perennial foxglove (*Digitalis grandiflora*), which grows three to four feet tall and blooms at the same time. Both plants look best in sizable groups, which are not difficult to attain. Be sure to cut the campanula stalks to the base of the plant after flowering so they won't wither in an unsightly manner that encourages your mate to say, "Why are we growing that ugly weed? I'm going to pull it out tomorrow." Chances are this won't happen, but why take the chance?

It is worth noting that 'Crown of Snow', a white-flowered cultivar of *Campanula glomerata*, does not spread invasively from the roots in our clay loam. One border planting has been in place for six years without need for division, whereas 'Superba' needs yearly division when grown as a border plant. Blooming as it does in late June and July, 'Crown of Snow' is fine for deflecting the heat from vermilion ruffians such as *Lychnis* × *arkwrightii* 'Vesuvius', *L.* × *haageana*, and Maltese-cross (*L. chalcedonica*). It would work as well in making the rose campion (*L. coronaria*) an almost respectable rose. This campion, incidentally, is prime material for a thug garden if it is allowed to go to seed, for germination is conspicuously triumphant.

The principal increase of the pale yellow foxglove is by seed too, which is sometimes overly successful. We always like to have young plants coming along, but not an army of them, so we cut about 80 percent of the stalks to the ground after bloom. *Digitalis grandiflora* is a fairly stable perennial compared with most foxgloves, which have biennial tendencies, though they are often capable of living an extra year or two, especially if deadheaded just after bloom.

I remember seeing a few plants of *Digitalis grandiflora* in flower the first June after we moved to Hillside, naturalized in a rough meadow near a stone wall. For the next ten years my father, who was then retired and almost looking forward to the grass growing so he could have an excuse to mow, inadvertently brought this area back to lawn. Then, in the last two or three years of his life, he was not as careful about cutting the verges. To my surprise the yellow foxgloves, present all that time but restrained to basal foliage by the mower,

In early summer, *Campanula glomerata* 'Superba' is lovely in large informal colonies with the pale yellow perennial foxglove (*Digitalis grandiflora*). They naturalize well, the first by stolons, the second by seeds. Both intend to take over the world.

started to bloom again. Although scorned by some because it is common, *Digitalis grandiflora* has given grace to many other kinds of plants. If you do not care to use this foxglove with *Campanula glomerata* 'Superba', try it with the taller, nonaggressive *C. latifolia* var. *macrantha*, which has violet bells. The two at their peak in June are stately and synergistic.

ARTEMIS LEAPS

Many good things, as well as bad, happen in the garden by accident. The difference between success and failure for some gardeners is to spot the good ones, wheel the losses — when possible — to the compost heap, and be silent. Your spouse may know that something worked because of your dumb luck, but you are not obliged to tell the visiting committee of the local garden club. What's more, don't call luck dumb, because you may be compromising your case, even to your mate. Luck is never dumb, especially when it is good.

Roman wormwood (*Artemisia pontica*) and *Geranium renardii* are a perennially attractive duo in the McGourty garden, provided we divide the wormwood yearly to keep it from conquering.

With that in mind, I would still like to make an admission, which, please note, is not a confession. Last year the finest new plant combination in our garden was based on an accident. From a midwestern nursery we had ordered some plants labeled *Artemisia michauxiana*. I am fond of artemisias in general and over the years have transported to the town dump only four kinds. These include the dreaded mugwort (*A. vulgaris*), whose common name should in perpetuity bear the harsh adjective. Also on my hit list have been wormwood (*A. absinthium*), which as absinthe pickled the brains of many artists and writers in Paris at the turn of the century, and *Artemisia annua*, a thug whose fresh green lace-doily foliage I originally admired on a very vacant lot in Outer Brooklyn. The annual artemisia was that borough's equivalent of fireweed (*Epilobium*) in the 1970s, as tenements were set ablaze with abandon, but few people's minds were on plants then.

The fourth artemisia was Roman wormwood (*A. pontica*), which has pretty, feathery gray foliage that is exceedingly refined. By most rights it should have been a superb edging plant, growing just a foot or so tall, setting off lawn and border perfectly. Upon my discovery that it was in fact a gladiator, I took our plants to the dump. Some years later a friend under the influence of herbs gave me a few more, unsolicited. I inspected the attractive foliage and mused that Roman wormwood might have mended its ways since its last, abbreviated stay with us. The prodigal was welcomed home, though planted in the confinement of a sunken bucket with drain holes. Several months later I caught the wormwood as it jumped pot, and I took it to the dump with a vow to my wife and Zeus that it would never reappear in our garden. Mary Ann let it be known that she had disdained this artemisia from the beginning.

Years passed and memories lapsed. The little package of *Artemisia michauxiana*, a northwestern species I had never seen, arrived from the mail-order nursery one fine spring day. The contents were in fine condition, and we were delighted with the beautiful lacy foliage. We decided that the little plants would be most advantageously displayed if we were to interplant them in our kitchen border among a grouping of *Geranium renardii*. This cranesbill from the Caucasus, unlike the common sorts with deeply cleft foliage, has leaves more or less rounded like those of a pelargonium, the common house plant known confusingly as geranium. However, the leaves of our cranesbill are smaller and sage green. The combination was like caviar and cream cheese on a Ritz cracker — perhaps not to the taste of purists, but it did good duty, and even Mary Ann liked it. Many of our friends even asked to be put on the reserved list for little snippets of the artemisia when we had a sufficient number for division.

Inevitably, and in slow, painful stages, we became aware at last that our *Artemisia michauxiana* was in fact *A. pontica*. A photograph of the true *michauxiana* in Rickett's wildflower volume for the Northwest confirmed the mistake. The Roman wormwood will be divided yearly as a measure of necessary restraint, a small price to pay for the beauty the plants generate in combination with the cranesbill, at least at this time.

BREWING WITH TANSY

I have always enjoyed groups of ferns with a background of pines, especially white pine (*Pinus strobus*), because of the neat contrast of foliage shape and color. Colonizers such as hay-scented fern (*Dennstaedtia punctilobula*) and even sensitive fern (*Onoclea sensibilis*) are much maligned because gardeners plant them in cramped quarters and expect them to behave as if they were at a black-tie dinner before the debutante ball. Both ferns, particularly the sensitive fern, can endure a fair amount of sun, but like most of their kind they are best in the shade. By and large this rules them out for use on the south and west sides of pines, unless other trees soften the afternoon sun.

Why not plant the fern-leaved tansy (*Tanacetum vulgare* 'Crispum') on such sites? It is a sun-loving colonizer with foliage that ranks with the most attractive in perennialdom. Fern-leaved tansy grows about four feet tall and has modestly attractive yellow flowers, resembling small buttons, in late summer. Plants hold up better in drought than many perennials; but if they become shaggy as the season progresses, you can cut them to the ground to encourage a round of fresh new foliage. The bright green crinoline leaves, when cut for the house, can serve as an excellent foil in flower arrangements. In the garden few insects or animals seem to take an interest in the foliage.

In sunny areas fern-leaved tansy can assume several roles that ferns play in the shade. For example, you can interplant daffodils among this colonizer for spring effect, when the new tansy foliage is particularly appealing. Later, as the daffodil foliage becomes dingy, the fully grown leaves of the tansy will hide the evidence.

Sounds like a fine plant? It is — like many other aggressors, when planted in the right spot, away from delicate border prey. As with Roman wormwood, I have taken fern-leaved tansy from genteel society to the dump several times. The Old World species from which it is derived, *Tanacetum vulgare*, is sometimes seen naturalized along roadsides, but without the ruffles it has little garden interest. I wonder if gardening mothers of an earlier time were trying to do it in when they brewed a tea of tansy leaves or made a tansy pudding at Easter. It is pretty foul-tasting stuff, indeed a very bitter herb, and as modern medicine discovered, it is toxic.

TYING THE RIBBON GRASS

Gary Koller, our good friend from the Arnold Arboretum near Boston, visits us occasionally, but he is always frisked as he emerges from the car. Gary's enthusiasm for all kinds of plants, especially thugs, is almost legend. His defense, as he drops a pesty petasites or a piranhic bamboo at the edge of the driveway, usually runs something like this: "Look, guys, I have a small city garden and it's not the easiest place to grow plants, so I'm always on the lookout for ones that will grow anywhere. Wait till you see this one." This sometimes gives us a slight pause, but unlike some of his confrères in the botanical world, Gary happens to be a very accomplished home gardener with a good aesthetic sense. Of his garden I will always remember a lovely May scene of the old-fashioned bleeding-heart (*Dicentra spectabilis*), with its valentines of flowers, rising above a shag rug of the variegated archangel (*Lamiastrum galeobdolon* 'Variegatum'), which is not an angelic plant. The house on one side and a brick wall on the other kept the archangel from flight.

On one of his visits Gary brought us with customary enthusiasm a hefty clump of ribbon grass (*Phalaris arundinacea* 'Picta'), known in bygone days as gardener's-garters. It is a beautiful rustic, with cooling silver-variegated leaves on stalks growing three to four feet tall. However, it is easy to keep plants lower by shears to encourage fresh foliage as the season progresses. This is important, because by midsummer the old leaves become tatty if there has been dry weather. At the Pepsico headquarters in Purchase, New York, I have even seen ribbon grass mowed in late summer to a few inches in height, forming a refreshing, dense carpet.

Knowing that Gary would eventually be back and no doubt would want a progress report, not an egress report, we planted the ribbon grass in our sun border, where it decided to engage all innocent bystanders. For two Aprils we tried subjugation by division, but by August the roots were on their way to new conquests. Finally Gary visited again that summer, and after the routine frisk, I asked with a forced smile if he might suggest an appropriate site for the ribbon grass. Immediately he replied, "Oh, I forgot to tell you, that plant can spread a bit. Why not put it at the base of that retaining wall, making a small border strip for it with the front side being the lawn?" This we did, and to this day mower and wall have kept the ribbon grass honest, pretty, and tied up.

We have discovered a few other relatively safe uses for ribbon grass. Its best performance is in broken sun, not hot, searing sun all day long. It does quite well in partial shade, bringing an injection of light to subdued areas that are too rough around the edges. In such conditions the growth habit of ribbon grass is more open, but roots are less aggressive. However, dense shade usually causes plants to wither away. For a winning combination, try ribbon grass near the trunks of birch trees.

I have mentioned a number of fine plants with one unfortunate flaw, which can often be put to advantage, but what about the eviction border at Hillside? The plants have fought it out for some years now, but they are all on the wane because of an unexpected alliance from the outside. No, it is not Mary Ann and Kathi sneaking out at night with flashlight to douse the area with herbicides. Rather, the winners are the native goldenrods, asters, and Joe-Pye weed. There may be a moral to this, but it is up to the reader to decide. Meanwhile, keep your eye on the trowel.

· 6 ·

Of Cabbages, Kings, and Kohlrabi

THERE SHE STOOD with tears in her eyes on a sunny August afternoon when all seemed right with the world. I tried to console her.

"But just think, Mary Ann. We can dry them in the sun, give them some shellac, and make baseball bats out of them."

The tears became sobs.

"I checked the zucchini just three days ago, and they seemed so small," she said. A dozen of the long green clubs were strewn around the vegetable garden. I knew very well that the compost heap would be the ultimate beneficiary.

"You could rise from that hammock once in a while and walk out to the vegetable garden to check the vegetables," she went on. "Besides, *real* men are supposed to take an interest in vegetable gardens." The key word here, veteran observers of such internecine horticultural scenes will note, is *out*. Here was my out.

"Dear, the real problem isn't you, it isn't even me, and it may not be the zucchini at all."

"What do you mean?" she asked suspiciously.

"It's distance, of course. The vegetable garden is so far from the house that no one can be expected to check the zucchini daily. Out of sight, out of mind. The answer is to get them down near the kitchen, where we can keep an eye on them. Two if necessary."

"But vegetable gardens are so boring," Mary Ann protested. "I don't want any ugly rectangular plot with plants lined up in rows as if at attention. Besides, around our house is so pretty, with the perennial borders nearby."

"Dear, I'm not suggesting we move the whole vegetable garden in. Just the zucchini, summer squash, and one or two other vegetables you really have to be alert about. We'll do a kidney-bean–shaped border on the lawn by the end of the driveway. There's good drainage and plenty of sun, just what most veggies need. And when we are preparing the bed, a truck can back up with a load of old cow manure and drop it without putting tracks on the lawn. Six by forty feet ought to be a respectable size for it."

"Well, zucchini has attractive foliage in a way, and summer squash isn't too bad," she mused. "Sort of like a hosta for sun."

The seed was sown, and I rushed to fertilize it. "And we can add some delphiniums and ligularias and cephalarias. They will complement the zucchini well — you know, the vertical with the horizontal, appropriate line material for the eye to feast on. Good gardening is good matchmaking, I always say."

A dark cloud came over her face, and she thundered, "You're a tricky one, McGourty! You're trying to get another perennial border into this garden. No way! I'd just end up having to take care of it."

"Oh, all right, love, I'll meet you more than halfway. I'll dig the bed and let you choose all the plants. Just include some vegetables that have really attractive foliage, and finish off the border with some handsome herbs, unusual ones if they fit in. Arrange everything as if you were doing a perennial border that size. Do groupings, too. We don't want visitors to think we run a roadside stand on the side."

Mary Ann did a rough plan, using zucchini and squash in the spine of the border, which had to be widened a foot (now seven feet all told), since a full-grown cucurbit usually has a girth several times the size of an over-aged fullback. We planned to use the front and rear verges of this island border for other plants with a hefty leaf texture that could hold up well with their husky companions.

COLES TO NEWCASTLE

Neither of us is unduly fond of cabbage, there being a limit to the amount of coleslaw (not to mention zucchini) that a small family can eat. However, the object of our visual affection was a red cabbage, which has more foliage interest than most hostas do. 'Ruby Perfecta' was the cultivar we planted, but any good slow-to-mature red sort would do. Five or six plants faced down the zucchini quite well, though Gertrude Jekyll probably turned over in her grave and whispered to Lutyens, "These Americans!"

To keep Miss Jekyll resting in peace by planting closely coordinated colors together and grading them appropriately, Mary Ann opted to put another kind

of cole plant, purple kohlrabi ('Early Purple Vienna'), next to the red cabbage as another frontal. It has soft purple-gray notched foliage and brightly colored "bulbs" (tubers, actually) that resemble little basketballs caught in hoops. This was a brave decision, because in one of the off-election years not long ago, a major national polling organization, having nothing better to do with its time, learned from its poll of some gardeners that kohlrabi was America's least popular vegetable. Of course, the pollsters were wrong about Dewey too, and it's possible that not enough Americans have given a fair taste test to kohlrabi, having eaten only the oversized, stringy tubers that get to the supermarkets. Purple kohlrabi has more eye appeal than its white counterpart. Plants grow ten to twelve inches tall, a good height for front-of-the border groupings, and they are spaced about six inches apart. Kohlrabi's one limitation in the ornamental vegetable border is that plants bear their tubers in forty-five days, then become world-weary, so you need two crops for a continuing display. Start a new batch of seedlings in a cold frame in late June and then move them onstage several weeks later to keep the circle unbroken. Adjust the sowing time to your climate, as we live in an area with moderately cool summers.

At the risk of bringing more coles to Newcastle, I should mention kale, ornamental ("flowering") kale, and ornamental cabbage too. Kale itself, if well grown, is an attractive plant, and Mary Ann sometimes incorporates a few plants in the front of the border, usually near cabbages because of the contrast in foliage texture. Kale has crinkled leaves (most notably along the edges), whereas cabbage has smooth foliage; new gardeners, though, might confuse the Savoy-type cabbage with puckered leaves, a good alternate for a frontal site, with kale.

Mary Ann is generous in her planting of this vegetable, usually setting out about fifteen seedlings of a dwarf (to fifteen inches) blue 'Vates' selection, whose young leaves we selectively pick in summer for salad mixings with some of the blander lettuces. Then, as the season progresses and plants get stockier, we cook the leaves as a spinach substitute or make soup. The harvest continues till November or so, when the remainder makes its way to the freezer. In milder climates and even in our own, a longer harvest is possible if the plants are covered with salt hay or evergreen boughs, but deer force the issue with us, ending the season by foraging the plants. On a cool, clear, late autumn night, if

Opposite, top: Silver sage (*Salvia argentea*) blends well with many plants, even culinary kale. *Bottom:* Ornamental kale (*Brassica oleracea* 'Red Peacock') is attractive in autumn and early winter even in a harsh climate.

it is very still, you can almost hear a sentinel buck sing out, "Gang, gang, the kale's all here!" in the McGourtys' vegetable garden.

Ornamental kale, or "flowering kale" as the catalogues call it (all kales flower, but not all are ornamental), is the scene stealer in autumn in the vegetable border. Although we set out young plants in late spring, they are inconspicuous until cool weather after Labor Day turns their centers vivid purplish pink or white. In the highly conspicuous 'Peacock' strain plants can be eighteen to twenty-four inches across, the deeply cut foliage presenting a mass of color that might be deemed vulgar in midsummer by some gardeners. I don't mind ornamental kale a bit in late fall, because it has the scene much to itself, with no competing colors nearby. This is autumn going out with a bang, weeks after tree leaves have fallen. In areas where the fourth season is relatively mild, the display can last far into winter. Oh yes, it's edible too — but a singularly unattractive gray when cooked.

There is no free lunch, except perhaps for insects, one in particular that must be mentioned when the cole vegetables are discussed. This is the imported cabbageworm, which looks like just another little white moth hovering over the garden. It is in fact sighting targets for egg laying in the ruffles and folds of kale and kin. Soon little green worms, as voracious as a group of hyperactive twelve-year-olds at a fast-food restaurant, devour the foliage. You can control them to an extent by hand picking, but over the summer several applications of Bt (*Bacillus thuringiensis*), a biological insecticide that works, may be necessary for good control. Of course, I grew ornamental kale over a period of ten years before the cabbage worms discovered it, but we live in a rural area without gardens nearby, and maybe the word is slow to get around to all the little critters.

As a footnote Mary Ann also chose to include sea-kale (*Crambe maritima*) in the border, mainly because we had a few young plants grown from seed we obtained in Europe, where it is native along the coast. It looks much like a nonheading cabbage, with large, coarse, gray-green, waxy leaves with waved and occasionally indented edges. Growing to at least a couple of feet in height and width in well-nourished soil, sea-kale, which is a perennial, is occasionally used as a frontal plant in large English borders. In our more modest-sized American ones, midborder placement is safest.

Graham Thomas, one of England's leading horticulturists, refers to sea-kale as having "perhaps the most beautiful of all large glaucous leaves" (*Perennial Garden Plants*). Thomas Jefferson thought of it in another manner: "I consider it among the most valuable garden plants. It stands our winter [at Monticello] unprotected, [and] furnishes a vast crop of sprouts from the beginning of December through the whole winter, which are remarkably sweet and delicious" (*Jefferson's Garden Book*). In fact, sea-kale is winter-hardy at least as far north as Vermont.

OTHER VEGETABLES

Lettuce is not the ideal plant for ornamental borders, because you need succession plantings through the season if you are to have a continuing display. Usually three or four plantings are required in our area, which has cooler summers than most, and we always seem to have seedlings coming along in window boxes for eventual transplanting to the border. Looseleaf kinds, not heading types such as 'Iceberg' (which has about as much taste as an iceberg), work best for us, because we can pick a few leaves of the former at a time without marring the display. 'Ruby' is the standard red for ornamental purposes, but it has all the flavor of boiled cardboard, so try 'Red Sails' or 'Red Rapids'. 'Green Ice' and 'Black Seeded Simpson' are green-leaved selections we come back to from year to year. Lettuce is a good vegetable to experiment with, because you lose only a brief period if a particular variety is a disappointment.

Spinach is an attractive vegetable but is for the short term, since it bolts with summer heat, so we give preference in the ornamental border to the Swiss chard known as rhubarb chard. With red midribs and leaves that turn from green to maroon as cooler nights come along in late summer, this is one of the most striking plants of its kind. We start this annual from seed in late April or May, either on the site or indoors for quicker results, and by midsummer it is two feet tall. A dozen or so plants enable us to pick leaves selectively through summer and autumn (sometimes to December) for salads and later for cooked greens. A number of quarts end up in the freezer, too. Occasionally we have leaf miner problems, and if they are severe we skip growing chard for a year or two to try to break the pest's life cycle.

Rhubarb (*Rheum rhabarbarum*) is a subject of at least dual disagreement for Mary Ann and me. I think of it as a bold foliage perennial with striking white flowers that would put a goatsbeard (*Aruncus*) to shame, but to me it is totally worthless in the kitchen — basic cause for a hunger strike. Mary Ann thinks of rhubarb as a superb dessert and a fine toner-upper at breakfast to get the taste buds in order for a spring day, but she also regards it as a coarse plant whose only redeeming landscape use is to face down a compost heap. So we compromised by choosing an ornamental rhubarb, *Rheum palmatum* var. *tanguticum*, which grows a good four feet in every direction and has sumptuous cut leaves.

Cardoon (*Cynara cardunculus*), a close relative of the globe artichoke, is another striking plant, with deeply incised, silvery, prickly leaves three to four feet long that combine well with plants having large uncut leaves. I like it in the border with rhubarb chard, and it is nice with plants of red cabbage too. We grow cardoon as an annual, but it is perennial where winters are mild, the bloom stalks rising the second year to a height of seven or eight feet and bearing violet thistles. Surprisingly often, plants will overwinter in the North.

I don't suggest growing cardoon as an edible in the ornamental garden, because this involves hilling soil around the stems in the same fashion as asparagus is blanched in Europe. The stalk has a mild, slightly nutty flavor but frequently has the texture of guitar strings. (In Switzerland, where the culture of cardoon is a finer art than in our own garden, it is even commercially tinned and sold in supermarkets.) But as an ornamental cardoon gets high marks, and no less a horticultural don than Graham Stuart Thomas refers to it as one of the most magnificent of all herbaceous plants. For a striking change from mundane plant fare, some spring set out three young cardoons in a half whiskey barrel on a sunny terrace and watch them take off. Growth will be quite full even if you forget an occasional watering, but for special lushness work a little slow-release fertilizer (such as Osmocote 14-14-14) into the soil mix at planting time.

Ornamental peppers, less than a foot tall and tidy in growth, are good candidates for the front of the border, because they are of interest during every stage of fruit maturation, which occurs over a long period in summer and early fall, until frost strikes them down. Depending on the selection, the fruit is round or rocket-shaped. 'Little Dickens', going from yellow to orange, is a good example of the latter, and it is quite edible. A pleasant change is 'Midnight Special', with purplish black foliage and bright red fruits. It is an excellent plant for containers too, mixed with annual dusty-miller for its gray foliage and with black mondo grass (*Ophiopogon planiscapus* 'Arabicus'), a perennial that we return to the ground or cold frame at the time of autumn frost. Sweet-alyssum in white- or purple-flowered selections is another good companion for 'Midnight Special'.

Okra doesn't get a good press very often, particularly from northerners, and even Mary Ann, who is from Virginia, prefers to be out of town when I am making a mess of it in the kitchen. Still, it has a place in the larger ornamental vegetable garden, especially the selection with red pods. These must be appreciated for their maroon color in the garden or as dried ornaments, for they turn green when cooked. Okra is a big plant in every respect, growing four feet tall. It is a member of the mallow family, and the yellow hibiscus-like flowers are among the most attractive in vegetabledom. Incidentally, the more okra pods you pick, the more flowers you get.

There are plenty of other ornamental vegetables, including Chinese cabbage

The ornamental vegetable border at Hillside in summer.

selections and eggplant, especially a variety with fruits that mimic chicken eggs. Jerusalem artichoke (*Helianthus tuberosus*) is a possibility for the rear of a large border. Its yellow sunflowers, borne on eight-foot stalks in late summer, give a floral dimension to the border, which is largely dependent on foliage boldness and contrast for effectiveness. However, this is a thug plant, and it is best to reset a few tubers in sunken containers each spring, so it doesn't take over the garden.

Our ornamental vegetable border varies from year to year, and we also include some herbs to round out the plantings. We usually grow parsley, bronze fennel, basil, salad burnet, garlic chives, purple-leaf perilla, catmint, and red orach. Latitude of choice exists, but there are limits. One spring when Mary Ann was late in planting, I gathered together a dozen seedlings of feverfew (*Chrysanthemum parthenium*) from the compost heap and planted them in the border, knowing they would give a good floral account for themselves. Despite my protest that the ancient Romans actually used feverfew foliage to add pungency to egg dishes, Mary Ann uprooted them, with the remark, "None of your weedy perennials here!" Oh well, I got my rhubarb in.

· 7 ·

Meadow Gardening

MEADOW GARDENING has come into its own, especially in parts of the country where brush does not quickly invade fields. It has not gained many followers in suburbia, where trim and tidy lawns reign, but a number of people elsewhere like the natural appearance it creates. Some maintenance is indeed required, namely mowing once a year in autumn and culling tree and shrub seedlings, as well as curbing certain aggressive weeds by hand or by spot treatment with herbicides. Perennial wildflowers must be rough-and-tumble sorts to cope with the competition, and they appreciate its absence the first year or two, until established.

Success depends in part on where you live and how much effort you are willing to put in. Meadow gardening is not a major task on the relatively dry and windy American prairie and its perimeter, where weed trees, let alone cultivated trees, have a difficult time becoming established. In the eastern states and the Pacific Northwest, which are areas of essentially high rainfall, woody growth — that is, the forest — is the natural course. There the meadow gardener must work harder.

Meadow gardening is not everyone's cup of tea, but it may be yours, especially as the conservation of petroleum-based products used in other forms of horticulture becomes a concern in the remaining years of this century (despite periodically depressed prices). Before launching a project, it helps first to see an area that has been given over to prairie "reconstitution" for some time, as the one at the University of Wisconsin in Madison, which is at its prettiest in summer. Books help too, particularly Laura C. Martin's *The Wildflower*

Meadow Book: A Gardener's Guide (Charlotte, N.C.: East Woods Press, 1986) and Warren G. Kenfield's *The Wild Gardener in the Wild Landscape* (New York: Hafner-Macmillan, 1966; out of print), a pioneer work based on original research. (A new edition is in preparation, to be published by Connecticut College Arboretum, New London.) Also valuable is the Connecticut Arboretum (New London) bulletin *Energy Conservation on the Homegrounds — The Role of Naturalistic Landscaping*, edited by William A. Niering and Richard H. Goodwin. However, meadow gardening is a rather young art (and even younger science). Also, each site has its own character, possibilities, and problems, and many fine points have to be learned by experience. This is as it should be, for the astute observer can make a valuable contribution to our knowledge of this field.

MAIN POINTS

Surely one of them is the advice to start small. Many worthwhile projects are abandoned because the energy of a gardener in August does not match his or her aspirations of the preceding April. Don't plan to change a field or home grounds all at one time. Choose a limited area, say a distant portion of the back yard that has been given to lawn, and keep the mower away from it until autumn. This will at least let you know what you have.

There will be pleasant surprises, perhaps some asters or yarrow you never knew were there. However, plants with a very great potential for spreading, such as bindweed and Canada thistle, should be repeatedly cropped by hand or spot-treated with a herbicide. A light but firm yank will take care of first-year tree or shrub seedlings. Don't delay pulling them, especially oaks.

Stable plant communities, such as they are, are made essentially by nature, not humans. Dig up a small patch of earth, and before much time has passed all sorts of plants, many unwanted, many unknown, will appear — unless you live in a semiarid part of the country or on a gravel bank. Seeds of some weeds can remain viable in the soil for more than one hundred years. What the meadow gardener is trying to do is to establish a desirable, fairly stable plant community, one with aesthetic appeal that requires, over the long run, moderately low maintenance. It is an uphill battle in most areas, a struggle where the bulldozer is no help, and you must even cast aside some old gardening tenets.

A cardinal principle is to disturb the soil no more than is necessary. This does not mean that you simply go out and scatter a few seeds from a packet of wildflowers (wild where?), then return to the porch, eat a granola bar, and

watch the plants grow. Nature doesn't work this way, at least not very efficiently, and you don't either. A friend has pointed out that there seem to be more cans in the meadow these days than meadows in a can.

Some soil disruption and plant tending will be necessary if you raise plants from seed on the site. If you set out young plants on the site in spring, they will also probably need care, especially watering, the first year. A two- or three-inch-deep mulch of wood chips, pine needles, or other organic material around them conserves moisture and discourages weeds, but keep it away from the plant crowns so as to minimize the chance of root rot. Bear in mind too that the majority of plants require well-drained soil.

Study the periphery of the site, whether the site is a meadow, small field, or

Above: Orange hawkweed (*Hieracium aurantiacum*) may be cursed in a lawn but is lovely in a meadow. It has upstaged more than one perennial garden.
Opposite, top: A June meadow of lupines (*Lupinus perennis*) on the Stoekel estate, home of the Yale Summer School of Art and Music in Norfolk, Connecticut.
Bottom: A meadow of black-eyed Susans (*Rudbeckia hirta*) and butterfly weed (*Asclepias tuberosa*) on Martha's Vineyard in July.

lawn to be abandoned, for this is where trouble is apt to originate, at least in the normally wooded parts of the country. If you have ash, maple, or oaks, you can expect a good number of seedlings. Some individual trees are much more prolific seeders than others of the same species, in part because their flowers may be all or mostly pistillate (female). These very trees will be troublesome over the years, and you might best give thought to their removal in the beginning, if the periphery is wooded and the trees won't be missed. Deciduous trees usually sprout from the base when cut, but an effective if slow method of making sure the roots die is to girdle the trunk with an ax and wait for it to die before cutting it down.

Black cherry (*Prunus serotina*) and chokecherry (*P. virginiana*), which are spread by wildlife, especially along stone walls, are also problem trees. Aggressors among shrubs vary from one part of the country to another; arrowwood viburnum (*V. dentatum*) and meadowsweet (*Spiraea latifolia*) can be bothersome in the East, ocean-spray (*Holodiscus discolor*) in the Northwest. Brush-killers applied to the cut stumps of some of these shrubs are not always effective. If you have only small colonies, resort to a pick, or cut the shrubs to the ground and spread black plastic over their bases, adding pine needles or nearby duff for aesthetics.

A dense stand of evergreen conifers adjacent to a meadow is very helpful, for their shade will discourage undergrowth that might eventually invade the meadow. In turn, if the conifers seed themselves into the meadow, a yearly mowing with a heavy-duty sickle bar mower will control them. Very few conifers are capable of sprouting from the roots when cut. (You can sometimes rent this type of mower from an equipment-rental store.)

Another stabilization technique is to encourage natural ground covers such as hay-scented or New York ferns along the periphery. Once they are established, their tightly knit root systems prevent virtually any other kind of plant from taking hold. The same is true, but only in a sunny borderland, of certain goldenrods, for example *Solidago rugosa*. Study the plants in nature in your area that form large clumps and keep out other plants. These can be big savers if you put them to work for you.

Sometimes they can also break a meadow, of course. For many Junes I have admired a planting of lupines (*Lupinus perennis*) in a nearby meadow that is upwards of thirty years old. The meadow has succeeded as long as it has because of evergreen trees on the periphery and a yearly mowing in autumn after the lupine seeds have ripened. Sensitive fern (*Onoclea sensibilis*), a colonizer, is gradually squeezing out the lupines and will probably win in five years' time.

The idea of the balance of nature originated with human beings, not with the ferns. But a run of one third of a century isn't a bad record in New England.

The range of appropriate plants for a horticultural meadow is wide, and it varies according to the part of the country. A lot of the best, including chicory and Queen Anne's lace, which make a lovely combination, are not even native to America. For additional ideas, see "A Garden of Thugs" on page 58. The following list is restricted to indigenous species of perennials. There are many others that should be tried.

Amsonia tabernaemontana, blue star. 2 ft., early summer
Anaphalis margaritacea, pearly everlasting. 12–18 in., white, late summer
Anemone canadensis. 1–2 ft., white, early summer
Aquilegia canadensis, columbine. 1–2 ft., red and yellow, spring
Asclepias tuberosa, butterfly weed. 1–2 ft., orange, summer
Aster spp. 2–6 ft., purple, pink, blue, or white, late summer to autumn
Baptisia australis, blue indigo. 3–5 ft., early summer
Cassia marilandica, wild senna. 4–6 ft., yellow, summer
Chelone spp., turtlehead. 3 ft., pink or white, late summer to autumn
Coreopsis spp. 1–3 ft., yellow daisies, summer
Echinacea purpurea, purple coneflower. 3–4 ft., pink or (less commonly) white, summer
Eupatorium spp., including *E. purpureum*, Joe-Pye weed, to 6 ft., pink; *E. rugosum*, 3–4 ft., white; and *E. coelestinum*, 2 ft., blue; all flower in late summer and autumn
Filipendula rubra, queen-of-the-prairie. 4–7 ft., pink plumes, summer
Gentiana andrewsii, closed gentian or bottle gentian. 1–2 ft., blue, autumn
Helenium autumnale, sneezeweed. 3–6 ft., red or yellow, late summer
Helianthus tuberosus, Jerusalem artichoke. 6–8 ft., yellow daisies, late summer
Heliopsis spp., false sunflower. 3–4 ft., yellow, long-blooming in summer
Liatris spp., gayfeather. 3–5 ft., purple or white spikes, summer
Lysimachia spp., loosestife. 1–3 ft., white or yellow, summer
Monarda didyma, bee balm. 3 ft., red, pink, or maroon, summer. The white-flowered cultivar is not vigorous enough to compete in a meadow
Monarda fistulosa, wild bergamot. 3–4 ft., lavender, summer
Oenothera tetragona, sundrops. 1 ft., yellow, summer

Physostegia virginiana, obedient plant. 2–4 ft., white or pink, late summer to
   autumn
Ratibida spp. 3–5 ft., yellow daisies, summer
Solidago spp. 1–6 ft., yellow, late summer
Thermopsis caroliniana, Carolina lupine. 3–4 ft., yellow, early summer
Vernonia noveboracensis, New York ironweed. 4–6 ft., purple, late summer to
   autumn

A selection of purple coneflower with flared instead of drooping rays. *Echinacea purpurea*
'Bright Star' makes a fine display for weeks in mid- and late summer in a meadow or a sunny
border. Appropriate border companions include globe thistle (*Echinops*) and *Phlox* 'Starfire'.

· 8 ·

Gardening in
Containers

CONTAINER GARDENING outdoors began for me about twenty years ago, when I started to grow a few annuals in redwood boxes. My color choices weren't especially good — hot-pants pink petunias, orange zinnias, and that sort of thing — but like most people who grow annuals I was interested in bright hues. It didn't really matter then if the various combinations shattered an occasional pair of sunglasses. That was the prepastel period of my gardening. I am sure I would have been drummed out of the local garden club.

In addition to my lapses on color coordination, I was but dimly aware that plants had different heights and that scale was not just an insect. Fortunately, giant sunflowers never appealed to me or I would have put them in containers, but there were a number of flops. One was *Salpiglossis*, which is a Texas-sized relative of the petunia, though it sounds more like a throat malady than a plant. It was only three inches tall when I bought it in a little tray from a garden center one Memorial Day, the traditional planting-out time for annuals in the Northeast. Within six weeks the two-foot-tall *Salpiglossis*, laden with bloom and weak of stem, followed Newton's Law. I scooped up the plants much like a dancer trying gracefully to hold his leading lady who has suddenly fainted. Stakes and strings didn't help much. *Salpiglossis* was in a five-inch-wide, five-inch-deep metal window box, moreover one that had no drainage holes. By the first of August Old Salpi, top-heavy and soggy-rooted, had given up the ghost, and American horticulture was the richer.

The metal window boxes held a certain fascination for me, mainly because they were cheap, light in weight, and lasted a few years if protected from winter.

They came in various lengths, too. I amassed one of New England's finest collections. After a while it occurred to me to use an ice pick to punch a few holes in the bottom for drainage, and plants grew better, even those rare ones that like the moist side of life. Why the manufacturers don't make the holes at the point of origin remains a mystery, for it would save gardeners a lot of woe.

In gardening one seldom has it all one's own way, and it became clear to me that the smaller the container, the greater the need for watering, regardless of whether you mix the currently popular chemical superabsorbents with soil or place a mulch on top. Summer drought is a more common occurrence than we like to think, and even with normal rainfall it is necessary in the cooler reaches of the country to water a metal window box at least once or twice a week. In warmer areas daily watering may be necessary, especially if plants are in full sun, as most annuals should in theory be. Man cannot garden by theory alone, however, and to cut down on the seemingly constant watering I learned the desirability of setting containers where they would receive morning sun and afternoon shade, since the summer sun from lunch time on is brutally drying. I am neither mad dog nor Englishman, nor are my plants.

In cities, where heat concentrations are greater, the matter of site is particularly important. In many instances the experienced urban gardener essentially looks upon shade from tall buildings not so much as a problem as an opportunity. If shade seems to come from all sides but light is fairly good, the container gardener can always rely on the Big Three of the shade-tolerant annuals — wax begonias, impatiens, and coleus. Luckily, each has many strains and colors from which to choose. Also, the gardener doesn't constantly have to remove the spent flowers to make these plants look tidy or to perpetuate bloom, as is the case with most other annuals.

It was in fact a miscalculation with impatiens that led me to dreams of glory with container gardening. Each spring for some years I bought a tray or two of impatiens to plant in compost in two large cement window boxes located under an old ash tree. My custom was to plant, water, and mulch them at the end of May, then return in late September to uproot them after the first frost had turned them to mush. They performed beautifully, and little or no watering was necessary, since they were shaded and the summers in our northern Connecticut village are cooler than in most areas. I thought container gardening was a cinch and couldn't understand why entire books had been written on the subject (mainly by Californians and/or city dwellers)!

Therefore, one winter I bought every window box on sale at every discount store in our part of the state, accumulating, to my wife's great horror, more than a hundred, which I placed on mostly sunny stone walls all over our property. We spent the next summer running about with hose and watering can, and we skipped the beach. By the end of July the petunias were peaked, and so were we.

Fortunately, there is a season called winter and it is a time in the northland for reflection, or, less kindly put, for figuring out what went wrong and resolving never to let it happen again.

Bigger containers (and grouping them to ease watering) seemed to make sense. By this time I decided to move up. Redwood tubs were out of the question, because although they are durable and attractive, they were beyond our budget, at least for the scale on which we wanted to garden. Also, Mary Ann objected to my scrounging through the greengrocer's garbage to retrieve bushel baskets, which don't make bad containers for a season if you partly line the interiors with black plastic (polyethylene).

Necessity is the mother of invention, and invention is the mother of discovery. In my wanderings through the discount stores I noticed that there were kitchen departments as well as gardening ones. The large, flexible plastic dishtubs that sold for $1.98 were ideal for my purposes, and I invested in a century's supply. They had no drainage holes either, but by this time I had become skilled with an ice pick, and this posed no problem. The tubs had two key assets apart from size — they were lightweight, and the plastic kept down evaporation. By good chance most of them were dull brown and would not steal the thunder from the plants. Mary Ann was lukewarm toward the tubs, and acidulous toward the few kelly green ones that crept in during my zeal to corner the market. Actually, they were a chlorotic kelly green and could have stood a shot of iron chelates. However, I assured her that we would plant euonymus vines around the base to soften their harshness. By and large they worked well, though one visiting landscape architect peered through the camouflage and asked sweetly, "Do you take in laundry too, Mr. McGourty?"

VEGETABLES

Rabbits forced us to increase our container gardening efforts. Our vegetable garden had been in a scrubby old pasture, which apart from the driveway was the only area of our property receiving all-day sun — a requirement for the best growth of food plants except the leaf crops (lettuce, chard, etc.). One year the pasture suddenly became a scene from *Watership Down*, with rabbits camped out every few feet, within hopping distance of the carrots. They even intimidated the woodchucks, who were also eyeing the carrots.

The logical response would have been a fence around the vegetable garden. I objected on aesthetic grounds, since old pastures in New England aren't meant to be cluttered, regardless of Robert Frost's comments about good fences and good neighbors. It struck me that the ideal spot to put the vegetable garden was at the end of the driveway — in containers. This was based largely on the theory that rabbits don't climb.

We located a half-dozen good-sized wooden packing crates and put two tomato plants in each, along with stakes cut from ash saplings in the nearby woods. Mary Ann marveled at my optimism. The stakes were nine feet tall, and even by the end of summer the tomatoes hadn't reached the top. The driveway resembled nineteenth-century Salem harbor with its masts shorn of sails.

We learned one thing about tomatoes: they are drunkards. Their thirst exceeds that of any other vegetable, except possibly cucumbers, which nature did not intend for little window boxes. We never needed a thermometer in summer because the tomatoes would tell us when it was more than 85° F. How well I remember the words, "Darling, the tomatoes are gasping again. Be a dear and give them a drop from the hose!" Half an hour later, after musing about tomatoes and how they learned from the old-time boxer called Fainting Phil Scott, who won his fights by dropping to the canvas shouting "Foul!" I would wind up the hose and wash myself down. Today a lot of greenhouses have miniature hoses aptly named spaghetti tubes, which run from individual containers to a central hose to a faucet. This would make sense adapted to the driveway vegetable garden, but then I wouldn't be able to think about Fainting Phil anymore. And spaghetti tubes aren't the prettiest system, either — even with sauced tomatoes.

Not all of our metal window boxes have rusted away yet, much to Mary Ann's disgust. We inherited several old tables that wouldn't be much worse for wear if left out during summer, and on these we placed boxes for green peppers, lettuce, eggplants, and minicarrots. Seed catalogues these days list a number of compact-growing varieties especially suited for containers. However, we needed extra space, so we added a couple of sawhorses and sturdy planks for more containers. Not a rabbit bothered to climb.

Our only problem in the driveway was with a raccoon, who one September evening raided the melons just as they were coming to the desired point of ripeness a few days before frost. Regardless of the catalogue talk, it is hard enough to grow melons in Connecticut because of cool summer nights and a short growing season, but like all home growers we felt like gambling a bit. We had started seed indoors under artificial light in April, moved young plants to wooden boxes in the driveway at May's end, and protected against cutworms with collars cut from paper cups. In the first couple of weeks we had placed a tarp of black plastic around the boxes to reflect heat. The crop exceeded our dreams — twenty-three beautiful muskmelons on their way to perfection. Then the raccoon struck, taking a single bite from each. We consoled ourselves with the thought that he might have developed a bad case of diarrhea later that night.

Melons — in fact almost every kind of container-grown plant — require some form of fertilizing as the season goes by, mainly because the frequent waterings wash away nutrients in the soil. We used to employ a water-soluble fertilizer every three weeks, and still put it to work on an occasional recalcitrant plant, but the special slow-release fertilizers that are mixed into the soil just before planting time save a lot of time and effort. No additional fertilizing is needed in the course of the summer. The slow-releasers are not inexpensive, but they allow us more hammock time than we used to get.

Containers by an old well in the McGourty garden include dusty-miller (*Senecio* 'Silverdust'), forms of kitchen sage (*Salvia officinalis*), and annual lobelia (*L. erinus*).

MIXING IT UP

There appear to be as many soil (or soilless) mixes for containers in America as there are gardeners. Specialty formulations (University of California, Cornell mix) exist mainly for the commercial grower, but can be adapted in the home garden. The city dweller might find it easiest to use a good grade of bagged potting soil with equal parts of coarse sand and peat, or to use an entirely soilless mix. The latter is particularly useful for hanging baskets because of its light weight, but you must give special attention to fertilizing and watering. Such mixes are more or less free of soil pathogens. They are based essentially on equal parts of ground peat moss and vermiculite and/or perlite, with a trace of dolomitic limestone. Our own mix is uncomplicated. It consists of year-old compost, in which some soil was incorporated during the composting process to hasten decomposition. This is approximately three quarters decomposed. Then we add two shovelsful of coarse-grade perlite per wheelbarrow load, a cup of lime, and a half cup of superphosphate, since our soil, like most in the Northeast, is deficient in phosphorus, an element that encourages root growth and flowering.

Unamended garden soil itself is not satisfactory for containers, because it almost invariably lacks the proper structure. If it is used in conjunction with peat and sand, some growers prefer to pasteurize it first. You can accomplish pasteurization, incorrectly called sterilization in many garden books, by cooking the moistened soil in small quantities in a 200° F oven for one hour. Close the doors and open the windows — there are nicer scents in the world than roasting soil. Also, it is a good practice to change the soil in garden containers every year.

All sorts of garden annuals, and some perennials, such as the hardiest, most rugged sedums, lend themselves to container use. Low height and compactness, or trailing nature, are important, and if you are just getting started it would be well to turn to a source such as the Brooklyn Botanic Garden Handbook *Gardening in Containers*, edited by George Taloumis.

Every container gardener has favorite annuals, including some that can be very different from the ones used in flower beds. Creeping zinnia (*Sanvitalia procumbens*), a little yellow daisy with a prominent dark eye, is a plant that comes to its best in containers, as does another miniature study in yellow, the Dahlberg daisy (*Dyssodia tenuiloba*). Both are nice with the electric blue of *Lobelia erinus* 'Crystal Palace Compacta' or the softness of *Lobelia* 'Cambridge Blue'.

We also like to start a container or two of Virginia stock (*Malcolmia maritima*), the flowers of which resemble arabis. They may be pink, lilac, or white, and plant height is only a few inches. Virginia stock, like sweet-alyssum, flowers in just five or six weeks from seed sown directly in the container. The bloom period lasts only a month or so during the heat of summer, but if you start seeds by August 1 you may have a long display during the cool days of autumn. One year I noticed that a November temperature of 17° F had not spoiled the flowers. Ornamental ("flowering") kale (*Brassica oleracea*) is one of the few other annuals that can tolerate such frost and look good in late fall. Snapdragons persist too.

Extending the season is important for anyone living in the cooler regions of the country, and container gardening can be singularly useful in this respect. Not only is it possible to hide the evidence if a container is in crisis and your mother-in-law or landscape architect happens to be coming for a visit, but it is also easy to grow fall bloomers such as cushion chrysanthemums in containers that are out of sight, perhaps on a distant stone wall, then bring them to the terrace or porch as they start to bloom. The flowers last a surprisingly long time, and if heavy frost threatens, it is no difficult task to place an old blanket over them, especially if the containers are grouped. Chrysanthemums cannot safely be left in containers in the open over winter in the North. We put them either in a cold frame or, removed from pots, into the garden, then place evergreen boughs on top after the ground freezes. The survival rate is fairly good with cushion mums, which are among the hardiest of the breed, but unusually wet winters take a toll.

Finally, good grooming is important, because containers are usually placed in conspicuous positions — by steps, doors, or terraces. You should remove spent blossoms several times a week. If some leaves are marred or scorched, remove them. Make sure containers are not beyond the reach of the hose! Certain annuals, such as petunias, look worse for wear as summer progresses. Pruning them back halfway, then feeding and watering them heavily, works well, but it makes aesthetic sense to get the containers out of sight until revival takes place. A hospital ward in a sunny spot behind a garage or tool shed makes the task easier and more enjoyable.

· PART II ·

THE PLANTS

· 9 ·

Long-Flowering
Perennials

A BLESSING and a curse of perennials is that most of them have a flowering period of just three weeks, which leaves forty-nine other weeks of the year to think about. This is a long time even if a gardener is good at anticipation. Indeed, the bloom time of some well-known perennials, including bearded irises and peonies, is much shorter, especially if there happens to be a spring thunderstorm when they are in flower.

Mary Ann and I remember leaving home in Connecticut one Memorial Day weekend for a five-day visit to Ontario. In our garden Oriental poppies were in bud, with promise of six-inch-wide flowers as bright as the vermilion bridges of Chinese gardens. The drive across rural New York was an unexpected pleasure, and not even the state Chamber of Commerce could have painted a more idyllic scene than nature did. The fields were aglow with oxeye daisies, soft pink ragged-robin (*Lychnis flos-cuculi*), and phloxy mauve dame's rocket (*Hesperis matronalis*), immigrants from Europe that lease the meadows of the northern states for a few weeks late each spring. The temperature was in the high eighties each day while we were gone. On our return home, there were no Oriental poppies to be seen.

Why then do we bother with them, the poppies, peonies, and bearded irises? Well, they do have a classic form that other flowers don't. A feral relative of bearded iris, the yellow flag (*Iris pseudacorus*), was even thought sufficiently worthy by the Bourbons to serve as the emblem of French royalty, the fleur-de-lis. I like always to have a few of these plants, but they should not form the basis of a garden if you are aiming for season-round interest.

Of course, if you would like flowers on the same plant through the season, annuals will do their thing in good stud fashion. A lot of people prefer to have the same kind of garden in September as in June. Depending on its arrangement, such a garden can be singularly boring, even more so than those that close their floral shop, after a brief sputter of neon azaleas, by June 1. In the case of the former, there is no hint of the coming season, nothing to look forward to except repetition of the present, until sudden death overtakes the plants on a frosty autumn night. These gardens are frequently riots of color, which is fine if they are kept from public view; but as the late Edward Hyams pointed out in this connection, a riot is by any account ugly.

Even though the hot tints of the tropics are all too often present in the constitutions of annuals, soft colors can be had by the score, especially in snap-dragons, petunias, and impatiens. Ironically, in many a garden the more sub-dued sorts of annuals can serve as a backbone, providing continual color through the mild months. At the same time, for vertebrae, a succession of perennials having fairly short bloom periods can provide variety, evoke the seasons, and give something to look forward to. In May there are columbines; in June, goatsbeard; in July, lilies; in August, liatris; in September, monkshood. This makes possible an ever-changing kaleidoscope, which is more interesting (and restful) than a riot.

MAINTENANCE AND TIME FACTORS

I am a lazy gardener, subscribing to the view that no man should have a garden larger than his wife can take care of. However, there has to be a compromise, for my spouse, curiously, feels that no woman should have a garden larger than her husband can tend. Annuals do require replanting each year, perennials don't (though some need more uprooting and shuffling about than the new grower suspects), so the greater part of our garden is devoted to perennials. It is almost as simple as that.

Our tastes evolve, and these are more or less reflected in the garden, though at times it seems to go its own stubborn way. For a better display and extra moments for croquet, we decided to give over a fairly sizable portion of our garden to long-blooming perennials, essentially those that bloom six weeks or more. The sense of continuity is now greater and we have less clutter, although I still trip over an occasional peony. Next summer I may even take up parachute jumping.

A list of selected stalwarts will vary according to where you live, as I discovered several years ago while visiting a friend in North Carolina. I spent some time extolling the merits of a perennial of southern origin, thread-leaved coreopsis (*Coreopsis verticillata*), including its lengthy bloom period. In northern Connecticut it averages six weeks in midsummer. On this September day in Winston-Salem the temperature was in the upper nineties, my friend's garden was wilted, and so were we. She gave me a blank stare and drawled, "My, you Yankee garden writers do go on! Give that coreopsis three weeks here, in a good year." With most perennials, the hotter the summer, the briefer the flowering, especially if they happen to be July or August bloomers. Even in a single garden the length of bloom varies according to the site of the border, an important factor being that bright afternoon sun accelerates the demise of flowers.

Certain plants that are native to warmer climates are exceptions. For example, gaillardia flowers for a remarkably long time in the heat of the southern summer, as does *Gaura lindheimeri,* though young plants of either are capable of a fairly extended bloom period in the North. Neither tends to be long-lived in the North, however, especially in heavy soils.

Green-and-gold (*Chrysogonum virginianum*) blooms for weeks in late spring and early summer, and sometimes repeats later in the season. It is best used in frontal groupings in a border or as an informal ground cover.

EVERBLOOMERS, SO TO SPEAK

I can think of only two or three perennials that bloom from spring until autumn in northern gardens, but generally even these are rebloomers rather than everbloomers. They are the native bleeding-heart (*Dicentra eximia*) and its very similar western relative *D. formosa*, and the diminutive southerner green-and-gold (*Chrysogonum virginianum*), especially in its upright, nonspreading form, *australis*. The typical eastern bleeding-heart is a slightly scruffy little thing that the eye wanders over, despite the plant's finely cut foliage and continual bloom. *Dicentra eximia* is usually relegated to the semiwoodland area but pops up from seed in odd places around the garden, even in sunny locations, where it can fend for itself tolerably well. One is not tempted to show it to neighbors. The flower color is pink, but the sort that has been through too many cycles in the washing machine. Over the years deeper tints have been distilled through hybridization and selection, but they fade to the color of a half-rotted apple, and you should remove the spent blossoms, if only for appearance's sake. This is a good practice with most perennials, and in some instances it extends the flowering period. 'Bountiful', 'Luxuriant', and 'Zestful', though they sound more like soaps than dicentras, are thought to be improvements, and are probably more common in gardens now than the species.

Fortunately, some plants, like people, overcome their humble origins, and the white-flowered form of *Dicentra eximia* is an excellent example. It blooms sporadically from spring to frost, fades well, and has attractive gray-green foliage. In addition, its young 'uns come essentially true from seed if no plants of the feckless pink-flowered type are around. The plants retain the ruggedness of the species, and they are remarkably shade-tolerant.

Dicentra eximia 'Alba' is for some reason considered a rock gardener's plant, the rock gardener's practical definition of a rock garden plant being one that he or she likes. (Butterfly weed and cardinal flower, regardless of height, are also adopted rock garden plants.) No matter; this white bleeding-heart fits well into a number of garden niches, as does a white counterpart of the western *D. formosa*. I like it as an informal edging to a shaded border or in small groups toward the front. Every so often you also encounter a fine white-and-light-pink-flowered variant of *D. formosa*, which adds grace to any woodland garden. Readers should not confuse any of these dicentras with the old-fashioned bleeding-heart that has lady's-locket flowers, *D. spectabilis*. This blooms briefly, if magnificently, in spring.

What a pity that it is mainly northerners and Californians who write garden books and sometimes give "common" names of their choice to plants of other areas, even though names for them may already be well established there. It's a bit like the touring British horticulturists on the Amercian lecture circuit who refer to giant sequoia as wellingtonia and are surprised when the audience looks confused. For years I was unaware that the little yellow daisy that botanists call *Chrysogonum virginianum* had any vernacular name but golden-star. Wyman told me so, and what's more, so did Bailey. What higher canonization could there be?

Then one day I happened to marry a southern girl, and we started to talk about plants. After a couple of months extolling the virtues of golden-star, which had been killed in my garden, after three years' prosperity, by a recent winter, I took my bride on a trip to Pennsylvania, which of course for many of us is the South. She had been largely unresponsive to my testimonials on behalf of this lovely plant, and then we finally saw it together in a garden there. With delight I exclaimed, "Hey, that's my old friend golden-star!" Mary Ann gave me a surprised look, then said, "Oh, you mean green-and-gold! That's what everyone in the South calls it."

Whatever name you choose to give it, *Chrysogonum virginianum* is a winner. It has a burst of bright yellow bloom in spring, then sporadic flowers through summer. Most plants of *Chrysogonum* in gardens are prostrate growers, seldom more than six or eight inches high, and they quickly form mats; but the upright, nonspreading form is the more dependable rebloomer. In fact, *Chrysogonum* is quite variable. Afternoon shade is beneficial, as is slightly more than the usual amount of compost incorporated in the soil. In the North, throw a few pine boughs on for winter protection, and hope.

Another long-flowering southerner, *Coreopsis auriculata*, is sometimes confused with *Chrysogonum*, but it has orange-yellow flowers whose color is hard to integrate with others. For a pleasing effect, however, try it with golden variegated kitchen sage (*Salvia officinalis* 'Icterina') and purple-flowered *Salvia* × *superba* 'East Friesland'.

A FEW DAISIES

Some people dislike feverfew (*Chrysanthemum parthenium*), and I confess that once in a while I have tried to evict this pungent, small-flowered white daisy from the garden. Attempts seem to be as futile as getting rid of johnny-jump-ups or cats once they are established. I suppose it can be done, with considerable effort and vigilance, at least as far as the plants are concerned, but one is apt sooner or later to ask why.

Feverfew is a lovely thing once you learn to love it. Notice that I call it a thing. Although this plant is what is euphemistically called a perennial in the manuals, it marches to its own fast drummer. Some individuals and strains are annual, others biennial, and still others refuse to give up the ghost for three or four years. This is the sort of species that irritates budding young taxonomists, because it does not fall into the neat little cubbyholes of classification. Once more nature mocks man's categories. Oh yes — the nurseries' too, because selections of feverfew are still listed in catalogues as "matricaria," though for many years feverfew has been known to be distinct from the true genus *Matricaria*. To confuse matters further, some taxonomists now put feverfew in the tansy genus, *Tanacetum*.

In this instance it doesn't matter much whether the thing is a perennial, biennial, or annual. The plants breed with the rapidity of slightly oversexed rabbits, and germination is close to 110 percent. This can be a serious problem for the laissez-faire gardener, but a judicious clip of the pruning shears as flowers fade nips it. When I am busy, or indolent, I use hedge clippers. In practice, some seeds always fall to the ground, and thus the survival of the species is ensured — as if there were ever any question.

Why bother to grow feverfew? Well, you will always have at least a handful of flowers in bloom from June until October, and often a large enough number to be modestly showy. It combines well in the garden with virtually any kind of perennial except overbred florist chrysanthemums, and it plays the role of straight man admirably. In addition to performing well in the sun, feverfew grows better in the shade than any other daisy with which I am familiar. It is a handy filler, too. If some part of the garden becomes a disaster area in midseason because of sickly scabiosa, dying digitalis, or wives who forget to water, you can summon feverfew seedlings from the periphery or compost heap on a moment's notice, and they will put on a show in a few weeks, especially if showered every seven days with a water-soluble commercial fertilizer.

For a particularly good display of feverfew, treat it like the chrysanthemum it is by pinching the shoots back halfway in spring when plants attain eight inches. Apply a water-soluble fertilizer. Repeat the pinching three weeks later and fertilize lightly again. Bloom period will be longest on relatively young plants.

Finally, feverfew is superb as a cut flower. Blossoms persist for a couple of weeks in the home and are particularly useful for this purpose in autumn, when most other garden plants have long since faded. Our old colonial house has small rooms, and these scaled-down daisies, in little pitchers, are ideal for compact dressers and nearly full bookcases. Feverfew keeps its demeanor among clutter.

Other members of the daisy or composite clan are among the long-flowering perennials. The cultivar of Shasta daisy (*Chrysanthemum × superbum*) called 'Silver Princess' starts to bloom for us in late June. If we divide plants every year or two — a good practice with most composites — and fertilize them lightly in spring and again in early summer, they repeatedly flower until the middle of September. Other Shastas vary in response to this treatment, and at least one seed firm offers separate strains of early, midseason, and late-blooming sorts. Grown from seed, these are somewhat variable, but the principal aim is to have a few of these classic field-daisy shapes in the garden for cutting purposes and to complement other, bolder perennials. One of our favorite long-in-bloom combinations for a sunny border is Pacific Giant delphiniums in the back-

Viki Ferreniea

Viki Ferreniea

Top, left: Coreopsis 'Moonbeam', which grows fifteen inches tall and needs a sunny site, is one of the few perennials to bloom from early summer till frost.
Right: Lenten-rose (*Helleborus orientalis*) may not be in bloom at Lent in many parts of America, but this more or less evergreen relative of the clematis and buttercup, growing about a foot tall, is early and long-flowering. Flowers are white or plum-colored, and the plants require shade.
Bottom, left: Long-blooming blue flax (*Linum perenne*), perennial foxglove, and euphorbia at Wave Hill, New York City.
Right: Bearded iris and *Veronica* 'Crater Lake Blue' at Old Westbury on Long Island. Some beardeds have been selected for rebloom.

ground, a yellow-flowered yarrow (*Achillea* 'Coronation Gold') in the fore-ground on one side, and the tallish, full-bodied Shasta daisy 'Star of Antwerp' on the other.

PREJUDICE

I know a few people who would rather eat pickled worms than grow yellow-flowered plants. My own culinary tastes are not as eclectic as theirs, but I do think they are missing out on something in the garden. There are a number of easy-to-grow, long-blooming yellow daisies, and one must exercise a certain restraint lest one has too much of a good thing, but to be without them alto-gether is to diminish the joy of gardening.

It is my intention some year quietly to construct a new perennial border in a sunny area and to devote it almost entirely to yellow-flowered plants, perhaps with a few orange ones for pepper and some white bloomers to intensify them. I will then invite every color snob I know from three counties to the unveiling, which will be in the guise of a cocktail party. Of course, appropriate tidbits from the garden will be served as appetizers. In the background the stereo will play the triumphant strains of the last movement of Beethoven's Ninth Sym-phony.

The backbone of such a border will be a native perennial, the false sunflower (*Heliopsis helianthoides*), which grows three or four feet tall and has several cultivars very high in butterfat content. One of them, 'Summer Sun', with good-sized, semidouble flowers and exceptional vigor, drips cholesterol from June until autumn frost. Another clump further along in the border will go to the fully double 'Gold Greenheart', a fine heliopsis with long bloom. Still further along will be a clump of 'Karat', a very large, single-flowered cultivar.

The 'Enchantment' lily, which has midsummer flowers of pure traffic-cop orange, with a constitution to match, will be liberally interspersed among the heliopsis. I should include some daylilies (*Hemerocallis*), especially 'Stella d'Oro', with its small, burnt-yellow flowers noted for a long bloom period. A few orange daylilies will fit in too. I will also plant perennial black-eyed Susans (*Rudbeckia fulgida* 'Goldsturm'), which always seem to be in flower in late summer. A few heleniums will provide a floral boost in copper for five weeks in late summer, followed by chrysanthemums.

Of course, the border will be some distance from the house.

BLUES AND PINK

I mentioned delphiniums earlier but did not give them their due, which is con-siderable. The Pacific Giants, six or seven feet tall when sober, are not good garden plants, although when well grown they are the most spectacular of all perennials. No blue can match the shades of some of their cultivars, particularly 'Summer Skies', a superb azure that combines well in June with the yellow daisies of *Coreopsis* × *grandiflora* or *C. lanceolata*. Deeper, true colors are to be had in 'Blue Bird' (with a white "bee" in the blossom center) and 'Blue Jay' (black "bee"). If you cut the initial flowering shoots to the ground promptly after the first wave of bloom in June, then nourish the plants with a 10-10-10 commercial fertilizer, new bloom stalks will appear in a few weeks, and in a cool climate produce flowers until frost. Delphiniums live longest and perform best in parts of the country with cool summers.

The tall delphiniums are exasperating plants, though, for they are exceedingly difficult to stake well. In particular, the woman gardener of average height feels as if she is dancing with a basketball player who has been fed growth hormones since youth. It is a struggle. The perfect delphinium stake has yet to be made. Some garden centers sell thin metal rods five feet tall with loops at the top end. These help, but at the summit of the plants there are still several feet of stalk that will bend or break in a good breeze. For this reason many gardeners have settled for lower-growing, less spectacular, but still attractive delphiniums such as the Connecticut Yankee strain and 'Blue Fountains'. Less is sometimes more, even in horticulture. The bad news is that these lower delphiniums are usually more short-lived than the Pacific Giants.

There are not many good blue-flowered perennials of moderate height, especially ones that bloom a long time, but stokesia (*Stokesia laevis*) comes quickly to mind. Although a few selections of this southern native with frilly white centers have been named, including dark 'Blue Danube', the plants in gardens are commonly grown from seeds. These germinate readily and produce flowering plants the first year if you start them indoors under artificial lights in January or February. Flower color varies from light blue to lavender, and fastidious growers may wish to do their own sorting out, selecting unusually attractive individual plants and propagating them by division. This is of little concern to me, because I have never seen an ugly stokesia. In fact, the only unattractive thing about the plant is an occasionally enountered "common" name, Stokes' aster.

In our garden stokesia blooms from July to September. In southern California flowering is intermittent through the year. Plants tend to be short-lived, especially in northern soils where drainage is slow in winter, so some gardeners as a matter of course have a few seedlings coming along in the cold frame. Stokesia looks good with just about anything, but it becomes very choice with silver-leaved plants.

Let's look briefly at other blues. Three short-lived, long-blooming, sun-loving plants are best treated as ephemerals to round out a garden, not to serve as a base. Blue flax (*Linum perenne*), which can be a pleasing counterpoint to bearded iris, flowers for several months on fifteen-inch stems. 'Sapphire', a bit shorter, is a good selection, as is the white-blooming 'Diamond'. Cupid's-dart (*Catananche caerulea*), a lovely blue with a dark center and papery calyx, ranges from one to two feet and flowers through summer. Fortunately, both *Linum* and *Catananche* are quick and easy from seed, and some gardeners plan to start a new batch under lights each year in late winter.

Aster × *frikartii*, mainly the selection 'Wonder of Staffa', has been widely promoted for years. 'Mönch' is fuller in flower and has a more even growth habit. Both are borderline hardy in the North and are particularly apt to die out if drainage is not excellent; they are a sounder choice in the mid-Atlantic states and milder areas. Height is three to four feet and bloom period is most of the summer, with a peak toward the end. *Aster* × *frikartii* is delightful with the white flowers of *Allium tuberosum* or *Artemisia lactiflora* and the pink ones of *Chelone obliqua* or *Physostegia* 'Bouquet Rose'. Mix in some silver foliage and the combinations can be memorable.

Catmint (*Nepeta* × *faassenii* and *N. mussinii*), European cornflower (*Centaurea montana*), and spiderwort, in this case *Tradescantia* × *andersoniana* 'J. C. Weguelin', all have a long flowering period if cut back two thirds or more right after the first wave of blue in late spring, then allowed to grow and rebloom. In areas with long, hot summers a second cutting may be indicated. Indeed, new gardeners timid with the shears should note that these are well-behaved plants only if cropped sharply when they start to get tatty.

Long-blooming perennials with pinkish hues? *Dianthus* × *allwoodii*, with a healthy life span only in free-draining soil, often repeats bloom if you faithfully deadhead it. Two cranesbills are also of note for longer-than-usual bloom. One is the Lancaster geranium (currently, and let's hope finally, *G. sanguineum* var. *striatum*), growing to one foot, with pale pink flowers beginning in late spring. The other is the more deeply colored *Geranium endressii* 'Wargrave Pink' of gardens, growing to two feet, blooming in late spring and early summer. Lancaster performs best in full sun and lean soil, 'Wargrave Pink' in dappled light or in afternoon shade with some additional organic matter in the soil.

Another pink we are fond of belongs to *Linaria purpurea* 'Canon Went', which grows to a wispy three feet or more and has flowers resembling dainty small snapdragons. Usually you can see a few clusters at any time in the mild months, even into October, provided you cut the plants back sharply once or twice in the growing season. They tend to self-sow, almost to benign weed status, so the circle is seldom broken, though plants are by nature short-lived. Sun and fairly dry, undernourished soil bring best floral results for this relative of butter-and-eggs. The good Canon usually self-sows true to color if the species from which it is derived is not present in the garden. *Linaria purpurea* itself has purple flowers, not at all unpleasant, but we prefer to keep the Canon pure.

YARROWS AND OTHERS

The various pink and red forms of common yarrow (*Achillea millefolium*), which grow two to three feet tall, bloom much of the summer, particularly if

Left, top: Linaria purpurea 'Canon Went' and Lancaster geranium (*G. sanguineum* var. *striatum*) are long bloomers at the Conservatory Garden in Central Park, New York. *Artemisia* 'Silver King' and pink foxglove (*Digitalis purpurea*) complete this June scene.

Bottom: The sun border at Hillside, actually an island bed, is at its peak in August and September. Long bloomers include *Sedum* 'Autumn Joy', *Helenium* 'Copper Spray', *Achillea* 'The Pearl', and *Phlox* 'Pinafore Pink'. Peegee hydrangea is in the rear.

Right: Artemisia lactiflora, the only artemisia grown for its flowers, attains four feet in average garden soil and makes a good late-summer companion in the sunny border for a grape-leaved anemone or *Aster* 'Alma Potschke'. All three bloom for many weeks.

plants are young and vigorous. In the border, they need division yearly so they don't take over. For this reason some gardeners prefer to consign these yarrows to the meadow.

The Galaxy series of hybrids between *Achillea millefolium* and *A. taygetea*, from Germany, has a very long summer bloom period, with colors ranging from red to pink, lilac, and sulfur. 'Hope' ('Hoffnung', 'Great Expectations'), a pale yellow sandstone tint, is one of the best, as are 'The Beacon' ('Fanal'), which is red, and 'Weser River Sandstone', a soft brick-pink sandstone fading to sulfur. Each should be deadheaded regularly and cut back severely once or twice in summer so it does not become floppy, ragged, or free-seeding. Still, the colors are refreshing.

Another choice for borders, though still in need of more frequent division than most perennials, is the white-flowered *Achillea ptarmica* 'Ballerina', a diminutive selection of 'The Pearl' for frontal positions. Unfortunately, bogus seed-raised plants resembling 'The Pearl', a rank grower, or even the ungainly wild species are often sold as 'Ballerina'. I think that *Achillea* 'Moonshine', with yellow flowers and good feathery gray foliage, is the best of the yarrows, growing to two feet, blooming most of the summer, and never invasive.

Summer phlox (*Phlox paniculata*) has had a bad name for years because of mildew and the washed-out purple-pink seedlings that appear in gardens that have been let go. You can control the mildew easily with Benomyl (Benlate), a systemic fungicide, and there are now a number of fine selections with no hint of mauve. My favorite is 'Sir John Falstaff', which has large salmon-pink flowers on four-foot stalks that do not require staking. The floral peak is July. After the first wave has passed you can remove the terminal trusses, and new flowers are then produced on axillary spurs until late September — just enough of them to provide a pleasant follow-up. Not all summer phloxes, including the striking cherry-red 'Starfire', which is currently popular, have as long a season. I am fond of 'Sir John Falstaff' bounded by two robust but stately growers with protracted bloom, globe thistle (*Echinops* 'Taplow Blue') and black snakeroot (*Cimicifuga racemosa*), which has tall wands of creamy white flowers. Purple coneflower (*Echinacea purpurea*), another long bloomer, is good nearby.

'Mt. Fuji', with white flowers, probably has the longest bloom period of any summer phlox, but in our garden it is more prone to mildew than most. *Phlox maculata* 'Omega' starts flowering several weeks earlier than summer phlox, pauses, then reblooms here in late summer. Flowers in the first wave are white with a small deep-pink center, but in the second wave they are all white, resembling a very tardy 'Miss Lingard'. The shiny, lance-shaped leaves of this phlox help make it a winner, too.

LATE STARTERS

In the North gardeners don't think of long bloomers starting in August, but three of them do — cushion chrysanthemums, *Sedum* 'Autumn Joy', and Canadian burnet (*Sanguisorba canadensis*). Of all garden mums, I esteem most highly one named 'Baby's Tears', which originated some years ago in Connecticut's Bristol Nurseries. In early August it begins to display little white buttons, which eventually change to lavender, but new flowers continue well into October. Since the color of the fading blossoms can be disconcerting if they are near strong yellows, we plant this cushion mum in front of false dragonhead (*Physostegia virginiana*), which is rosy pink with a hint of light purple.

It is nice to have a few chrysanthemums like 'Baby's Tears' that are truly good garden plants, but the popular modern kinds are often short-lived. I wish that the growing season in interior New England were long enough to accommodate to its fullest *Chrysanthemum nipponicum*, a shrubby white daisy that adorns coastal gardens with its flowers for months at a time. On Long Island this plant is called the Montauk daisy. It blooms briefly for us in October (some years not at all), then frost mars the beauty, so we have consigned our plants to the compost heap. Oh well, there are plenty of other good plants to grow in autumn, and not all of them are chrysanthemums.

A favorite combination of ours, effective usually from August until November, is *Sedum* 'Autumn Joy' planted in front of Canadian burnet. The latter has bottlebrush spikes of white flowers on strong, five-foot stalks, and from a distance they remind one of autumn-blooming snakeroot (*Cimicifuga simplex*), whose flowers are often killed by frost in the colder reaches. The burnet is a better performer in New England, while the snakeroot is superior in the mid-Atlantic states.

Sedum 'Autumn Joy', which grows about two feet tall and has stubby light-green leaves of interest all through the growing season, undergoes a floral transition that is of note. Flower buds form in late July or August and resemble pink broccoli as they open. In September they become dark, approaching Indian red. This is actually the beginning of the seed-head stage. By October's end they are mahogany. In some years they finish the season with a straw color, unless you cut them first for dried arrangements in the home. Such chameleons are welcome in the garden. Fortunately, this one happens to be a good garden plant, as indestructible as one of its alleged parents, the showy stonecrop (*S. spectabile*), but longer-lasting in bloom and without the cotton-candy pink that flaws the species. 'Autumn Joy' is one of the best perennials. For most profuse bloom in fall, shear the plants back halfway in spring when they are eight inches tall.

· IO ·

Perennials
Out of the Ordinary

OUR FRIEND Chuck has a plant collection, not a garden, and he seldom grows more than one plant of a kind, because in his words, that takes valuable space. But somehow he finds room for everything, even if it means putting a six-inch-tall dianthus in the middle of a border behind the plume poppy (*Macleaya cordata*), which makes an imposing frontal at seven feet.

We visited Chuck not long ago. He had been in England earlier in the year and had brought home from nurseries there, with his specially laminated USDA import permit, a number of plants that he had never seen before, ones that were no doubt introductions to America. He wanted us to see them all, even to give us offsets, because a few of them were already well established beyond his wildest expectations and starting to consume valuable space.

Chuck was especially proud of the progress made by the speckled cress (*Barbarea vulgaris* 'Variegata'), which looked to me as though it had 2,4-D injury. I started to remark on this curious coincidence when a very short, very swift kick in the shins by Mary Ann deflected my attention to a double-flowered lady's-smock (*Cardamine pratensis* 'Flore-Pleno'). Nearby a variegated horseradish (*Armoracia rusticana* 'Variegata') was thriving, and Mary Ann ventured the thought that Chuck would have a fine supply to accompany roast beef next winter. This drew a stare from him that matched the gaze of a mackerel that has been dead for a week.

Finally we approached the *pièce de résistance,* and my heart began to sink. In front of us was a plump little purple-leaved plant with familiar spikes of closely set seeds. Chuck was beaming. "Now, just look at this wonderful form of plantain," he said. "Do you realize it's one of the rarest plants in the garden, and it is already sending out pups? I am going to give you one to take home!" I had just spent part of that very morning trying to eradicate from one of our borders the green-leaved plantain, from which this purple specimen was derived.

THE OTHER SIDE

That is one side of the story. Having worked one third of my life for a botanical institution, I am keenly aware that in the garden the term *rare* is not necessarily synonymous with *valuable*. Many plants are deservedly obscure. In reality only a small percentage of the plants of the world are worth candidacy as garden ornamentals. However, even this relative basketful gives us magnificent possibilities.

I remember a discussion I had with Gus Mehlquist a few years ago when we were walking around a garden that was not very interesting because the plantings were totally predictable. We had a sense of déjà vu all over again, to use

Lamiastrum galeobdolon 'Herman's Pride', simply dubbed Herman by some gardeners, is a distinctive new ground cover for shaded sites.

the phrase attributed to Yogi Berra. Dr. Mehlquist had recently retired from a distinguished teaching career at the University of Connecticut and was feeling rather crusty about the garden. I casually mentioned my regard for bridalwreath spirea or some such common plant and said that at least we were seeing a well-grown one.

Dr. Mehlquist's response, delivered with some intensity, was to this effect: "Why bother with the common? If you see the same plant half a dozen times on your way to town, you have visual ownership of it and can enjoy it along the way. Save your own garden for something special, with plants you won't run across everywhere. Make your own garden different from everyone else's." I still wink at a pretty bridalwreath and wouldn't tear it out of the garden on the basis of its commonness, but I basically agree with the Mehlquist view.

My interest happens to be in perennials that are out of the ordinary. When I think of the number that have become available in the past decade or so, I marvel at the possibilities they pose for garden diversity. Perhaps I am also lucky not to be a collector of trees or shrubs, for new varieties of them frequently take years to become available. A woody plant nurseryman is also by nature conservative. He has to be, when choosing new plants to grow, because a substantial investment in time and space, and therefore money, is involved. He cannot simply dump a block of six-year-old yews because housing starts are down. A little anecdote illustrates the difference between him and perennials nurserymen.

One autumn a few years ago my friend Pierre, a wholesale nurseryman in perennials, invited us to dinner. We get together every few months, and per custom Mary Ann and I brought along a few plants, as normal people might bring a bouquet of flowers or a bottle of wine. One of the gifts was a new silver foliage plant for shaded areas, *Lamium maculatum* 'White Nancy', which Allen Bush, a North Carolina nurseryman, had brought back a year or two before from Beth Chatto's delightful nursery in England. Allen gave a cutting or a young plant to Pamela Harper, who shortly gave me one. I rooted a few from this and looked forward to seeing how 'White Nancy' would perform for us.

After our dinner with Pierre I did not see him again until the following spring, six months later. When our paths finally crossed, he had a long face, and I asked the reason. "Do you remember that lamium you gave me? It died!" I promised I would give him another. He retorted, "That's not necessary. I made one thousand cuttings from it and its offspring. And we gave the original plant a proper funeral!"

Granted, not many perennials are nearly so easy to propagate and grow on for sale, but this story does help to explain the revolution that has taken place in the availability of perennials, not counting the development of tissue culture techniques for propagation. Many of the new perennials will fade away in a few years, to be replaced with still others, and a sorting-out process will take place in the marketplace and in home gardens. The garden will probably benefit, but I suspect the near future will be a particularly tumultuous period for designers who are truly interested in plants and must learn rather quickly what the new ones can and cannot do in the landscape. There are so many choices now, and without a certain restraint on the part of both designer and home grower, our gardens stand a chance of becoming hopelessly cluttered and disjointed. But it is a risk we must take if we are going to have a richer American horticulture.

LUSTING FOR LAMIUMS

Lamium 'White Nancy' is the best introduction among ground covers for shade that I have seen in the past twenty-five years. There are very few silverlings for shade, and their value is high because of their ability to inject light into dark places — and after all, darkness is the visual drawback of shaded areas. In addition, the white flowers, which are borne in early summer, inject light. No plant is perfect, however, and 'White Nancy' does have a weakness. By midsummer the growth habit becomes open and leaves often get world-weary, but not as severely as in the similar cultivar 'Beacon Silver', which has purplish pink flowers.

In either case, cutting back the stems almost to the ground with hedge shears, or in large areas even with a string trimmer, does wonders. Within several weeks the plant has a flush of vigorous new growth, which carries it well into December. Although a layer of snow has kept *Lamium* 'White Nancy' in leaf here several winters, the selection is more persistent-leaved than evergreen, with a new surge of growth in early spring. Height during the growing season is about ten inches, and plants, while vigorous, are not weedy like some of the lamium brethren. Normal garden soil suffices quite well, with some peat moss mixed in at planting time.

What about the landscape uses of 'White Nancy'? There are dozens, but one that appeals to me is interplanting with small spring-blooming bulbs, especially scillas and chionodoxas, in areas that receive sun in spring but are shaded by trees in summer. The lamium foliage very nicely covers the evidence of bulbs going dormant. 'White Nancy' is also attractive with the lacy leaves of the fringed bleeding-heart (*Dicentra eximia*) or its hybrids, or with the dark green foliage of European wild-ginger (*Asarum europaeum*) or Lenten-rose (*Helleborus orientalis*).

There are almost as many uses for *Lamiastrum* 'Herman's Pride' as there are

Lamium maculatum 'Beacon Silver' is a valuable ground cover for shade, as is its white-flowered counterpart, 'White Nancy'. Both retain their foliage till early winter or longer.

for *Lamium* 'White Nancy'. A rugged but uninvasive, shade-loving ground cover growing about ten inches tall, this superior *Lamiastrum* has silver-speckled foliage persisting into winter. Like *Lamium* 'White Nancy', it injects light into a dark corner, even into fairly deep shade. Moderately attractive yellow flowers appear in late spring and early summer, but this is above all a foliage plant.

Herman, for lack of a common name, makes a good contrast with the dark, leathery green hellebores, especially with the deeply fingered leaves of *Helleborus foetidus,* or in a slightly milder climate than here in Connecticut, with the scalloped, wider foliage segments of *H. lividus* var. *corsicus.* Herman is also a good mate for *H. atrorubens,* which is one of only two plants I recall ever seeing in flower here in January — a pretty good flip of nature, since our mean temperature for that month is 9° F. Usually the maroon-plum flowers start in late February or March and continue for a couple of months.

Helleborus atrorubens, which grows about one foot tall and has evergreen or deciduous leaves depending on the winter, isn't a problem plant. The basic conditions it needs are shade, compost or peat moss mixed well with the plant-ing soil, and reasonable absence of tree root competition. I have not noticed seeds on *H. atrorubens,* but plants divide in spring without difficulty compared with other hellebores, especially the Christmas-rose (*H. niger*). In fact, our orig-inal clump, heavily laced with mugwort, was given to us during a July heat wave, and I immediately bare-rooted it to remove this garden-busting weed. On the theory that it's just as well to be hanged for stealing a sheep as for stealing a goat, I then divided the clump. Every piece lived; but I don't recommend the practice.

Another combination I like with 'Herman's Pride' or 'White Nancy' is the black mondo grass (*Ophiopogon planiscapus* 'Arabicus'), which grows about ten inches tall. Although we have had plants on a shaded slope for ten years, black mondo, whose leaves are as black as asphalt, is much more robust and at home in milder areas, especially California. It gives its best performance here when we overwinter a few plants in the cold frame and use them in a large container with Herman or Nancy. Few things in horticulture are so black and white as this combination. To accentuate the effect, we could add a few rooted cuttings of *Pilea* 'Silver Tree', a house plant with slightly puckered black-and-silver foliage suggesting a lamium dipped in tar.

DEINANTHE AND ASTRANTIA

Deinanthe bifida, a Japanese member of the saxifrage family (Saxifragaceae) with no common name, is at two feet a larger, coarser plant than any of the above. We are tempted to pass it by quickly in search of the many little gems of the shaded garden; but sooner or later our peripheral vision catches it and we stop dead in our tracks, wondering if nature is playing games with our idea of what foliage should look like. The hydrangea-like leaves have a deep cleft at the tip, creating a butterfly effect. The nodding white flowers are exquisite but inconspicuous, and they grace our garden for only a few days in midsummer.

We grow another interesting species, *Deinanthe caerulea,* from China, whose ice-blue flowers were described by nineteenth-century plant hunter Robert For-tune as "like that of some monstrous waxier Pyrola that has known sorrow both wisely and well." Both the Chinese and the Japanese deinanthe have chunky foliage that suggests lacy-leaved perennials for companions. Because nothing should upstage the special flowers, ferns in the same general height range, especially Christmas or lady ferns, are logical choices. Another possibility is astilbes that have bloomed earlier, and that includes most of them. However, if you want companionate bloom, *Geranium* 'Wargrave Pink' and masterwort

(*Astrantia major*) are fairly delicate in appearance and have appropriately incised leaves.

People, especially mates, don't always see plants the same way. When Mary Ann asked what *Deinanthe* meant, I smiled beatifically and said, "Now, remembering my schoolboy Latin and Greek, *deus* refers to a god, and *anthos* means flower. Clearly, my dear, *Deinanthe* signifies 'flowers of the gods,' so let's have a little respect for them." In the manner of the best Thurberian female, she gave a sniff and said, "Well, they look like bio plants to me." (*Bio* is a British botanic garden shorthand phrase meaning "of botanical interest only.")

However, even Mary Ann had enthusiasm for masterwort (*Astrantia major*), a plant that hasn't appeared in many American gardens, perhaps because of its relatively slow growth for a perennial. It takes two or even three years to come into its own, demanding unusual patience from a society that gets fidgety in the fourth and final minute of a potato baking in the microwave oven. Still, the beautiful little white or pink pincushion flowers are worth the wait. They begin to open here in mid-June, and most years some are still coming along in August. The clusters are an inch or so across, with a series of tiny flowers arranged like stars over a dome (an astrodome, at that), which in turn sits on a plate composed of bracts (modified leaves). They have the natural complexity and simplicity of a snowflake. Although their carrying power in the garden is only twenty-five or thirty feet, the sensitive viewer, especially the flower arranger, is apt to stop short when seeing astrantias for the first time.

Astrantia major, which grows about two feet tall and has much-divided foliage at maturity, performs well in any part of the garden that is not exceptionally sunny and dry or deeply shaded. It thrives in light shade and moist, woodsy soil, self-sowing freely but not to the point of aggrandizement once it becomes established. Not much cultivar selection has taken place, but several good ones are available for gardeners who develop more than a passing interest. They are 'Rose Symphony', 'Sunningdale Variegated' (old-cream-and-green leaves in spring, green in summer), and 'Shaggy' ('Margery Fish'), which has somewhat larger bracts.

Another masterwort, *A. maxima*, with fewer leaf segments and rose-pink flowers, is less often encountered, and indeed much of what we have grown from seed as that species has turned out to be *A. major*, which is quite variable. Often a similar misattribution occurs with *A. carniolica*, which is a dwarf. *Astrantia*, which belongs to the parsley family (Umbelliferae), germinates readily from seed and is a surprisingly good plant for new sowers to begin with, provided they don't get jittery the last minute the potatoes are being nuked in the microwave.

ANEMONOPSIS AND FRIENDS

Anemonopsis macrophylla is another perennial without a solid common name, though a literal translation of the genus name is "anemone-like." What ignominy it must be for a plant to go through life always being compared with others! Human beings would never put up with it; and if you don't believe this, when was the last time you saw an entry for John Smith-like in the telephone directory? Actually, the situation is more depressing for *Anemonopsis*, for the specific epithet *macrophylla* means "big-leaved," and the plant does not have particularly large foliage compared with other *Anemonopsis* (there are none), the border anemones, or, come to think of it, lots of other perennials. In context, the botanical epithet seems to approach a real everyday epithet, and I am reminded of Banana Nose Bonura, who managed the Stamford Pioneers in the Class D baseball league when I was a boy. Banana Nose couldn't do much complaining either, but for another reason. His real name was Zeke.

The Pioneers were losers, as were, in my opinion, the botanical christeners of *Anemonopsis*, Siebold and Zuccarini. They sound more like a turn-of-the-century Chicago vaudeville team than reputable botanists. Regardless, our plant is a quiet winner, a good mate for *Astrantia* in the lightly shaded garden. It grows about two and a half feet tall and blooms with pendant pale violet or rose flowers just over an inch across. Like other plants with flowers that face down, *Anemonopsis* is ideally planted on top of a wall so you can see the action better. I have even used it as a hanging-basket plant in a shaded spot on the porch. The flower buds, which resemble reddish brown grapes, have a month-long pregnancy and add much to the appeal of the plant. The flowers open here in August. Anemones resemble them a bit.

Several other perennials look their best when planted on a rise. One is *Tricyrtis macrantha*, a yellow-flowered toad-lily with lax stems that the gardener is tempted to stake early in the season; but the plant never has a natural grace when treated that way. This toad-lily blooms on two-foot-long stems in September and October and should be grown in compost-laced soil in the shade. There is also the *Codonopsis* genus. The one I like best is *C. ovata*, which has musk-scented white bell-shaped flowers in midsummer. They are related to campanulas but with attractive dark markings on the inside of the corolla. *Codonopsis* is taprooted, and if you disturb the root in transplanting, the plant may go dormant for a couple of months or even the remainder of the season. On several occasions I thought I had killed some in transplanting, only to see them grow quite normally the next year. We have used *Codonopsis* for summer display in a hanging basket, too. Plants grow well here in partial shade or sun but in mild climates should get at least afternoon shade.

FOR THE SUN

Euphorbia myrsinites, a sun lover with prostrate, ropelike stems, usually looks best when planted on top of a wall and allowed to cascade over. Here we have a difficult plant to incorporate in the garden, because it is so distinctly subtropical in appearance and always seems to be saying, "Look at me, look at me." This euphorbia, which has yellow flowers in spring, otherwise resembles a gray-shingled florist's eucalyptus that nature forgot to starch. Mary Ann, who is less kindly disposed, says it looks like an octopus with psoriasis. Plants tend to be short-lived, but they self-sow freely. They should be grown in lean soil, because they have a tendency toward baldness in the center if their diet is at all epicurean.

Although I have seen *Euphorbia myrsinites* thrive in northern Vermont and even self-sow prodigiously there, it is most impressive in the mid-Atlantic states in late winter, when there is little else of interest in the garden. We have killed it here with mediocre drainage, which Mary Ann considers a blessing in this instance.

Site, soil conditions, and nutrients can make or break most perennials as ornamentals, but this is especially true for many of the less common sorts, most notably ones of Mediterranean origin grown in cool, moist regions. Asphodel (*Asphodeline lutea*), a beautiful member of the lily family (Lilaceae) from Sicily, with spikes of clear yellow flowers in late spring and narrow blue-gray leaves, is a prime example. Grow it in full sun in well-drained hardscrabble soil, and it's a charmer even as far north as Ontario, where I saw it thriving at the Niagara School of Horticulture. However, put it in a deeply dug, humus-rich border with extra nutrients, a thick mulch, and a little afternoon shade — the horticultural equivalent of a meal ticket to Lutèce or The Four Seasons — and it will become so loose and ungainly a three-footer that you'll wonder why anyone would bother to grow the plant.

Occasionally I come across a perennial that stands best by itself instead of being berthed among others in the border. *Phlomis russeliana,* the most aristocratic member of the mint family (Labiatae) I know of, is a good example. Plants grow about three and one-half feet tall and have sumptuous sage-green felt pads that pose as leaves. The hooded light yellow flowers are arranged in clusters along the leaf axils, giving a candelabra appearance that strikes the viewer as

Phlomis russeliana grows about three feet tall and bears yellow flowers in early summer. Save it for a specimen position because of its handsome foliage.

subtropical, or at least Corinthian. Some gardeners are surprised that this phlomis is winter-hardy here in Connecticut, for it is native to Asia Minor. We have lost no plants to cold in the past ten years, and I have seen them thrive even in northern Vermont. However, good drainage is important, as is plenty of sun. Ideal placement is near a door, with nothing tall nearby, or as a shrub substitute to replace one of the many banalities in foundation plantings.

Knautia macedonica, a member of the teasel family (Dipsacaceae) with pin-cushion flowers of oxblood color, will probably be seen more in gardens when word spreads about its several good traits. The flowers, which are about two inches across, are borne on chunky plants that grow a couple of feet tall. Apart from their unusual color, they have an exceptionally long bloom period, six to eight weeks, spanning the best part of summer. *Knautia* is a sun worshiper, as you might expect of a plant from Macedonia. It mixes well in the garden with a variety of plants. Try it, for example, with a lower-growing Shasta daisy such as *Chrysanthemum* × *superbum* 'Silver Princess', *Veronica spicata* 'Alba', *Allium cernuum,* which has nodding pink flowers, or with pale yellow *Coreopsis* 'Moonbeam'. In our climate, *Knautia* requires a winter mulch of evergreen boughs or salt hay.

The genus *Lychnis* is not apt to win accolades at the annual dinner meeting of the Plant Connoisseurs Society, but two or three kinds rise above the proletarian pack of hot pink or flaming vermilion types. *Lychnis coronaria* 'Alba', the white-flowered variant of the tawdry rose campion, is a fine upstanding gray-leaved plant with pristine flowers borne on three-foot stalks in early summer. True, it is not a Methuselah among perennials, but if you cut the flowering stalks to the ground right after bloom, longevity will increase, and plants will not self-sow.

Because a wet winter can take a toll, it is an insurance policy to let one stalk go to seed, then harvest some of the seeds to scatter around the base of the planting in late summer. If we spot any young plants with pink flowers in our garden, we discard them immediately to keep the progeny true to color. This is an excellent strain for border designs in the sun, because gray foliage and white flowers complement virtually everything. *Lychnis coronaria* 'Oculata', which is identical except for a pink eye, is also uncommon and useful.

Another good gray-leaved lychnis not often seen is the flower-of-Jove, *L. flos-jovis,* the best form being 'Hort's Variety', which has clear pink flowers on fifteen-inch stalks in early summer. 'Hort's', incidentally, has nothing to do with horticulture; rather, the variant was found by a fine British plantsman of the early part of this century, Sir Arthur Hort. It breeds rather dependably true from seed as the others do, provided the species from which it is derived and similar variants are not nearby. The chances are you would not like to have the species around anyway, as it has reddish purple flowers. Try 'Hort's Variety' with the blue flowers of *Aquilegia alpina* or the white of *Geranium sanguineum* 'Album'.

AN OLDIE BUT GOODIE

With the flood of new perennials, some lesser-known older sorts are apt to be overlooked. One of the soundest in the three-foot height range is *Centranthus ruber* 'Albus', the white-flowered variant of the common Jupiter's beard, a familiar British garden subject that is even a denizen of the sidewalk cracks in Los Angeles. Neither presents cultural problems, provided you can give them sun and reasonably good drainage.

Both *Centranthus* grow especially well in alkaline soil, although they don't require it. Overly rich soil brings lanky growth and less bloom. The small pink flowers of the common kind appear a bit staid even in the deepest color forms, and the white-flowered variant has better carrying power from a distance. The bloom period, which you can prolong considerably by deadheading, is early to midsummer in cool parts of the country, late spring in mild areas. Because of another common name, red valerian (it is neither a valerian nor often a real red), *Centranthus ruber* is often confused with *Valeriana officinalis*, a much taller plant with deeply cut green leaves.

SOURCES

Lots of other good out-of-the-ordinary perennials deserve a mention — enough to fill a book or two — but one of the passing frustrations is availability of sources. We have fewer problems in obtaining such plants today than gardeners in the past did, but by their nature these varieties are not going to appear like *Sedum spurium* in every catalogue. Here are a few catalogues with a good selection:

KURT BLUEMEL, 2740 Greene Lane, Baldwin, MD 21013
BUSSE GARDENS, 635 E. 7th St., Rt. 2, Box 13, Cokato, MN 55321
CARROLL GARDENS, Box 310, 444 E. Main St., Westminster, MD 21157
GARDEN PLACE, 6780 Heisley Rd., Box 388, Mentor, OH 44061
HILLSIDE GARDENS, 515 Litchfield Rd., Norfolk, CT 06058 (no shipping)
HOLBROOK FARM AND NURSERY, Rt. 2, Box 223B, Fletcher, NC 28732
CHAS. KLEHM & SON NURSERY, 2E Algonquin Rd., Arlington Heights, IL 60005
PRAIRIE NURSERY, Box 365, Westfield, WI 53964
RICE CREEK GARDENS, 1315 66th Ave. NE, Minneapolis, MN 55432
SISKIYOU RARE PLANT NURSERY, 2825 Cummings Rd., Medford, OR 97501
ANDRE VIETTE FARM & NURSERY, Rt. 1, Box 16, Fishersville, VA 22939
WAYSIDE GARDENS, 1 Garden Lane, Hodges, SC 29695
WE-DU NURSERIES, Rt. 5, Box 724, Marion, NC 28752
WESTON NURSERIES, Rt. 135, Box 186, Hopkinton, MA 01748 (no shipping)
WHITE FLOWER FARM, Litchfield, CT 06759
WOODLANDERS, INC., 1128 Colleton Ave., Aiken, SC 29801

A fuller list appears in the back of *Perennials: How to Select, Grow & Enjoy*, by Pamela Harper and Frederick McGourty (HP Books, Tucson, AZ 85703).

The annual seed exchange list of the American Rock Garden Society (Buffy Parker, Membership Secretary, 15 Fairmead Rd., Darien, CT 06820), which is sent to members each winter, is an excellent source of perennials from seed. The Hardy Plant Society also issues a good list (Mr. S. M. Wills, Membership Secretary, The Manor House, Walton-in-Gordano, Clevedon, Avon BS21 7AN, England). An extensive commercial source based in England is Thompson & Morgan, Box 1308, Jackson, NJ 08527. The firm also lists many uncommon annuals.

· 11 ·

Combining
Perennials

IN THE UNITED STATES, the cultivation of plants takes many forms. There are African violet hobbyists, gladiolus growers, hosta lovers, bonsai buffs, greenhouse plant gurus, orchid and rhododendron specialists, primulologists, cannaphiles, devoted students of the genus *Saxifraga,* gerbera groupies, and many veterans of the vegetable patch. More than sixty plant societies are active these days, not to mention ten societies devoted specifically to irises.

On occasion I have attended the meetings of such organizations and found them fascinating, not only for the animated and detailed discussion of special plants, but also for the human participants, many of whom are quite special in their dedication. If a hemerocallis meeting had taken place on the last voyage of the *Titanic,* its members would have been oblivious of the main problem at hand, at least until the last stanza of "Nearer My God To Thee" was sung. Lifelong friendships are made at such get-togethers, and a certain number of lasting enmities, too. I remember one speaker showing 140 consecutive slide close-ups of gentians. As a result, I have developed what will probably be a lifelong coolness toward this otherwise innocuous group of plants.

But is all this emphasis on individual plant groups really gardening? Perhaps it is, if we consider gardening in a very strict sense, as the collecting of cultivars. To me, however, the subject has always implied something more: the creation of aesthetically pleasing arrangements of plants, as well as the culture of those plants. It is the combination of different forms — the coarse with the refined, the light with the dark — as well as their synergistic effects, that truly makes a garden distinct from a collection of plants.

The late Vita Sackville-West put it another way. She once remarked that successful gardening was largely a matter of good marriages, albeit arranged ones for the most part. She was referring, of course, to plant combinations. Some are not lasting affairs, despite impeccable lineage and spectacular honeymoons. A shocking number were just never meant to be because of the roving nature of one of the partners. In some cases there can be no recourse but divorce, by yanking out one or more of the incompatible parties. (*Ménage à trois* — or *à quatre* — requires extra-special circumspection in the floral kingdom.)

Our own garden is full of divorces, as are the gardens of friends who also care about the compatible display of plants. We don't like to talk about skeletons in the family closet, at least not in print. If we are dealing with trees and shrubs, we can inflict permanent scars on the landscape by the wrong combinations. Fortunately, with perennials the simple corrective is a trowel. Perennials can be moved! Many of them have traveled long distances in our garden. Had they belonged to a frequent-flyer club, I am sure a few would have earned a trip to Hawaii by now.

COLOR AND TIMING

Mixing flower colors from different parts of the spectrum, such as yellows and pinks, frequently causes squabbles. Oranges and pinks always bring about pitched battles while the gardener looks on helplessly. Counseling doesn't work under such circumstances, though buffering the contending parties with plenty of silver foliage, white or blue flowers, or green foliage can turn adversity into diversity.

Timing is of the essence in avoiding some fierce battles. Each year there is a near collision in one of our lightly shaded borders between two sound perennials — *Astilbe* 'Rheinland', which has lovely eighteen-inch-tall steeples of clear pink flowers, and the common 'Enchantment' lily, whose flower color has been described as vermilion or nasturtium red by polite authors. Actually, it is traffic-cop orange, which is a hard tint to use in the garden, though there is hope if you keep it several hundred feet from the house. Fortunately, in the half-dozen years of this partnership, the astilbe has finished doing its thing two or three days before the lily has started. Someday the weather conditions may cause the blooms to overlap, and if they do, I will be prepared to scythe the astilbe in one fell swoop. Being a peace-keeper forces one to make difficult decisions.

In some parts of the country, climatic conditions routinely cause the astilbe and lily to overlap. Clearly, some of the floral combinations that work for us in New England don't in Georgia or California, even though the plants may grow well there. The United States is a large country, and gardeners must work out their own plant marriages according to their regions and indeed the microclimates in their gardens.

But suppose Mary Ann and I would like to avoid going down to the wire with color clashes in our garden. One way might be for us to plant *Astilbe* 'Rheinland' with other astilbes having slightly different tints of pink. In another part of our garden, in fact, we alternate the mid-pink 'Rheinland' with another cultivar, 'Peach Blossom', which has pale pink flowers. Usually, colors close to each other combine quite well. (The summer phloxes, which some gardeners are apt to dismiss with the epithet *magenta*, are a good example.) One exception is red; if one tint is orange-red, as in the Maltese-cross (*Lychnis chalcedonica*), and the other is pinkish red, as in the rose campion (*Lychnis coronaria*), the combination can be like squeaky chalk on a blackboard.

IF IN DOUBT, USE SILVER

An increasing number of gardeners are beginning to appreciate silver foliage for its value in bringing out the best flower color in other plants. These days, probably the most widely sold perennial in the Northeast is a plant called silver mound, *Artemisia schmidtiana* 'Nana' of the trade. In one section of our garden we use it as an edging for a drift of *Astilbe* 'Peach Blossom'. It provides early summer elegance, but then silver mound would complement anything except a giant sequoia. Even brassy yellows and oranges look dignified in its presence.

Silver mound performs best in the cooler parts of the country, but even there it has a tendency to flop open halfway through the season, resembling a silver cloud — sometimes a cirrus one at that. If you like tight little mounds, grow it in very sandy soil in full sun. I don't mind the former effect as long as the cloud has a silver lining, but in some situations you should prune this plant sharply in midsummer if it is to look good the rest of the growing season. If summers in your area are very hot, consider substituting lavender cotton (*Santolina chamae-cyparissus*) for the same silvery effect, but be aware that this delightful subshrub has yellow flowers in summer that will clash with pinks. Some gardeners routinely remove these flowers, as they do the flowering stalks of another useful silver-leaved plant, lamb's-ears (*Stachys byzantina*), but the discord that results from leaving them on is not serious.

Lynden B. Miller

Top, left: Astilbes and hostas are a fitting combination for shaded areas. This June scene at New York Botanical Garden shows *Astilbe* 'Peach Blossom' with *A.* 'Fanal', whose red flowers shine like a beacon.

Right: Pacific Giant delphiniums, pink climbing roses, and green foliage soften the harsh tint of rose campion (*Lychnis coronaria*) in the Van Vlack garden.

Bottom, left: Gray foliage makes green seem greener and purple purpler. *Artemisia* 'Silver King', gray santolina (*S. chamaecyparissus*), and *Artemisia schmidtiana* accompany pale pink Lancaster geranium (*G. sanguineum* var. *striatum*) and *Salvia* × *superba*.

Right: Variegated Japanese Solomon's-seal (*Polygonatum odoratum* 'Variegatum'), which is sparse in lower foliage, benefits from a skirt of blue-eyed Mary (*Omphalodes verna*). Both are spring bloomers for shaded sites.

A ROSE IS NOT NECESSARILY A ROSE

Let us return for a moment to rose campion (*Lychnis coronaria*). There is precious little that is "rose" about it. It has a color that because of its vulgar loudness appeals mainly to people with tin eyes. We evicted this old-time, free-seeding, short-lived perennial from our garden with a vengeance after discovering young plants cavorting with 'Enchantment' lilies. The first-year foliage rosette is a wonderfully seductive satiny gray, but we can have that in a white-flowered form with *L. coronaria* 'Alba', which comes true from seed if you keep it away from the loud type.

No flower color is intrinsically bad, but I have the highest regard for any gardener who uses rose campion well. Such a person is Mildred Van Vlack. Mrs. Van Vlack's Connecticut garden is at its peak in the latter part of June, when old roses and the first wave of delphiniums are in fine fettle. The rose campion has a backdrop of good, pink old roses, and there are several perennnials nearby with good green foliage, as well as a smattering of plants with white flowers. It is a winning combination, and I often think of it, though I have never actually tried it. Mrs. Van Vlack is a bolder person than I am.

STRETCHING IT OUT

Floral combinations with perennials are transient, because most plants bloom for just three weeks or so. Perhaps that is just as well, because we can have a succession of combinations through the season, with something new to look forward to as the months go by. Lately I have had a special interest in extending the period in which the garden is attractive further into autumn. Normal people admire sugar maples or watch football games in fall. My taste runs more toward combating seasonal senescence in the garden, delaying the inevitable, and more positively, preserving beauty. Summer in the North is too short, and I don't see any reason to throw in the trowel on Labor Day, particularly when some of the year's best weather is yet to come.

Of course, there is always the chrysanthemum, which seems to be a tyrant of fall gardens. When I visit a garden center in September, I get the uneasy feeling that every flower in the world has a rounded form. Chrysanthemums have become events rather than garden plants. In recent years they have evolved apart from the garden and are now to many people just an extension of a florist crop. It is hard to classify the autumn chrysanthemum taxonomically and even season-ally; it is not quite a perennial, it is not an annual, and many of the cultivars start to flower by late July. Of course, if we want such flowers programmed into bloom, we can go to a florist even in March.

I do not really care to see a chrysanthemum in March or in July, and I do not think that excessive hybridization has made the plant prettier. Do not mistake me: I am fond of the chrysanthemum — single-flowered and pompom sorts that will bloom in September and October and maybe even November in the severe land where I live, and ones that will survive winter in good shape and not need yearly division or staking. A dream, you say? No, I see these in older gardens from time to time, and ask for cuttings. Unfortunately, they do not seem to be in the trade anymore.

How much richer our gardens would be if we thought of the chrysanthemum as *one* of autumn's plants rather than its *exclusive* one. That time of year may be top-heavy with daisy flower forms, but other plants can relieve the possible monotony. Foremost are the spikes of the late-blooming snakeroot (*Cimicifuga simplex*), whose pure white bottlebrushes on three- to six-foot-tall stems rise from the sea of chrysanthemums, each complementing the other. The spikes of a September-flowering false dragonhead (*Physostegia virginiana* 'Bouquet Rose') are useful with white chrysanthemums, since the latter are apt to fade to a purplish pink and need some visual support so as not to appear tatty. Chrysanthemums, like most plants, should have their spent flowers removed. In this case, removing the flowers can extend the season of effective bloom considerably. Pink turtlehead (*Chelone lyonii*) can serve much the same function as false dragonhead, though its individual flowers are hunchbacked.

My favorite combination for autumn doesn't include a chrysanthemum, and the blooms last a long time. This is a *ménage à trois* combining *Sedum* 'Autumn Joy', with flat clusters of Indian-red flowers on two-foot-tall stalks; Canadian burnet (*Sanguisorba canadensis*), whose five-foot-tall stalks topped by white bottlebrushes are less showy but more frost-resistant than those of *Cimicifuga simplex;* and the fall monkshood (*Aconitum carmichaelii*, sometimes listed as *A. fischeri*), with clear blue flowers on stalks that usually attain three feet. A

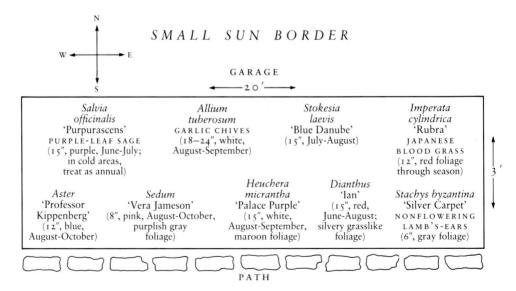

SMALL SUN BORDER

Salvia officinalis 'Purpurascens' PURPLE-LEAF SAGE (15", purple, June-July; in cold areas, treat as annual)	Allium tuberosum GARLIC CHIVES (18–24", white, August-September)	Stokesia laevis 'Blue Danube' (15", July-August)	Imperata cylindrica 'Rubra' JAPANESE BLOOD GRASS (12", red foliage through season)
Aster 'Professor Kippenberg' (12", blue, August-October)	Sedum 'Vera Jameson' (8", pink, August-October, purplish gray foliage)	Heuchera micrantha 'Palace Purple' (15", white, August-September, maroon foliage)	Dianthus 'Ian' (15", red, June-August; silvery grasslike foliage)	Stachys byzantina 'Silver Carpet' NONFLOWERING LAMB'S-EARS (6", gray foliage)

PATH

fourth partner is evident in the background if a cool summer has delayed flowering. This is *Helenium* 'Copper Spray', which is four to five feet tall, yellow-orange, and showy. Off to another side is *Rudbeckia nitida* 'Goldquelle', with yellow flowers that are fully double. This plant resembles a scaled-down version of golden-glow, *R. laciniata* 'Hortensia', the dowdy, turn-of-the-century matron one still encounters near old farmhouses. A few New England asters, the white-flowered *Boltonia asteroides* 'Snowbank', and a tall ornamental grass or two (for example, *Miscanthus sinensis* 'Silver Feather', or zebra grass, *M. sinensis* 'Zebrinus', with its horizontal yellow bands) would provide a quite tolerable autumn border — enough to wean all but die-hard machos away from the television set on a Saturday afternoon in October. They probably wouldn't even notice that chrysanthemums were missing.

SHADE

To the innovative gardener, shade is an opportunity, not a problem, and in warmer parts of the country it is a blessing for plants as well as for people. Approximately 40 percent of the best-known perennials demand shade or are shade-tolerant (there is a difference between the two). This gives the gardener who is looking for aesthetically pleasing combinations plenty of plants with which to experiment. The warmer the area, the greater the number of plants that welcome some shade, especially in the afternoon.

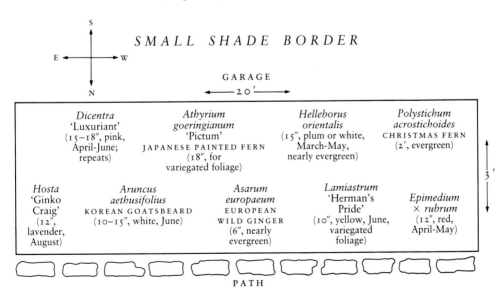

SMALL SHADE BORDER

Plant partnerships are not forever, but one I like very much is the European wild-ginger (*Asarum europaeum*) planted in front of maidenhair fern (*Adiantum pedatum*). The deep green, leathery, chunky foliage of the former is enhanced by the light-textured, delicate green of the latter. In time the fern grows too tall, and so you must rework the combination periodically. If you can obtain the more compact-growing Aleutian form of maidenhair fern (*A. pedatum* var. *aleuticum*) from a rock garden nursery, you might use it as a substitute. Another variation on the theme is to substitute one of the southern wild-gingers — either *Asarum shuttleworthii* or *A. virginicum,* with their attractively marbled foliage — for the European species.

Foliage combinations are more durable than floral ones because the leaves are present throughout the growing season. In the case of the three wild gingers I have mentioned, the leaves are in fact evergreen. Should you want to add an attractive floral partner, Korean goatsbeard (*Aruncus aethusifolius*), with feathery, astilbe-like foliage and eight-inch-tall stalks of white flowers, is a fitting companion. The foliage itself is winning, and the plant makes a fine ground cover in a small area.

Another low-growing foliage combination for the shade is *Hosta venusta* and a dwarf meadow-rue, *Thalictrum minus,* which grows only one foot tall in its better forms and has small, lacy foliage that looks best after a rain, when beads of water cling to it. *H. venusta* is the smallest true species of hosta (only a couple of inches high), but with a blocky effect. One variant even smaller than that, *H. venusta* 'Minus', is useful for rock garden troughs. Both the thalictrum and the

Opposite, top left (from front): European wild-ginger (*Asarum europaeum*), variegated fairy-bells (*Disporum sessile* 'Variegatum'), and Korean goatsbeard (*Aruncus aethusifolius*) in a deeply shaded part of the McGourty garden. Contrast in foliage is noticeable through the season.
Top right: Shasta daisy (*Chrysanthemum* × *superbum* 'Alaska') and *Veronica longifolia* represent the two most common flower types found in gardens, the rounded or daisy form and the spike. Good border design usually includes a mixture of the two plus the loose airy form, as found in baby's-breath (*Gypsophila*) or statice (*Limonium*), as a change of pace.
Middle left: Japanese painted fern (*Athyrium goeringianum* 'Pictum'), valued for its lacy gray fronds, which inject light into shaded areas, is an appropriate mate for European wild-ginger (*Asarum europaeum*).
Middle right: A low meadow-rue, *Thalictrum minus,* guards the smallest of the *Hosta* species, *H. venusta.* Foliage contrast keeps the eye coming back for more. Forget the flowers; they are excess visual baggage.
Bottom: Blue and yellow usually combine well in the garden. In a roughly informal border at Hillside, *Veronica* 'Crater Lake Blue' consorts with yellow flag (*Iris pseudacorus*). After bloom in early summer we cut back the veronica sharply to improve the growth habit, and we remove seed pods from the iris so plants won't self-sow.

hosta bloom, but the flowers are irrelevant, except perhaps to the plants and to the sort of gardener who judges plants only by blossoms.

These combinations are satisfactory in fairly deep shade, but the number of choices increases in light shade. The focal point in July and August in our main border, in a section that receives less than five hours of sun each day, is a grouping of five plants of a largely neglected American woodlander, the black snakeroot (*Cimicifuga racemosa*). These were planted in a woodsy, moisture-retentive soil in 1964 and have not been divided since, nor have they been fertilized more than two or three times over the years.

The actual flowering period of the black snakeroot in our garden is no longer than a month, but the six- or seven-foot-tall stalks are prominent for two weeks before the pearl-shaped white buds open, and the stalks have architectural merit for several more weeks after flowering. I was not much of a gardener in 1964, and my immediate aim then was to hide a statue of a little girl that my mother left me. The snakeroot did not perform its task very well, though it did soften the statue, and the main beneficiaries have been the surrounding plants that I selected for summer bloom: *Heliopsis* 'Gold Greenheart', magnificently scented regal lilies, and clear pink summer phlox 'Sir John Falstaff', which will linger in bloom until September if we remove the old flower heads and if we have been conscientious in applying the fungicide Benomyl to control mildew.

· 12 ·

In Praise of
Common Plants

THREE OR FOUR TIMES a year I am dragged, kicking and screaming, to a cocktail party by a wife who accuses me of becoming a hermit. I am not very good at such affairs and usually retreat to study a bookcase if I think I can get away with it. No one bothers a bibliophile, especially one who reads books. Every so often there is no bookcase, and I have to stand by the brie talking with someone whose eye reaches beyond my shoulder as soon as I answer her question about my occupation — a horticulturist. Not surprisingly, the conversation turns to cheese, and I remark about my fondness for brie, even when it is heated and has almonds on it, which seems increasingly the case in this complicated age. At the last bash this brought a swift retort: "But it's *so* common. Nobody serves it at the better parties anymore. Everyone's into chèvre now, with shredded macadamias on top." I almost spilled my Campari and soda.

The same sort of thing happens when I attend plant meetings these days, too. Recently one speaker complained about the glaring ubiquity of annuals; another railed against hostas as the ornamental cabbages that are taking over America. People utter these sneers with the sort of fervor that turf specialists reserve for lawns that have dandelions in them. I happen to be fond of dandelions, and once suggested to a lawn man that the world would be a better place if we let the dandelions grow and pulled out the grass, which gets in the way of the climax lawn. What is the sin of a dandelion except commonness? It is a beautiful plant. My turf friend realized at once that he was in the presence of an unregenerate American crank.

The fact is, it's a trendy country, and gardening, like any other field, has its share of "in" plants and "out" plants. Paperbark maple, Japanese painted fern, variegated Solomon's-seal, and European wild-ginger are "in" plants, of course. "Out" plants, which may have been "in" at one time, include cannas, gladioli (except the species, which are "in"), *Catalpa, Strelitzia,* and *Kolkwitzia.* Regional variations occur, especially in California. In general, the number of "out" plants is greater in the Northeast and Northwest than in other parts of the country. There are not many in the Plains states.

Occasionally a plant is "in" in one place, "out" in another. An example is crape myrtle, which is as common in the South as watermelon but undependably hardy in New York, hence valued. I know a person who grows one of the hardier palms, *Rhapidophyllum hystrix,* on an island off the Massachusetts coast. This specimen is a far cry from one grown in Ireland or Cornwall or even Norfolk, Virginia, but it is treasure in the eye of the owner-beholder. A few advanced plantsmen like *Gaura lindheimeri,* a perennial wildflower from Texas with white flowers resembling moths who have been through a hailstorm. It is not very well known among gardeners, and it is not intended to be. *Gaura* is one of those plants with quiet grace. "Quiet grace," of course, is a horticultural euphemism for secondary elegance. The *Gaura* cult has grown.

A MULTINATIONAL THISTLE

Along with nine or ten other people in America, I am fond of the Scotch thistle (*Onopordum acanthium*), whose prickly silver rosettes give rise the second year to very prickly, eight-foot-tall stalks. As they reach toward the heavens, these become candelabra bearing reddish purple flowers, much like those of the globe artichoke, in July. Scotch thistle isn't really Scottish at all, and it was probably an Englishman who first called it Scotch, as an epithet. It is native from Europe to central Asia but has moved around in its own exuberant way. In South America it is called the Argentine thistle, probably by the Chileans.

Stately biennials such as the Scotch thistle are not easy to use in the landscape, especially ours. My wife expressed her opinion on the subject in no uncertain terms: "You'll plant those thistles in my garden over my dead body!" Mary Ann is not one of the nine or ten Onopordophiles on this side of the Atlantic, and my efforts at plant sensitivity training have not been entirely successful.

Much of the success of a garden has to do with the proper placement of plants, and I ascertained that there was room for compromise, or at least maneuvering, since Mary Ann had specifically referred to the garden, not the property. In this give-and-take, I was given the driveway as part of the settlement, with the understanding that early each August Mary Ann's son would be allowed to chop down the Scotch thistles with an ax before the seeds ripened fully and spilled over into the next county. Steven spends most of July sharpening the ax. He is not an Onopordophile either.

Fortunately, the large driveway of our old farm is unpaved, though the soil has been compacted by two centuries of pressure from cows, horses, stagecoaches, wagons, tractors, cars, trucks, backhoes, and overweight Labrador retrievers. The evidence is covered by an inch or two of battleship gray pebbles called trap rock.

I carefully chose a planting spot away from wheels, human feet, cat runs, and potential home plates of preteen baseball crazies. As I believe that Scotch thistles should go first class, I selected a southerly location next to our barn, between a garage door that opens to a tool storage area and another door that leads to an old stable where pots are stored. There is considerable traffic between the two. When wife, young 'uns, and our nursery staff go by, they can all admire the

Johnny-jump-ups (*Viola tricolor*) are good spring mates for daffodils — common but winning.

Scotch thistles, I thought. Well, they at least look at the thistles, though not with the kind of warmth these noble plants deserve. Each person except me looks forward to early August, and there is an irreverent celebration on the appointed day of felling.

Growing Scotch thistle in gravel is a bit of an art. The improvement of the soil, as it were, consisted of incorporating several shovelsful of peat moss, worked in by pick until the pick broke. Good sendoffs are vital, so I added some superphosphate and lime, too. Actually the sendoff was more like a takeoff, and I, for one, am pleased to report that a modest naturalizing has taken place. With biennials, one must leave a few seeds to ripen *in situ* lest the species should die out, which my wife thinks an unlikely occurrence with Scotch thistle. We also let a few first-year plants remain at the base of the clump — more than we need, perhaps, but the silver rosettes are pretty and form a pleasant contrast with the gray trap rock and the barn-red barn. *Genius loci,* I always say. "Barnyard plants," Mary Ann mutters.

JOHNNY-JUMP-UPS

I have always had a sneaking admiration for Johnny-jump-ups (*Viola tricolor*), the European wild pansy that must have come to America in the wake of the *Mayflower.* Few plants have had more names over the years — some sixty in English alone, including herb trinity, three-faces-in-a-hood, love-in-idleness, cull-me-to-you, and heart's-ease, a name that later rubbed off on the garden pansy, which is a nineteenth-century hybrid of *V. tricolor* and one or two other species. It is not good form to admit strong fondness for Johnny-jump-ups, but they have won more friends over the years than, say, *Acanthophyllum gypso-philoides.*

Our first gardening encounter with Johnny-jump-ups occurred some years ago when Throckmorton, a quintessentially Yankee bachelor friend, dropped by with a couple of flats that had just been given to him by an older lady for whom he occasionally gardened. There were all sorts of variations in flower color, running the gamut of purple, yellow, and white, the three tints that make up the "tricolor" in the species name. Throckmorton made a point of picking them over and reserving the most colorful for himself. In fact, we were left with the purple ones, pretty enough but not what we had anticipated.

The Johnny-jump-ups were planted in one of our perennial borders, and they flowered beautifully all through the season. I began to wonder why no one gave them prime spots in the garden. The next year the reason became abundantly clear. They had increased their space to half the border, and we realized that something had to be done.

One day a visiting rock gardener who thought we should have a rock garden too suggested that we turn the far end of our driveway, away from the Scotch thistles, into a scree. Well, water certainly does run through, under, and over the driveway in late winter, and there is no shortage of small stones.

I gathered that the conditions would not have quite met with the approval of Farrer (author of *The English Rock Garden*), so I decided on a fantasy scree in the driveway. We sprigged in a few young plants of Johnny-jump-ups, and nature took over in its inimitable way, despite the occasional intercession of automobile wheels and snowplows. Each spring we have a veritable cavalry unit of new seedlings, and we let them gallop to their heart's content, or ease, so to speak. They are still mostly purple, which doesn't really bother us, but when we visit the gardens of friends who have good tricolor Johnnys, Mary Ann and I take a moment to admire them, which brings an odd stare from our hosts. They would rather have us appreciate their *Acanthophyllum gypsophiloides*.

THE MARIGOLD PEACE SETTLEMENT

I am in my postmarigold period of gardening, but that does not mean that I cannot stop and wink at one from time to time, particularly when no one else is around. Visitors are sometimes surprised to see them in our garden. I gently point to my wife (if she is not looking), and they understand as I hustle them off to another border. Marigolds, you see, are part of the marital compromise.

One June, a day or two after returning from our honeymoon, Mary Ann asked when we were going to put in the annuals. The garden looked rather complete to me, and with a guarded tone I asked what annuals she had in mind. I hoped she was planning for next year, and for color in the vegetable garden in the meadow beyond our house, out of sight.

"Love me, love my marigolds!" she exclaimed. "I want them up front, right by the door. Orange ones, yellow ones, maybe some white ones, too."

I took the offensive. "Mary Ann, this is a quiet residential area. What will the neighbors think? Besides, there may be zoning regulations. And what do you expect me to tell the president of the International Meconopsis Society when he drops by for lunch?"

She replied, "Tell him David Burpee is coming for dinner."

That settled it. I lost.

I may have lost the war, but I was determined to win the peace. If one is going

Garlic chives (*Allium tuberosum*), variegated moor grass (*Molinia caerulea* 'Variegata'), and French marigold (*Tagetes* 'Sparky') in an August scene in the kitchen border at Hillside.

to plant marigolds, one should at least go about it properly. Concessions were exacted. In return for limiting the planting by the back door to one area and with surrounding plants of my choice, I conceded to Mary Ann's color selection, 'Sunkist' orange. In addition, I agreed to give several window boxes by our old well to marigolds, but they had to be small, yellow, single-flowered French types such as 'Dainty Marietta', or signet types, which for marigolds are refined, especially when mixed with dusty-millers and *Nierembergia*. We agreed some-day to try the low-growing foliage marigold called Irish-lace, *Tagetes filifolia*, which late in the season bears tiny whitish flowers that cannot be seen from a speeding car. Essentially, it is a marigold for people who don't like marigolds. You don't see it around much, but it is available.

But what we are really talking about is orange. It is a difficult color to get around, particularly 'Sunkist' orange. Actually, not many plants have it: some cultivars of *Kniphofia*, zinnias, and calendulas; also California poppies (*Esch-scholzia* sp.) and butterfly weed (*Asclepias tuberosa*), which is not the hard electric shade because the flowers are small. I thought of the times I had seen these plants displayed well in gardens, and it was usually with yellow flowers or golden-foliaged plants.

Just around this time Tom Dilatush, a nurseryman friend who was trying to interest us in ornamental grasses, gave us a mature plant of variegated moor grass (*Molinia caerulea* 'Variegata'), which has leaves striped green and pale yellow. It makes a tidy clump about two feet tall when the airy flowers appear in late summer. What we did not know then was that *Molinia* is one of the most beautiful of all perennial grasses and looks good even in November, when the leaves become light buff. Tom suggested that we plant the *Molinia* near the door so we would be aware of its presence then.

The moor grass has served as the catalyst for a grouping of low-growing 'Sunkist' orange marigolds we planted in front of and alongside it. Also, it cools while they enhance, and the combination works. For a complement, we planted some ornamental onions with gray leaves and soft yellow flowers, *Allium carinatum* var. *flavum*, nearby. Their flowers open in a fascinating manner near but not at the top of the scape, from a long beak that encloses them. They bloom for a number of weeks in midsummer. This is one of the prettiest alliums, and it almost takes the minds of curmudgeons off marigolds.

EVER SO SWEET ALYSSUM

There are few banal plants, just banal sites or banal combinations. One annual that I have never found banal in any way or location is a low-growing plant from the Mediterranean world that most gardeners take for granted — sweet-alyssum (*Lobularia maritima*). There is no need to describe it here except to say that purple- and rosy pink-flowered variants of the usual white-flowered mat, 'Carpet of Snow', are available. As an edging plant, the last has bound down many a border that otherwise would have been strident red or yellow clouds floating in space.

I like sweet-alyssum best, however, as individual specimens planted among low-growing foliage plants of patrician but slightly obese form, such as *Bergenia* or the first-year rosettes of the wonderfully felty silver sage, *Salvia argentea*. One pleasant use of 'Royal Carpet' sweet-alyssum, which has purple flowers with a bit of white, is to intersperse it among plants of this superb sage, where the alyssum provides textural change but color compatibility. The two in turn are guarded as a distinct garden scenario by a background of lavender-blue *Stokesia*, in turn overseen by purple coneflower (*Echinacea purpurea*). The flanks are safe from invasion if you have some grays, pinks, and whites defending them. There is no shortage of choices. These are cool, lingering scenes for the beach days of summer.

Sweet-alyssum differs from most annuals because it is frost-tolerant, and even in our wretched New England climate it may have some flowers as late as November. It also self-sows, and each year usually brings a new batch of seedlings near where plants were the year before. I simply spend a few minutes each spring rearranging them and discarding the excess.

One of the loveliest uses of sweet-alyssum is simple abandonment. A few years ago a landscape designer friend took me on a tour of gardens in Beverly Hills. We stopped at a posh hotel where there were fine, rather elaborate designs with many plants I knew only from straitjacket culture in greenhouses. I don't relate to such plants very well but was aware that praise, or at least gentle comment, was expected. Then, off to one side appeared a brick terrace covered with low white mounds. Sometime before, someone had given the area between the bricks to sweet-alyssum instead of the customary mother-of-thyme, and it had filled the openings beautifully and lavishly. My friend was disappointed that I was focusing my attention on such common plants, so I made a point of speaking favorably about some lantanas nearby, which made matters worse. But then, even the cracks of Los Angeles sidewalks are fascinating to northeasterners whose plants of red valerian (*Centranthus ruber*) or Mexican fleabane (*Erigeron karvinskianus*) have faded away. One man's garden flower is another man's weed.

· 13 ·

Annuals for
Perennial Borders

"PLEASE TELL US what your favorite white-flowered plant is for the back of the border," she said.

I had just finished speaking to the Outer Humpton Garden Club on "Perennials of Distinction." Perhaps it was the blue corn tortillas with melted yak cheese and slivered pignoli that rarefied my taste, but I blurted, "*Cleome* 'Helen Campbell'."

The silence was so still I could hear the Perrier fizz on the other side of the living room. With slight amusement and a flick of her Gucci handbag, the lady protested, "But that's an *annual*, not a serious plant."

This sort of exchange was common in the better clubs I encountered on the lecture circuit several years ago, with allowance of course for different cheeses and their carriers. In Peoria or Paducah perhaps the cleome would never have been questioned, since annuals have always been "in" there, but not so at the Outer Humptons of the East. Even in this inhibited atmosphere, I am frankly glad to say, annuals are at last emerging again in gardens. Certain kinds are the perfect accompaniments for perennial borders endangered by midsummer lag.

Most perennials, as I have said, have a bloom period of just three weeks, whereas the majority of annuals bloom all summer. I do not feel this is a drawback of perennials, because with careful selection a gardener can have an ever-changing scene through the season, but incorporating a few annuals can transform a slightly stodgy perennial border into a fresh, crisp summer blend that will continue to draw the eye until frost.

Not all annuals are appropriate, and it helps to have a few criteria for choosing ones that will work best. Electric colors, ones of neon intensity that are associated with some of the better-known annuals, are best left to those gardeners who like pep rallies in the garden. It seems to me that there are enough ordinary challenges in displaying colors at their best for us to avoid the classic troublemaking tints of ruffian red, sunset orange, and yahoo pink. Admittedly, some selections of zinnia, marigold, and gazania have subdued colors, but those aren't basically their nature, and that isn't why we grow those plants. In the main, they have showboating colors, and a shouting match is inevitable if too many of them are together. In my own garden I prefer no shouting, though in good-sized borders some firmness of plant voice is needed if the whole is to be effective. This is one reason that bright colors predominate in park plantings.

It is better to look to annuals not so much for vivid color accompaniments for perennial gardens, but for those traits that are a bit short in perennialdom. Spiky flowers aren't numerous among the perennials, compared with the rounded or daisy forms we encounter increasingly as summer progresses. True, there are lots of sentinel veronicas and some cultivars of *Salvia × superba*, as well as lythrum and liatris, but no spiky perennial matches *Salvia farinacea* in general garden utility. In mild climates it is more or less perennial, but in areas with a real winter it is grown as an annual. 'Victoria', a good lavender-blue, grows eighteen to twenty-four inches tall and blooms from June to frost. It supersedes 'Blue Bedder', whose narrow spikes appear anorexic by comparison. 'Victoria' combines well with a wide range of perennials with rounded or daisy shapes, including the border yarrows in yellow, such as the long-blooming *Achillea* 'Moonshine' (two feet) or *Achillea* 'Coronation Gold' (three feet). In the whiskey-tub planters that have become popular in recent years, a single plant of *Salvia farinacea* 'Victoria' makes a fine centerpiece faced down with pale yellow *Coreopsis* 'Moonbeam', which blooms all summer, and silver sage (*Salvia argentea*), a perennial that goes on for only three or four years for us but that has the most sumptuous gray foliage rosette of any hardy perennial I know.

Opposite, top: Salvia farinacea 'Victoria' is a superior selection of mealy-cup sage. It grows about eighteen inches tall and consorts well with other annuals, such as cosmos, and with a wide range of perennials.
Bottom: St. Joseph's sage (*Salvia viridis;* formerly *S. horminum*) is a low-key annual with attractive bracts in deep blue, rose pink, or white. Height is eighteen inches, and plants need sun to do their best.

←——— 50' ———→

Caryopteris × clandonensis BLUE MIST SHRUB (4', August-September; prune back to the ground in early spring)	Cassia marilandica (5', yellow, July)	Echinops 'Taplow Blue' (5½', June-August)	Achillea 'Coronation Gold' (4', June-July)	Cleome 'Helen Campbell' (6', white, June-October, annual)

7' ↕

Veronica incana (12", blue, June)	Lavatera 'Mont Blanc' (3', white, July-September, annual)	Kniphofia Royal Castle Hybrids RED-HOT-POKER (3', orange & yellow, July-August)	Sedum 'Autumn Joy' (2', reddish pink, August-November)	Salvia farinacea 'Victoria' (18', deep blue, June-October, annual)

Santolina chamaecyparissus LAVENDER COTTON (15", yellow, July, silver foliage)	Salvia officinalis 'Icterina' GOLDEN VARIEGATED SAGE (15", for foliage) interplanted with Dyssodia tenuiloba DAHLBERG DAISY (6", yellow, May-August, annual)	Dianthus 'Aqua' (12", white, May-July)	Geranium sanguineum striatum LANCASTER GERANIUM (10", pale pink, June; repeats)	Linum perenne 'Diamond' (12", white, May-July)

DROUGHT-RESISTANT MIXED BORDER
(Full Sun — Very Little Watering Through Summer.
Plants are perennial unless otherwise noted.)

All of these plants are sun worshipers and drought resisters, though they shouldn't be pushed to the desert limit, which is a temptation when dealing with such plants. White-flowered selections of *Salvia farinacea* exist, including 'White Porcelain'. Though useful for schemes with silver-leaved perennials, or ones with pink flowers, they are not usually as attractive or floriferous as the typical lavender-blue form of this sage. Bear in mind that they all make excellent cut flowers.

SNAPDRAGONS AND BELLS-OF-IRELAND

Since we hear a lot more about the importance of low maintenance than about beauty as an ultimate aim in gardens these days, I will hesitate for a split second before recommending a plant that needs staking. However, the tall, full-bodied spikes of the Rocket series of snapdragons, in separate color selections that are quite refined, deserve more than a passing mention and are better performers over a long period than the dwarf strains. Among the Rocket tints are buffered

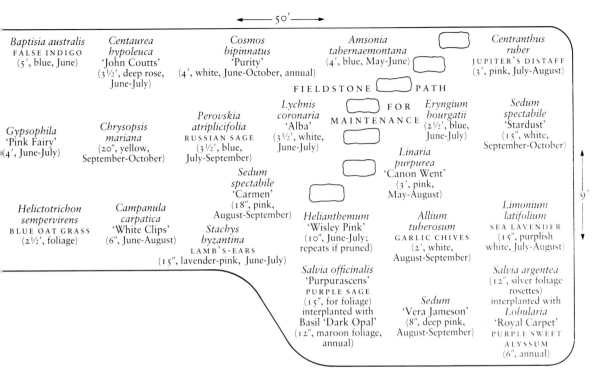

←——— 50' ———→

Baptisia australis
FALSE INDIGO
(5', blue, June)

Centaurea
hypoleuca
'John Coutts'
(3½', deep rose,
June-July)

Cosmos
bipinnatus
'Purity'
(4', white, June-October, annual)

Amsonia
tabernaemontana
(4', blue, May-June)

Centranthus
ruber
JUPITER'S DISTAFF
(3', pink, July-August)

FIELDSTONE   PATH

Gypsophila
'Pink Fairy'
(4', June-July)

Chrysopsis
mariana
(20", yellow,
September-October)

Perovskia
atriplicifolia
RUSSIAN SAGE
(3½', blue,
July-September)

Lychnis
coronaria
'Alba'
(3½', white,
June-July)

FOR
MAINTENANCE

Eryngium
bourgatii
(2½', blue,
June-July)

Sedum
spectabile
'Stardust'
(15", white,
September-October)

Linaria
purpurea
'Canon Went'
(3', pink,
May-August)

9'

Helictotrichon
sempervirens
BLUE OAT GRASS
(2½', foliage)

Campanula
carpatica
'White Clips'
(6", June-August)

Sedum
spectabile
'Carmen'
(18", pink,
August-September)

Stachys
byzantina
LAMB'S-EARS
(15", lavender-pink, June-July)

Helianthemum
'Wisley Pink'
(10", June-July;
repeats if pruned)

Allium
tuberosum
GARLIC CHIVES
(2', white,
August-September)

Limonium
latifolium
SEA LAVENDER
(15", purplish
white, July-August)

Salvia officinalis
'Purpurascens'
PURPLE SAGE
(15", for foliage)
interplanted with
Basil 'Dark Opal'
(12", maroon foliage,
annual)

Sedum
'Vera Jameson'
(8", deep pink,
August-September)

Salvia argentea
(12", silver foliage
rosettes)
interplanted with
Lobularia
'Royal Carpet'
PURPLE SWEET
ALYSSUM
(6", annual)

yellow and apricot-bronze, as well as a good soft pink and glistening white. Snapdragon flowers, which occur sporadically through the season, are at their finest in autumn. They often survive a few hard frosts and are effective some years until early December, enduring after most annuals have become skeletons or dust. They can even yield some good cut flowers then, and it is no great surprise to have a few plants live over winter.

Judicious placement is important for snapdragons, especially the Rocket series, which may be three and one-half feet tall by season's end. A sunny site protected from wind is called for, as with any plant that needs support, and it helps to have a solid deep green background such as a yew, which still looks fresh late in the season. For a long-lasting garden scene, accompany the snapdragons with gray-leaved perennials such as lamb's-ears (*Stachys byzantina*) or with coralbells (*Heuchera*), whose foliage improves with cool weather and looks nicely marbled until winter descends hard. Late-flowering chrysanthemums in complementary colors help complete the picture.

Incidentally, the taller snapdragons will need less rigid support if you set the seedlings, when you plant them out in May, an inch or two deeper than normal in the soil so they can develop prop roots. Pinching the tips early also helps them distribute their eventual weight more evenly. Try to support the plants so you won't be unduly conscious of the stakes, which is difficult in the case of a spiky bloom; or simply place a few twiggy dead stems from birch or blueberry around the base just after planting, to provide support that will become inconspicuous as the snaps fill out.

Bells-of-Ireland (*Moluccella laevis*), a sun-demanding annual with attractive green bracts in spikes borne on plants that may reach three and one-half feet, is grown more in cut-flower gardens than in borders. Frequently it requires light staking too, but this annual makes a delightful change of pace in perennial borders when planted near the brassy yellow false sunflower (*Heliopsis helianthoides*), especially 'Gold Greenheart', a good durable perennial in the same height range. Both bloom for the better part of summer.

WHITE FLOWERS AND COMBINATIONS

Good white-flowered plants with a long bloom period are at a premium, because they blend well with everything. They also keep possibly warring flower color factions at bay in the garden, and stand out especially at dusk, when many of us have the only moments of the day to contemplate gardens leisurely. New gardeners tend to ignore white; experienced ones regret they don't have more.

Because a properly planted perennial border of some size can entail an expense that is the match for that of a new subcompact car (but the border will probably last longer if well maintained), a few annuals of good dimension go far to alleviate the nervousness of the family treasurer. They can also particularly complement the display of perennials, some of which are slower to fill in than others. "Space filler" is an ignominious horticultural term, but two large-growing kinds of annuals come to the aid when aspiration has exceeded budget. One is *Cleome* 'Helen Campbell', whose stalks of white flower clusters may attain seven feet by September in well-tended soil with a sunny exposure. Despite the height, plants are neither broad nor heavy-textured but airy and somewhat refined. My friends in Outer Humpton would object to an old vernacular name for the plant, cat's whiskers, an allusion to the conspicuous long stipes from older blooms, which persist below the new flowers as the season progresses.

Cosmos bipinnatus, in its white-flowered selections, is harder to find in garden centers than it was ten years ago, but it is worth the search. The numerous small, saucerlike flowers borne above deeply cut foliage are attractive through the season, though a light shearing in midsummer will improve appearance and bloom. Height may be four or five feet, depending on soil and site, and individual plants spread well over several feet. As with most annuals, it is best to avoid mixed colors, which give a spotty or busy appearance in a border. Separate pink-flowered selections are available too. All are sun worshipers, and none is fussy about soil.

Want a lower, stockier white for midborder? *Lavatera* 'Mont Blanc', with flowers like a small hibiscus but more refined, is a sound choice, especially where summers are hot and long. Height is usually three feet and plant habit broadly rounded. The only principal pest in our experience is the Japanese beetle, which afflicts the mallow family (Malvaceae) as badly as the rose family (Rosaceae). Hand picking the little beasts is the logical control if you have planted only several *Lavatera*, and you need only several for a good display.

Gray foliage is at least as useful as white flowers in the garden, and for the

Cosmos bipinnatus usually comes in mixed colors these days, but a good white is worth the search.

same reasons. There are, of course, perennials that can provide this, but some are going to die if winter is especially wet or drainage is unsatisfactory, and others self-destruct in summer heat. Still others are Cossacks, ready to invade their neighbors. One of the annual dusty-millers, *Senecio* 'Silverdust', gets around these problems and always looks fresh, even in November. Don't be surprised if a few plants live over the winter, for the selection is a tender perennial, though we like to start with new plants each year for uniformity of display. More finely cut dusty-millers exist, but 'Silverdust', which has a sound constitution, is superior if only because the gray leaves have more surface area, and the eye picks it up at a distance. Height varies by season's end, sometimes exceeding fifteen inches, but 'Silverdust' is basically a frontal plant in the border. It is also very handy for tub or container plantings. In late autumn it makes a nice foil for a month or two with cut twigs of the winterberry holly (*Ilex verticillata*) inserted in the potting soil, because their red fruits gleam in its company.

BLUE FLOWERS

Good clear blue is an uncommon flower color among both perennials and annuals, yet valuable for much the same reason as is white — it complements almost everything. I am more interested in what a plant can do in the garden in relation to other plants than I am in its actuarial table, so I seek the good blues whence they come. The most popular annual lobelia, 'Crystal Palace Compacta', is an intense, nearly psychedelic blue and perhaps best reserved for bright combinations in containers, but 'Cambridge Blue', the color of a clear Dakota sky on a spring day, is a delightfully cooling front-of-the-border plant. Even an Oxonian might smile at it. Plants may not bloom as profusely in dappled light as in full sun, but their flower substance is better and bloom period longer. In fact, lobelia usually looks its best early and late in the growing season, as strong summer heat and sun bring about semidormancy or worse.

The Chinese forget-me-not (*Cynoglossum amabile* 'Firmament') is a change of pace when you are chasing the horticultural blues. The fifteen-inch plants, with grayish green foliage and midblue flowers about one-half inch wide, are best not planted together in large groups, because the density of flowers is not great and their bloom period is slightly erratic, whether the summer is hot or cool. You would do better to sandwich Chinese forget-me-nots in informal drifts between frontal and midborder groupings of other plants in the sun. If arranged this way, they are inconspicuous when they are out of bloom; in flower they are a pleasant surprise, even enchanting, especially with white-flowered perennials such as *Veronica* 'Icicle' in the background. Chinese forget-me-nots tend to self-sow, and an occasional plant will overwinter for an early start. *Cynoglossum* 'Firmament' doesn't take up much space, but it is one of those plants that is capable of transforming a plant collection into a garden.

Also in the quest for good blues, don't overlook the gentian sage (*Salvia patens*), a tender Mexican perennial that grows roughly two feet tall in the average summer. You may have a better chance of obtaining it from a greenhouse or herb nursery than from a garden center. In autumn before a killing frost you should remember to bring it indoors, to be wintered over in a cool, sunny room, and to take cuttings along the way for thrifty young plants the following season. It is fine in midborder with the soft pink midsummer perennials, such as *Phlox paniculata* 'Fairest One', and the white of Shasta daisies or the pale yellow of *Coreopsis* 'Moonbeam'. It combines well with roses of white or soft pink hue, too.

Mary Ann and I disagree about the merits of a number of plants, but the bush morning-glory (*Convolvulus tricolor* 'Dwarf Royal Ensign'), which has erect stems about a foot tall, is not one of them. When gardeners first see its pristine blue flowers, accented by yellow and white throats, they realize that although the word *blue* has been used with utmost license for all sorts of plants, this is the real thing. Because I have spent a fair portion of my horticultural life doing in — or attempting to do in — another *Convolvulus*, the field bindweed (*C. arvensis*), whose roots can be embedded nine feet deep in the soil, I had considerable prejudice to overcome. Fortunately, in the five or six summers we have grown the dwarf morning-glory, we have not noticed any chance seedlings. Still, we have no difficulty germinating store-bought seeds, which we start indoors about six weeks before planting out. 'Dwarf Royal Ensign' makes a lovely tub plant when combined with dusty-miller or creeping zinnia (*Sanvitalia procumbens*) on a sunny terrace, but there are many possible companions for this agreeable annual from southern Europe.

I suppose most gardeners have a soft spot for the annual bachelor's-button (*Centaurea cyanus*). My objection is that it has tall, floppy stems and needs more than the usual deadheading to look good. Still, bachelor's-button is a rough-and-tumble plant, and I wouldn't be without it for too many summers. Although it may not be considered prime boutonnière material anymore, it still makes a fine cut flower, and it tolerates poor soil better than most other annuals do. 'Jubilee Gem', a dwarf fifteen-inch cultivar, is relatively tidy and a true blue. You can extend the bloom period, shorter than that of many annuals, by sowing a second batch of seeds directly in the garden in early summer. Germination is high, and young plants grow to flowering stage in about six weeks. 'Jubilee Gem' also makes a pleasing, unusual tub plant in a sunny spot.

We are also fond of an annual woodruff with small but generously borne heads of light blue flowers — *Asperula orientalis*. It grows a foot tall and has an informal (but not lax) habit, unless it is overwatered. Plants perform well in sun or partial shade. They do not flower all summer, but when they start to fade in five or six weeks, we shear them halfway back and fertilize them for another round. There is no harm if you forget to do this, for the seed heads, resembling the fruits of a small clematis, have ornamental value too. A grouping of annual woodruff makes a fine, out-of-the-ordinary display in a container or tub. Seed sown outdoors directly in the container, or indoors for an early start, germinates readily. It takes seven or eight weeks for the initial flowers to appear.

One selection of nemesia, *Nemesia strumosa* 'Blue Gem', has blue flowers, but most American gardeners know this South African wildflower only in mixed colors, usually shades of yellow, orange, and red, plus white. Normally we refrain from mixed colors because they give a spotty effect in the garden. Still, perhaps because the nemesia tints (except for an occasional cherry-pink) are all compatible, their garden effect can be winning.

Nemesia is a sun worshiper belonging to the Scrophulariaceae, the botanical family that includes the snapdragon. It is usually less than a foot tall in gardens, and like delphinium, performs best in areas with cool summers. In mild climates, it is better to grow it as a spring or autumn annual. We estimate eight or ten weeks from seed to flower. Sometimes you can find nemesia in garden centers, but such uncommon charmers are seldom found on the increasingly scrawny lists of the huge bedding-plant growers who dominate the market today. Economics wins, and gardens are the poorer in variety as a result.

REDS, YELLOWS, AND ORANGES

The reddish orange seen in Maltese-cross (*Lychnis chalcedonica*), a couple of other *Lychnis* species, and some daylilies is a difficult hue to find in perennials, so we turn mainly to annuals when we require it. However, most annuals with this tint have large flowers of electric intensity that overwhelm other plants. Shock waves aren't usually necessary for garden effect, except conceivably in parks or very large borders, but the restrained use of reddish orange can sometimes save a dull border from tromping by somnambulists. A little-known annual from South America called mask flower (*Alonsoa warscewiczii* 'Compacta'), which grows ten to twelve inches tall, solves the problem for small borders and is a topnotch container plant for sunny areas, particularly with white sweet-alyssum or the smaller single-flowered kinds of yellow marigolds.

Mask flower, also a member of the Scrophulariaceae, was somewhat popular in gardens of the 1920s and '30s, and was included in Alfred C. Hottes's *The Book of Annuals,* which was the standard work on the subject in those days. In this country, the less common sort of plant has become scarce over the years, and this is one example. We saw this species for the first time a few years ago at Great Dixter, the garden of Christopher Lloyd, in England, and were so taken with mask flower's felicitous combination of bright color and refinement that we sought it out and have grown it with pleasure since then. The individual flowers, just over a half-inch wide, project themselves considerably further than other annuals with flowers of a similar size but a more delicate hue. As with a number of uncommon annuals, gardeners must turn to overseas sources for *Alonsoa* seed. Although some packets are incorrectly sold as the compact form and contain seed that results in much taller and less graceful plants, the chase for this engaging pixie is worth it.

Perennials with yellow daisies for flowers are about as rare as wasps at a Labor Day picnic, and the same can be said for annuals. However, there *is* one of the latter that Mary Ann particularly esteems, and I had better mention it if I am going to persuade her to start our *Alonsoa* seed indoors under artificial light this season. This is calliopsis (*Coreopsis tinctoria*), a native wildflower in many parts of the United States. The species itself, which grows up to four feet tall, is a little unkempt and would benefit from an injection of laundry starch in the lax stems, but dwarf strains in mixed colors have well-behaved growth habits. The flowers tell the story, though — profuse little daisies, often less than an inch across, in bicolor shades of yellow, bronze, and mahogany, or sometimes all one color or the other. It is difficult even for a curmudgeon to dislike them.

Calliopsis grows well in a variety of soils, including those that are relatively poor and dry. A more important requirement is a bright, sunny exposure. If you do not remove the spent flowers, the bloom period won't extend all summer. Deadheading is a tedious task because of the numerous small flowers, so we shear plants lightly after the first wave of flowers, then apply a mild dose of water-soluble fertilizer.

A good way to grow the dwarf forms, which reach ten inches or so in height, is in containers; after shearing the plants, we whisk the containers out of sight to a sunny rehabilitation area for a couple of weeks, then bring them back on stage. Seed germination is fast and good, and there isn't much point in starting calliopsis indoors. We start seeds in the ground or in planters in early May (thinning them as if they were radishes) and can usually expect flowers toward the end of June. If you really like calliopsis, try a second sowing in the latter part of July (later in areas with long, hot summers). Fresh, young plants are usually more attractive in bloom than older ones that have been rehabilitated.

THE ART OF COMPROMISE

Gardening with spouses is a horticultural give-and-take that may lead to his-and-her gardens. One of our gardens is of course dominated by calliopsis and similar yellow daisies of modest account — *Baileya, Dyssodia, Layia,* and their ilk — and the other will perhaps ultimately be the same, but we have not quite reached that point. There are always bargaining cards; my diamond is St. Mary's thistle (*Silybum marianum*), also known as holy thistle or blessed thistle. Regrettably, Mary Ann chooses to call it by its genus name, accenting each syllable in a deliberately slow manner. The bold and clasping bright green leaves of this "divine" plant have conspicuous white veins, as if marbled with milk, or even silver. In midsummer, sturdy stalks rise ethereally to four feet and bear classic white- to rose-purple thistles, representing pure elegance when planted among the summer phloxes of similar tint.

Despite my fondness for the plant, old silly-bum is not allowed to cross the border into California because it is a thistle, and my wife would like to see it banned in our state too. This is because of an unfortunate incident that took place in our garden. Once, during a temporary absence on my part, Mary Ann decided to tidy the borders and threw all sorts of plant refuse, including the spent flower stalks of the thistle, onto the compost heap. The next year some two thousand seedlings germinated on the heap; another two thousand germinated around the garden because of a spring top-dressing of compost we had given to several borders. She ultimately rogued all of them, except for a few seedlings over which I stood, saying delicately but firmly, "If these go, so do the calliopsis." Marriage is a series of compromises, and I won that one.

Many people have tried to talk me out of my fascination with annuals. To those who are skeptical, beware. Someday you may find yourself fascinated with *Phacelia, Nigella,* and *Didiscus,* and before long, *Oxypetalum.* You may even find the various seed catalogues to be good reading. May you have sweet dreams of mignonette.

· 14 ·

Hostas—Valentines
Among Ground Covers

A CHANGING ROLE for hostas has quietly been taking place in American gardens. Years ago, the plantain-lilies or funkias, as they were often called, were considered mundane plants, all right to plunk here and there as accents when the landscaper ran out of ideas. They usually ended up on sunny, gravelly banks where the foliage would start to scorch about the first of June, or perhaps they were used to face down the north side of an outhouse that had seen better days. After all, who could take seriously a plant named funkia?

The prejudice was international, and it still goes on in some areas — but not in Japan, where most of the species are native and many of the early cultivars originated. A few years ago in England I was trapped on a long journey in the same car with a well-known but very opinionated garden writer of that country, who felt it important to prattle on when there was danger of silence from the other passengers, which was frequent. Out of the corner of his eye he spotted some hostas and blurted, "Ornamental cabbages, really — the only sad difference being that they don't die after the first season. Don't understand what you Americans see in them!" I didn't know quite how to respond, for up to a point I respect cabbages of various kinds, including the soup they can make in the right hands, so I remained silent and continued to read the landscape.

Obviously, not all of the English have as cool a regard for hostas as the garden writer, and in fact one of the leading breeders, Eric Smith (the *tardiana* hybrids), was English, but these plants are associated more with American gardens. England, because of its benign and relatively uniform climate, has the choice of a wide number of foliage perennials from mild parts of the world, ranging from

acanthus to melianthus and from phormium to zantedeschia. It is easy to understand why a colorful new hosta draws yawns from the surfeited.

The harshness of the diverse and complex climates of America reduces the
variety of foliage perennials from which to choose, unless you live along the
Pacific coast or in the deepest South. For the rest of us there are hostas. These
days there is no particular need to lament this fact, for many fine new cultivars
are rapidly becoming available, in part because of the wonders of tissue culture
propagation. Maybe someday we will even have totally slug-resistant hostas,
and deer-resistant ones as well.

My main interest in hostas is not so much in the individual plants, although
they are fundamental, as in how they can be used to complement other kinds of
plants in the garden. This is different from the approach followed by the hosta
collector, who takes the same delight in obtaining a pretty new cultivar as a
stamp collector does in obtaining a special issue of Bulgarian rose commemora-
tives during the reign of King Boris. To each his own, my own being the garden,
which depends on the plant.

My eye turned to hostas years ago, when we first moved to Hillside. At one
side of a driveway, beyond a split-rail fence, was a group of thirty luxuriant
large-leaved hostas near an ash tree that has a four-foot diameter. Not a weed
was around, and the hosta foliage looked in good condition despite the drought
of that summer, the summer of 1963. New owners always want to change a
property, to put their own stamp on it, and it seemed to me that rambling roses
along the fence would be in order. I bought some and started to dig the planting
holes. Within a minute my fingers were numb from trying to make a dent in the
compacted gravel that I had thought was soil. As it turned out, the area had
once been part of a much larger driveway. The shovel eventually broke, and the
roses, scrunched into their abbreviated holes, died, but the hostas continued to
thrive. Places exist on earth, indeed in our garden, for such plants, and right
then and there I decided that hostas were too important to leave to the collectors.

The hosta in question didn't seem all that uncommon, and I saw it performing
well as a ground cover in a number of other gardens, but it was years before I
was able to discover its valid name, *Hosta undulata* 'Erromena'. I too decided
to try it as a ground cover, in some rough parts of our property where elaborate
soil improvement or total weed removal was impractical. In early spring as new
growth started, plants in the former driveway yielded readily to division by pick,
and I soon had enough young crowns with which to work. Over the years,
despite the dozens of kinds of ground covers we have tried, none has been a

better weed smotherer or has required less maintenance than 'Erromena'. In its own quiet way, it is a great plant.

But one cannot live by 'Erromena' alone, and I began to look at other hostas as possible ground covers. High prices ruled out many of the newest sorts for immediate use, but I discovered that the price tag usually dropped within a few years of the new cultivar's introduction. If I like one enough, I am willing to settle for a single plant or two, which after several years of regular division will yield enough for ground cover purposes, unless it is a particularly slow-growing hosta, such as *H. tokudama*. Let us look at some of the possibilities.

SILVER VARIEGATED

Dozens of hostas have variegation. Many of them differ but slightly, and I suspect some are impossible for even the hosta expert to identify if their labels

Lynden B. Miller

White astilbe, *Hosta fortunei* 'Aureo-marginata', and a Japanese tree lilac stand out in early summer at the Conservatory Garden in Central Park.

are removed. I once did just that, with malicious pleasure, to bring a visiting, very self-assured, humorless don of the genus down to earth. However, given the clutter that the name game has caused in recent years, gardeners should not overlook some variegated hostas that are very fine indeed.

Nomenclature is improving, too. Just a few years ago it was possible to find three distinct variegated cultivars named 'Thomas Hogg', in honor of a United States marshal in Japan, appointed in 1862 by Abraham Lincoln. Mr. Hogg, who with his brother had a nursery on East 79th Street near the East River in Manhattan, was America's first certified hosta buff. He was probably responsible for the introduction of a number of cultivars, though not the hosta genus. It is too bad that there does not seem to be a hosta left that is validly named for him.

Large areas in the shade often call for big-leaved hostas with silvery margins. 'Antioch', with oversized, heavy-textured leaves, is excellent, as is the smaller, sturdy, fast-growing cultivar that these days is called *Hosta undulata* 'Albo-marginata'. To confound neophytes, who may have some odd notion that nomenclature is intended to bring order out of chaos, this cultivar is not at all similar to the thin-leaved, wavy-edged variegated hosta known as *H. undulata*. *H. u.* 'Albo-marginata' is a larger plant with waxier leaves whose variegation lasts well through the season. *Hosta undulata* itself, one of the prettiest of all variegated plants in spring, especially when forget-me-nots (*Myosotis scorpioides* var. *semperflorens*) and ferns are nearby, has variegation that frequently becomes dull or even disappears by August, which makes new gardeners wonder if they have bought a pig in a poke. The next spring good variegated foliage emerges again. *Hosta undulata* makes an acceptable ground cover mainly if you plan to be away on vacation all summer.

Hosta undulata 'Albo-marginata' fares better in a wide range of conditions, including moderate dryness, than most hostas. Such adaptability is welcome in ground covers, for these are often the last plants one remembers to water. Provided the soil is well laced with peat moss to the depth of eight or ten inches (as you should do for all hostas), 'Albo-marginata' is one of the most rapid growers. It will probably fill in nicely by the end of the first growing season if you set individual plants two and one-half feet apart, then mulch them, water regularly, and give them slug bait occasionally.

Hosta crispula, which looks like a larger, thicker-textured version of *H. undulata* 'Albo-marginata', is one of the handsomest for ground cover in a large area. In our garden we have pressed it almost to the cultural limit by planting it under a mature red-leaved Japanese maple, whose copious surface roots carry on silent wars against many plants. Yet *Hosta crispula* holds its own, and the foliage contrast is lovely through the summer.

Sometimes a smaller silver-variegated hosta is called for. 'Louisa', unlike the hostas I just mentioned, which bear lavender bells in midsummer, has white ones appearing in August and September. A fast grower and quick on the buildup from division, it is one of the most valuable of the new generation of hostas for ground cover purposes. White-flowered variegated hostas are rare, and the usefulness these two traits pose for light injection into shaded areas is quite evident. 'Louisa' is derived from *Hosta albomarginata* (which should not be confused with *H. undulata* 'Albo-Marginata') and has lance-shaped leaves about six inches long by two and one-half inches broad.

You may want a more diminutive hosta for ground cover under small-leaved shrubs. One excellent possibility is 'Ginko Craig', a lavender-flowered sort with variegated leaves not much more than two inches wide. It is quick to establish itself after division and will probably become a popular hosta, because it serves a specific landscape purpose. Somewhat leaner is *H. gracillima* 'Variegated', which is useful under well-established dwarf conifers that are no longer really dwarf. Other, even smaller hostas, mainly in the toy category, are available for rock gardeners who become bored with little buns.

GOLDEN VARIEGATED

Golden-variegated hostas are usually at their best in light shade. We don't have as large a choice as with silver-variegated sorts, but there are some handsome ones.

Among the best when it is true to name and grown in partial shade is 'Gold Standard'. This is a large-leaved plant with light yellow-green leaves unevenly edged in green. Unfortunately, when tissue culture first became a widespread means of propagation in the big nurseries, the progeny of this cultivar was very uneven. Aberrant young plants that should have been culled by the nurseries were distributed to thousands of gardeners, who puzzled over the difference between the glitzy catalogue photographs and the actual plants. To compound the dissatisfaction, light factors have to be just right for 'Gold Standard' to do its proper stint in the garden. If it gets too little shade, the chartreuse center bleaches and becomes ugly. Too much shade results in dull variegation. Because of these factors and the still fairly steep price for this otherwise fine hosta, many gardeners hesitate to use it for ground cover. Nevertheless, it makes a nice combination with pale orange hemerocallis (not the roadside sort) off to a

Left: Hosta undulata 'Albo-marginata' helps set off the toad-lily (*Tricyrtis*). The latter usually needs visual support for its small, intricate flowers, which bloom in the shade late in the season. *T. hirta*, perhaps the hardiest species, has survived a dozen winters at Hillside.
Right, top: A ground cover of *Hosta crispula* serves as a light anchor for red-leaved Japanese maple (*Acer palmatum* 'Atropurpureum').
Bottom: Hosta fortunei 'Aureo-marginata' and lady fern (*Athyrium filix-femina*) are attractive, durable partners in light shade.

slightly sunnier flank, along with the soft yellow perennial foxglove (*Digitalis grandiflora*).

Our most attractive golden-variegated hosta for spring coloration is the large-leaved *H. fortunei* 'Albo-picta' (a misnomer), which is a delight planted near leopard's-bane (*Doronicum*) and *Trollius* × *cultorum* 'Orange Globe'. The latter two can take a little shade in summer, provided they have sun at bloom time in spring. Unfortunately, the foliage of 'Albo-picta' becomes all green by the end of June, and the gardener's eye skips over it for the remainder of the season. Of greater value, though less spectacular in spring, is *H. fortunei* 'Aureo-marginata' ('Obscura-marginata'), which is pretty with nearby groupings of primulas of yellow or orange hue, blue-flowered Jacob's-ladder (*Polemonium caeruleum*), and a brightly colored sedge (*Carex stricta* 'Bowles' Golden').

A much smaller golden-variegated hosta for ground cover use is 'Kabitan', which is derived from *H. albomarginata* and has the good late-summer lavender flowers associated with that species. However, the foliage of 'Kabitan' is the real winner, for it is a rich, almost oily chartreuse with a thin green margin. The right exposure is important to bring out the best in this plant, for it is often grown in too bright light, which bleaches the special leaf color. An interesting combination can be had with apricot-colored *Viola* 'Chantreyland' and the orange form of the Welsh poppy (*Meconopsis cambrica* 'Aurantiaca'). If the lance-shaped leaves of 'Kabitan' don't provide enough body for the situation, try 'Golden Tiara', which has neat, heart-shaped green leaves edged in gold.

EIGHTEEN-KARAT GOLD

From the chartreuse center of 'Kabitan' to the entirely golden-leaved hostas is not a long jump. 'Sum and Substance' is the largest and thickest-textured we have come across. This is probably best treated as a specimen plant, for a ground cover planting would be in scale only at Versailles, if hostas were permitted there. It tolerates more sun than most golden-leaved hostas do. A number of other golden-leaved forms of varying stature exist, but after a certain point even the collector must ask how distinct one is from the others. I am tempted to paraphrase Ronald Reagan's curious remark about redwoods, "Once you have seen one, you have seen them all."

Still, a couple of gold-leaved hostas stand apart from the pack, one being 'Piedmont Gold', of rather large leaf size. The other, 'Wogon', is smaller. In a distant part of our garden, hidden from view until the visitor turns a corner around a wall, is a group of brightly hued 'Piedmont Gold' from which rise the nearly black leaves of a selected form of *Cimicifuga ramosa* 'Atropurpurea'. (*C. ramosa* appears very similar to *C. americana*.) The combination is arresting because you come upon it by surprise. I would not care to have it in full view all the time, because it would monopolize the eye to the detriment of the garden.

In a quite different part of the garden, 'Wogon' forms a bright buttery carpet under a mature spreading hybrid yew (*Taxus × media*), which has a very dark, almost somber green appearance much of the growing season, except during the flush of chartreuse new growth in May and June. Then the role of 'Wogon' changes from contrast to complement. As with variegated plants, you must use restraint for the gold combinations to have their greatest effect. An even more important reason is to keep the garden from looking like a horticultural zoo.

GRAY VALENTINES AMONG THE GOLD

Gardeners often overlook a key use of glaucous-leaved hostas, because the prime example of this group (and one of the world's great plants), *Hosta sieboldiana* 'Elegans', is gainfully employed much of the time as a specimen plant. It serves this role admirably when planted by the back door — never by the front door, which is unused in America except by process servers, Girl Scouts selling cookies, and strangers who are lost, none of whom merit such a hosta. Consider it, too, for a good-sized grouping in a shaded far corner of the garden, where light injection is important.

There are precious few gray-leaved plants for shade, and the immense soup-spoon leaves of a well-established, well-nourished 'Elegans' will perform their function true to name. The lighter the shade (within reason), the stronger the leaf coloration. Also bear in mind that the cupped foliage, which may be as much as eighteen inches across on a mature plant that is several feet wide, can trap a certain amount of litter in woodland conditions. It is best to situate groupings in more open parts of the woodland, especially away from trashy ashes and punky poplars.

I am not sure I have ever seen a bad *Hosta sieboldiana* 'Elegans', but as known in the trade it is variable, and the foliage takes two or three years to come into its own. I once asked a candid English nurseryman what he perceived as the difference between *Hosta sieboldiana* and *H. s.* 'Elegans'. He winked and said the former is a first-year plant, the latter a second-year one. The truth is that some are more elegant than others.

Hosta sieboldiana is one of the few hostas to come reasonably true from seed. It is in fact one of the few genuine, unaltered species of *Hosta* grown in gardens, so we can expect a degree of unevenness. This can be a detriment, because gardeners don't always know what they are purchasing at the garden center. But it can also be a benefit, since any good observer can make selections that might lead to presumably better, more distinct, very even cultivars. As a result, in recent years we have seen a plethora of choices, the "new" cultivars commanding a good price, then fading into the background as yet another batch emerges with the latest catalogue. It is like the candy freak who discovers that M & M's suddenly come in five new colors. At first, euphoria. But they cost a bit more, and next year . . . As happens in Hollywood, the unique becomes "very unique."

Despite its massive size, which few perennials can upstage, *Hosta sieboldiana* 'Elegans' combines well with a variety of plants. One thought is to have adjacent groups of 'Elegans' and a golden-leaved hosta with large foliage of a different shape, such as 'Sun Power', which has tapered leaves. There are golden forms of *Hosta sieboldiana* itself, but unless you pair them with 'Elegans' in a large garden, the partners may resemble two Japanese sumo wrestlers eyeing each other uneasily. Other companions for 'Elegans' include the larger silver- and golden-variegated sorts of hostas. Selections of *Hosta fortunei* with dark green leaves are also good. Because most hostas have large horizontal planes of foliage as the season progresses, interlocking ground covers of them have the greatest impact when viewed from a higher elevation, such as a second story or the top of a vale.

You hardly need be restricted to other hostas for foliage combinations for 'Elegans'. Lenten-rose (*Helleborus orientalis*) and *H. atrorubens*, as well as the less versatile Christmas-rose (*H. niger*), provide good, leathery, dark green leaf contrast, and their winter or early spring flowers are an eagerly awaited sign that winter will someday end. Even nicer in foliage, but more for the mid-Atlantic and southern states than the colder reaches of the North, are *H. foetidus* and *H. argutifolius* (*lividus corsicus*).

Rodgersia pinnata, with leaves resembling those of a horse chestnut, and *R. podophylla*, with wedge-shaped foliage, are possibilities. I even recall an effective interplanting years ago with the common mayapple (*Podophyllum peltatum*), whose large foliage is at its best in spring before 'Elegans', a late riser, comes into its own. By July, when the mayapple leaves were tatty and about to wither, potentially leaving a big gap, the foliage of 'Elegans' was dominating the scene. A less sophisticated combination, but not a less beautiful one, is sweeps of good-sized ferns in the background of hosta groupings. Interrupted and cinnamon ferns (*Osmunda claytoniana, O. cinnamomea*) are as good choices as any, but *Dryopteris erythrosora* with its red-tinged new growth is appropriate too. You may be tempted to include a smaller fern, such as Japanese painted fern (*Athyrium goeringianum* 'Pictum'), but this choice is more in scale with *Hosta tokudama*, nature's diminutive version of *Hosta sieboldiana* 'Elegans'.

The flowers of 'Elegans', like the flowers of all other *Hosta sieboldiana* cultivars, are afterthoughts of nature. Hidden in the foliage or rising on scapes just slightly above it, they are usually an overlaundered pale lavender striving for white. A plant can't have everything, regardless of claims made in moments of enthusiasm, but this hosta's magnificent foliage enables us to overlook what new gardeners might consider a flaw.

Think of the leaves of 'Elegans' as a suitable foil for virtually any flower color

Hosta sieboldiana 'Elegans' and *Geranium endressii* 'Wargrave Pink' are handsome mates over a long season. Light to medium shade is best.

sported by a nearby perennial. I particularly enjoy it with the pink or mauve tints of some of the larger cranesbills, the true genus *Geranium,* not the ubiquitous windowsill plants from South Africa known botanically as *Pelargonium.* In light shade try this hosta with *Geranium* 'Claridge Druce', *G. psilostemon,* or perhaps nicest of all, *G. endressii* 'Wargrave Pink'. Other suitable companions of similar color range include *Astilbe taquetii* 'Superba', fringed bleeding-heart (*Dicentra eximia*) or the hybrid *D.* 'Luxuriant', *Digitalis* × *mertonensis, D. purpurea,* and various phlox, particularly *P. maculata* 'Alpha'.

GREEN IS THE COLOR

Hostas with entirely green leaves haven't enjoyed the same popularity in recent years as the variegated sorts, but a number are very sound garden plants. We turn to them for particular traits as well as for relief from some of the variegated cultivars that seem like four-year-olds vying for attention at a party for adults. After a certain point they become very difficult to accommodate, and one wonders whether they shouldn't be hustled off to a playpen, out of the hearing of all but the deer, who may be amused by them momentarily.

For fragrance you can still choose the hosta known to previous generations of gardeners as the August-lily, *Hosta plantaginea.* Indeed, the immense, intensely scented flowers of its cultivar 'Grandiflora' suggest a *Lilium,* to which larger botanical family, the Liliaceae, hostas belong. This hosta, like *H. sieboldiana,* also has a nostalgic association with the English designer Gertrude Jekyll, who planted groups of them in large tubs. The idea is worth resuscitation along shaded entrances and terraces, especially if you get the hefty, inexpensive, half-barrel whiskey tubs that have become Kentucky's and Tennessee's second most valuable export. If you want a bigger bang from the barrel than the hosta can provide alone, plant a few divisons of *Lamium maculatum* 'White Nancy', with silvery foliage, just inside the rim. But save your appreciation for the design until the sun slips over the horizon, a time of day when the hosta and the lamium are at their ghostly best.

As fond as I am of *Hosta plantaginea,* one of its hybrid offspring, 'Royal Standard', is a better plant for ground cover purposes, because it fills in more quickly and is very adaptable to a wide range of growing conditions. Also, because it has been around for years and is rapid on the buildup from division, it is relatively inexpensive. 'Royal Standard' has rather showy, fragrant white flowers in late summer. 'Honeybells' is similar, but its flowers are pale lavender. Foliage of both is light green and late to appear in spring, like that of *H. plantaginea.* This last characteristic, late appearance, makes these hostas good candidates for interplanting with spring bulbs in light shade. The bulbs bloom early and their leaves begin to yellow; then the hosta foliage emerges and hides the dying evidence. Aesthetically pleasing companions in partial shade include pink turtlehead (*Chelone lyonii*) and the various August-September blooming anemones. Summer phlox cultivars that flower a bit later than the pack, including the shell-pink-and-white 'Fairest One', are also nice.

I also like to have a group planting of *Hosta lancifolia,* with glossy green leaves and rich lavender flowers that bloom in the latter part of summer, in a shaded spot near several clumps of *Astilbe taquetii* 'Superba', which grows three to four feet tall and has steeple-shaped clusters of flowers the color of black raspberry ice cream. Their bloom periods sometimes overlap, as does that of *Astilbe* 'William Buchanan', a lovely, shiny, cut-leaved plant that has eight-inch-tall clusters of white flowers. This is one of the most vigorous of the really dwarf astilbes and is itself a candidate for ground cover in a small area.

I have made a fair number of divisions of *Hosta lancifolia* over the years for our own garden as well as for the nursery. Toward the end of one spring afternoon several years ago, my fingers were almost numb from breaking up large clumbs of this hosta, and the barn floor was littered with its fresh young leaves. The telephone rang. It was Mary Ann, delayed in a neighboring town and asking me to get dinner started. She said that some spinach was in the refrigerator.

It was a cold day, and I needed little prodding to enter the kitchen. Meal preparation went well once my thumbs had thawed, but we were short on spinach. Not long before, a gardening acquaintance versed in ways Japanese had casually mentioned to me that hostas were used occasionally in the Orient for cooking. Inspired, I dashed to the barn, picked up the afternoon's leavings, and returned to the kitchen. After washing the foliage carefully and removing the pithy midrib, I mixed the hosta leaves with the spinach.

Cooking was brief, and I was busy chopping the greens as Mary Ann came into the driveway. Dinner was on the table in a flash. I surreptitiously watched her as she ate the concoction, because she is usually able to detect anything out of the ordinary, down to the tiniest anchovy or scungilli I might add to spaghetti sauce. The "spinach" passed muster, or at least went without comment, and I eventually took a few bites too. Hosta greens probably don't have much of a future in the American kitchen, but they're nice to know about if you run short on spinach or have too many lancifolias in the garden.

Several other green-leaved hostas with good flowers deserve a mention. My driveway hosta, *H. undulata* 'Erromena', a large grower making a first-rate cover, has profuse lavender bells on four-foot scapes in July. *H. fortunei* 'Hyacinthina', with gray-green leaves, is a solid old cultivar for ground cover. Another big old-timer, *H. ventricosa,* has arresting violet bells also in July and glossy dark green foliage. It is an apomict, reproducing true from seed without sex — nothing promiscuous here!

Much smaller hostas worth consideration for our purpose are 'Sweet Susan' and *H. nakaiana. Hosta tardiflora,* an even smaller species with good deep mauve bells on scapes about ten inches tall, is indeed very tardy to bloom — September and October. Try it in light shade with one of the late coralbells, *Heuchera micrantha,* which has small white flowers, and *Allium stellatum,* which has pink ones; or use it with toad lily (*Tricyrtis hirta*), which has curious white flowers with lavender markings. Toad lilies strike me as being at their best when interplanted with silver-variegated hostas.

Because there are so many valuable hostas, it is difficult to know where to stop. I could even mention a cultivar selected because it is more stoloniferous than others, 'Ground Master', but I am not sure it is more beautiful. So let us end with *Hosta la vista* . . .

· 15 ·

Packing Old Sandra

WHEN I WAS a boy growing up in Fairfield County, Connecticut, in the 1940s and '50s, there was only one ground cover, pachysandra (*Pachysandra terminalis*). Even the least knowledgeable gardener called it that, never Japanese spurge, the purportedly common name used for it in books. Pachysandra had quite some esteem and was considered to be a new plant find, though it had first come to America in the 1880s. When people were remodeling gardens along with houses after the war, they streamlined. Out went the big borders with their miscellany of flowers that were difficult to maintain, if not a yoke of the past. The new look was green, and it seemed a good idea then for gardens to look as green in winter as they did in summer. Above all, they were to be care-free, so that valuable golf-course time would not be eroded. This is where pachysandra came in. Men in particular loved it, especially if they were not gardeners.

I am not sure there were really pachysandra parties, but I do recall friends of my parents visiting and carefully noting the nice carpet of pachysandra that was emerging in the darker recesses of our garden. In turn, my parents, when visiting their friends, took time to admire their respective stands of pachysandra. Even by the privet and under the big maple did it grow, though more slowly. By the age of fourteen I had learned how to admire a good patch of pachysandra. Or at least to feign admiration.

SIGNS OF MATURITY

Years passed and I began to travel, first to the mid-Atlantic states, where I noticed that their equivalent of pachysandra was English ivy (*Hedera helix*). In the South mondo grass (*Ophiopogon japonicus*) was the ground cover of choice, or at least immediate last resort, because it would grow anywhere. In California the standard was the Canary Island ivy (*Hedera canariensis*), which looks like an English ivy that should have dieted. Even England, a land of horticultural diversity, had its ubiquitous ground cover, *Euphorbia robbiae*, which doesn't look like much of anything either. For reasons of climate each of these ground covers reigned supreme in its area, with only one upstart, periwinkle (*Vinca minor*), showing up in all regions with any frequency. They were good soldiers — too good, in fact. When a plant has virtually no flaws in the growing, it becomes a cliché in the landscape by overuse. In Japan, the homeland of pachysandra, there is no danger of this. People grow it once in a while as a potted plant, but almost never as a ground cover.

As we prepared to move from trim and tidy Fairfield County to the wilds of northern Connecticut in the early 1960s, a thought occurred to me: Since our long-standing home was to be superseded by a gas station, where pachysandra is generally unwelcome, why not bring some of the plants along with us? About twenty-five flats of pachysandra made it onto the moving van, much to the bemusement of the burly driver, who had seen a great deal in his day but not this, and off we went.

That summer I spent hours preparing soil with peat moss and planting the spaghetti-like stolons of pachysandra in the far reaches of our new property, between shrubs, around shaded boulders, over exposed tree roots, and in nooks and crannies where John Deere in his wildest moments never intended a lawn mower to go. The areas were then dutifully mulched, fertilized once or twice, weeded regularly for the first season, and watered weekly. In a year's time the pachysandra filled in perfectly and did what it was intended to do — lower the overall maintenance to give me more time for gardening. The pachysandra lukewarmed the cockles of my heart, and I went on to mostly other things. In some twenty-five years we have spent perhaps ten hours tending the pachysandra — raking tree leaves off in autumn, pulling an occasional weed, and trimming the ground cover back when it threatens to seize a walkway.

But the past never disappears completely in one's own garden. A few years ago, after the pachysandra digested some Goldie's ferns (*Dryopteris goldiana*), one of my wife's favorites, Mary Ann coolly inquired why, when we had moved, I hadn't also brought along the ground cover junipers and variegated euonymus that also afflict the suburban New York landscape. Twisting the ice pick, she asked whether my former girlfriends had been called Biffy, Buffy, and Muffy, all good Fairfield County names. My murmurs of protest that ferns were in fact botanically lower plants did not help. Nor did the visit of an English horticultural don, who politely suggested, tweaking his mustache, that some *Euphorbia robbiae* planted among the pachysandra might be an improvement. I told him I had once obtained a snippet overseas, but that the second or third frost of winter had blackened it irrevocably.

The low point occurred during a visit from a professor of horticulture at a nearby state university. A few years before, when we had both been speaking at a symposium on ground covers, a moment of rashness had led me to say to the congregation that I was the president of the Help Stamp Out Pachysandra Movement of America. Each autumn at the university since then, in his course on ground covers, the good professor had referred to the movement and said that its president actually lived in the state. Now, upon visiting our garden for perhaps the tenth time, he finally noticed pachysandra all over the place. Perplexed, the professor asked for an explanation. Equally perplexed, because my wife was standing nearby and a detailed answer was not in order, I blurted, "Previous owners, you know. Must have come from Fairfield County."

I occasionally had good company. One spring at daffodil time I visited John and Gertrude Wister at their home in Pennsylvania. Dr. Wister was then in his later years, an unofficial dean of American horticulture winding down from a remarkable career, which included the founding of or inspiration for many plant societies. We had enjoyed a lengthy and lively correspondence, during which he had proffered advice on which cultivars of hemerocallis, iris, hosta, and other genera I should be planting. Never once did he mention pachysandra.

Upon visiting the Wisters I noticed a carpet of pachysandra beyond the front door and was surprised to see a number of healthy, vigorous daffodils coexisting very nicely. My impression had been that nothing short of a catalpa could thrive for long with pachysandra applying its tourniquet. Dr. Wister said, "I thought that too, but I became tired of seeing just pachysandra. The key is to select the most rugged kinds of daffodils and to fertilize them periodically. These are often the least expensive ones too, but don't buy mixtures, because a solid block is usually prettier." Because of its low height, pachysandra doesn't do as good a job as ferns of hiding ripening foliage of daffodils after bloom; at least the foliage is less conspicuous than with most other ground covers, though.

One of the aesthetic benefits of a ground cover is a sense of unity it gives through simplicity, and I am not suggesting that gardeners should underplant pachysandra with a wide range of other plants, most of which would be ill-adapted to cope anyway. However, in a large planting you may find it desirable to ripple the carpet a bit to avoid monotony. Among the strongest candidates for this purpose are hemerocallis, Siberian iris, hostas, mayapples, lady ferns, and sweet cicely (*Myrrhis odorata*). The last is particularly nice, because the licorice-scented foliage resembles a fern but plants bear moderately showy clusters of white flowers in May, followed by heads of seeds, initially green, then black, which prolong the period of interest.

MAKING IT DIFFERENT

There are other pachysandras. My favorite is the Alleghany spurge (*P. procumbens*), which is not very well known, though it is the only native American pachysandra. Depending on the severity of the winter, it is evergreen or at least persistent-leaved with matte green foliage that is larger than in the Japanese species, giving the plant a squat appearance. The name *pachysandra* means "thick (or fat) man," an allusion to stamen width. Granted, no one grows pachysandra for its flowers, but Alleghany spurge is rather attractive when its creamy or pinky-white spikes appear in spring. It makes a very dense, slow-growing ground cover about ten inches tall that is not likely ever to give you any trouble. A counterpart from the Himalayas with shiny evergreen foliage, *P. stylosa,* is perhaps the best species for foliage, but plants suffer in our garden over winter and are better adapted to the mid-Atlantic states. The last thing a gardener wants is a borderline-hardy ground cover.

Two Japanese pachysandra cultivars are worth a mention. One is 'Green Carpet', deeper green and slightly more compact than the species. The other, 'Variegata' ('Silver Edge'), is more likely to catch the eye. Like most variegated forms, this is slower-growing than the species from which it is derived, but it makes a serviceable ground cover in small areas where you can easily remove the occasional shoots that revert to green. In our garden a doughnut-shaped planting of 'Variegata' in light shade around the base of an old mountain-laurel (*Kalmia latifolia*) provides excellent foliage contrast and gives this shallow-rooted evergreen shrub a living mulch. From a distance 'Silver Edge' presents a light gray appearance, as do all variegated plants, bringing light to dark areas like a beacon. The neighbors probably won't even take it for a pachysandra.

· 16 ·

Up with
Ornamental Grasses

IT WAS a warm spring day, and while I was moving pots of perennials around in our driveway, which serves as a sales area, I became aware of a man looking at the ornamental grasses. He was in neutral, shifting from foot to foot, while his wife was in high gear up in the garden, taking more moments to look at plants than he felt was appropriate. Clearly the visit was eating into valuable golf time. As I passed by, he gave me a curious look and asked, "Do you actually sell these things?" I assured him that we did. He shot back, "Well, they look like crabgrass to me, and if I were you, I'd put some Scotts Plus Two on them so they don't get around the lawn!" I bit my tongue and silently hoped that he would make a hole in forty.

Of course ornamental grasses are not everyone's cup of tea, but they have appealed to enough people to cause a ripple in horticulture in recent years. My own first encounter with them long ago, at the Brooklyn Botanic Garden, was a happier one than with my would-be golfer. It was on a November day, after chrysanthemums had withered and tree leaves had fallen. One doesn't expect a group of plants to be coming to its best at that time of year, and perhaps the element of surprise increased the impact of my first-time view of what was then called, in good botanicalese, the monocot bed. A few years before, as the institution was evolving from a botany garden into a horticultural one, this "teaching" border had been reshaped by landscape architect Alice Ireys to display plants in a more pleasing aesthetic manner. I was lucky to see it in the backlighting of a late autumn afternoon, just as the plants had been dipped in evanescent gold by the low angle of the sun.

Miscanthus sinensis 'Gracillimus', in flower in September, is one of the most graceful ornamental grasses even in winter, when the leaves become parchment-colored. Height is about five feet.

There was Ravenna grass (*Erianthus ravennae*), rising to a twelve-foot height to dominate the border with its attractive plumes, which are often confused with those of pampas grass (*Cortaderia selloana*), a plant not dependably winter-hardy north of Washington, D.C. The back of the border was given largely to the miscanthus grasses (*M. sinensis*), most of them growing to seven feet. Older books call them eulalia, but I have never heard them called that by any gardener. They include several standard cultivars, including 'Variegatus', with white stripes on the leaves; zebra grass ('Zebrinus'), with horizontal yellow bands; and 'Gracillimus', with remarkably graceful narrow leaves on plants that are usually a couple of feet shorter than the pack. All of them are late bloomers, bearing feathery beige fans in September and October.

Other grasses were included too. The one that had proliferated the most was switch-grass (*Panicum virgatum*), with airy heads of pale brown flowers floating above arched leaves, growing to a total height of five or six feet. Nearly half the border consisted of it. Also present was ribbon grass (*Phalaris arundinacea* 'Picta'), worse for wear in the full sun and in need of a haircut and a shave around the roots. But most of the grasses were well behaved and performing well despite the prolonged drought that passed for summer in New York in the 1960s.

THE GERMAN CONNECTION

My regard for ornamental grasses has, if anything, increased with the years, as I have gotten to know them better and discovered what they can do in the landscape. We have many more in America today, thanks in good part to the astute introductions of Kurt Bluemel, a very fine Maryland grower whose origins are in the Sudetenland, now a part of Czechoslovakia. He came to the United States in the 1950s and eventually became a citizen. While nearly all of

Calamagrostis acutiflora 'Karl Foerster', named for a noted German horticulturist, grows four or five feet tall and blooms earlier in summer than most of the other tall ornamental grasses. Give it sun.

the American nursery growers who were searching abroad for new plants focused on England, Holland, and Japan, Bluemel looked to Germany.

He did so with good reason. Language was important; few German nurserymen speak English well, and few American ones speak German. Also Bluemel soon learned, in the early years of his nursery, when landscaping was particularly important to his firm, what German perennials were not available here. We had, of course, the Arends astilbes and *Sedum* 'Autumn Joy', but few others. Indeed, it seemed almost as if the horticulture of the two countries in this century had been separated by a wall that was scaled only by an occasional helenium or rudbeckia, maverick American plants that went to Potsdam instead of to Oxford for their pedigrees before returning in cultivar form to the United States. The two wars had much to do with this separation, but it continued well into the 1970s, when the current perennials boom in America began. Gardeners whose Spartan regimen had for years consisted of junipers, yews, and look-alike broad-leaved evergreens suddenly had an appetite for new plants that matched that of a dieting piranha.

The Germans have a passion for ornamental grasses, and nowhere in the world has there been such extensive selection and systematic testing of cultivars. Wherever you go in Germany — except in the small villages, where sunflowers and ivy-leaved geraniums still reign supreme — you find the grasses, and not just in ones and twos. They are a dominant feature especially in parks, where groups of them often approach thirty or forty plants of a kind. Among the most common is the feather reed grass (*Calamagrostis acutiflora* 'Stricta'), which grows about six feet tall and blooms in late summer, and the slightly shorter cultivar 'Karl Foerster'. The latter blooms earlier and has attractive light cinnamon-colored heads through the summer. They are especially striking with the rusty foxglove (*Digitalis ferruginea*), because cinnamon is an out-of-season color, one usually associated more with late autumn. The genus *Calamagrostis* is not even listed in Cornell University's *Hortus Third* (1976), the most comprehensive plant encyclopedia in the United States.

Several years ago, when Mary Ann and I were visiting gardens in Germany with our friends Eberhart and Peggy Altmann, we visited Fritz Koehlein. Koehlein is vice president of the German Perennials Society as well as an author and hybridist whose monographs on various plant groups have been translated into several languages. I asked him why he thought ornamental grasses were so widely used in Germany.

An energetic person who is not at a loss for words, Koehlein was quiet for a minute, then he said, "Karl Foerster." Foerster's name is unknown to most American perennial gardeners, but his book *Gräser und Farne*, one of twenty-eight he wrote, has been widely read in Germany. It was the man himself who had the real impact, though. Foerster lived from 1874 to 1970. For Germany he was the equivalent of Liberty Hyde Bailey, John Wister (both of whom were also productive into their nineties), and Charles Sprague Sargent, all rolled into one.

Foerster was responsible for naming more than five hundred kinds of perennials, many with fanciful or poetic appellations, such as 'Goldsturm' (storm of yellow) for a popular rudbeckia. His nursery and test garden at Potsdam-Bornim became a mecca for German gardeners seeking delphinium, helenium, ornamental grasses, and a host of other perennials, including phlox, of which he named 128 cultivars. In fact, his most quoted remark was "Life without phlox is an error."

Foerster set the stage for the "environmental" gardens that became popular in Germany in the 1960s and '70s. Essentially, these were based on the idea of planting large numbers of particular kinds of perennials, especially grasses, in groups, along with others according to their cultural requirements. Such gardens became central to German park schemes. Display is usually enhanced by numbers, and maintenance becomes proportionately lower if all plants in a certain area have the same needs. People also sometimes claim that plants of the same environmental background usually blend well aesthetically. Fundamentally, these gardens evoke the prairie, or the prairie as interpreted by the Germans, which seems to incorporate pampas and steppes as well.

This thought is sometimes amusing to an American visitor seeing *Verbena bonariensis, Cleome hasslerana, Cosmos bipinnatus,* and other south-of-the-border plants among the northern grasses, perennial sunflowers, liatris, and various coneflowers; but this does not necessarily abnegate the idea for many people. Indeed, isn't the American dream of a meadow-in-the-can, with plenty of European wildflowers among the grasses, somewhat akin? (True, the American version includes a young lady in a Maidenform bra sipping a Diet Pepsi as she prances across the meadow.)

However, ornamental grasses probably would not have come into their own in America except for the high-visibility gardens designed by two landscape architects with close connections to Kurt Bluemel. They are Wolfgang Oehme and James van Sweden. Their imaginative plantings around various public buildings in Washington, D.C., which scale the German "environmental" gardens to American conditions, were a breath of fresh air for a landscape that had turned stale with age and banality of design. Though other plants are represented in Oehme–van Sweden gardens, the larger ornamental grasses dominate, along with *Sedum* 'Autumn Joy' and *Rudbeckia fulgida* 'Goldsturm'. The gardens are informally harmonious in summer and autumn and possess some winter interest, although they strike the compulsively tidy gardener as in need of a vacuum cleaner in the cold months. In addition, they usually require less upkeep than traditional borders, though as usual Americans confuse low maintenance with no maintenance. One Oehme–van Sweden garden I saw recently in the Baltimore-Washington area showed that it is every bit as susceptible to weeds as any other if it becomes neglected.

Our country is prone to trendiness, and Oehme and van Sweden's Teutonic prairie approach has appealed to so many people, including marginally interested gardeners, that it is already on its way to becoming a cliché in a few neighborhoods. Some even hail it as "the new American garden," an interesting claim of singularity for a diverse land that does not lend itself to just one kind of garden. Even if some of the plants employed are able to grow well in several climatic regions, what is the point of a single American garden? To many gardeners the joy of American horticulture is its diversity. I do not care to go to Los Angeles and see a photocopy of a garden down the road from me in Connecticut, although it might satisfy the sense of uniformity needed by those who feel most comfortable putting gardens into a mold. It is like painting by numbers, I suppose, and welcomed especially by designers who fear originality, or by those who are too involved with structures to learn a variety of plants.

Whatever one's reservations may be about the Oehme–van Sweden gardens, they have at least brought attention to an overlooked group of plants — the grasses. My own preference is to use them as occasional components of a border, not the dominant theme. An excess of linear foliage (or excess of any other kind) destroys a visual balance of form and causes the eye to skip to other parts of the landscape. It is like driving across Kansas — after a certain point, it is best to be done as quickly as possible. With that in mind, here are some of my favorite grasses for border uses. I will leave the prairie to others.

SINGING THE BLUES

Blue oat grass (*Helictotrichon sempervirens*) grows about two feet tall (up to an airy four feet when flowers appear in early summer). It is lovely toward the front of the sunny border, just a single plant with a backdrop of a taller pink-flowered perennial such as *Chrysanthemum* 'Clara Curtis', *Phlox* 'Sir John Falstaff', *Physostegia* 'Bouquet Rose', *Monarda* 'Croftway Pink', or *Lythrum* 'Rob-

Opposite (from front): blue oat grass (*Helictotrichon sempervirens*), *Chrysanthemum* 'Clara Curtis', *Phlox* 'Sir John Falstaff', and *Eupatorium rugosum* in the main border at Hillside in August.

ert'. Blue oat grass does best in our garden if we divide it every two or three springs. Cut back the spiky foliage mounds, which more or less persist over winter, only halfway in spring, otherwise plants may succumb. Given well-drained soil, this grass with its narrow blue-gray foliage resembles a refined yucca, but without the stiffness. It is hardy as far north as Montreal, though not as long-lived as some grasses.

Blue fescue (*Festuca ovina* var. *glauca*) is another useful grass, looking its best along a brick terrace or as an edging plant for a border fronting on a flagstone path. Its low height (eight inches) and tufted habit make it a candidate for interplanting with a purple-flowered annual sweet-alyssum (*Lobularia maritima* 'Royal Carpet'). Or use a generous grouping to face down several dwarf purple barberries (*Berberis thunbergii* 'Crimson Pygmy'). Blue fescue needs the same conditions as *Helictotrichon* and seems to grow best in circumneutral or alkaline soil. Division is called for every several years.

Germany provides a number of superior selections of *Festuca* with varying heights and hues. 'Sea Urchin' is an attractive one. *Festuca amethystina*, several inches taller than *F. ovina*, is also a useful plant. We are fond of another blue-leafer, *Koeleria glauca*, which grows about fifteen inches tall and has a greater life expectancy than *Festuca* in acid soils. Both combine well with sky-blue annuals such as *Cynoglossum* 'Firmament' or *Lobelia erinus* 'Cambridge Blue'.

Anglophile gardeners who take Gertrude Jekyll too seriously often get into trouble with a larger blue-leaved grass, *Elymus arenarius*. It was Miss Jekyll's favorite grass, but the plant requires a retinue of gardeners to keep it properly straitjacketed in a border because of its propensity to spread from the root. A colonizer, especially in sandy soils, the blue lyme grass, as this *Elymus* is some-times called, is best in a meadow or among shrubs where it can romp a bit, as it does in the Montreal Botanical Garden among a sea of low junipers. As a large-scale ground cover with several plants of purple-leaved smoke bush (*Cotinus coggygria* 'Royal Purple' or similar cultivar) in the background, it can be arrest-ing. Lyme grass grows three to four feet tall and has leaves that are half an inch wide.

RATING THE REDS

Red-leaved grasses are not as common as blue-leaved sorts, but they are striking if properly used. Japanese blood grass (*Imperata cylindrica* 'Rubra' or 'Red Baron') grows a foot tall and has red foliage all season. It is most beautiful in autumn, especially if placed to take advantage of backlighting effects in late afternoon, when plants look as though they are on fire. Full sun brings out the greatest color intensity. Blood grass can be grown as far north as Vermont, but sharp drainage and a light cover of evergreen boughs in winter are important in the colder reaches of the North. This is also one of the last plants to make growth in spring, and it is very easy for the impatient gardener to consign blood grass to the compost heap prematurely.

The best grouping of Japanese blood grass I have seen is in the Columbus, Ohio, garden of plantsman Dick Meyer, who is a master of pleasing combinations. This consists of blood grass clumps set at intervals in a ground cover of *Orostachys furusei* (*iwarenge*), a gray-leaved, ground-hugging sedum relative from Japan. In fact, low sedums themselves are good companions, notably *S. cauticola*, *S. dasyphyllum*, and *S. sieboldii*. As a backdrop, *Sedum* 'Autumn Joy', to two feet, is also appropriate. However, blood grass is eminently a design plant, and any gardener with imagination can have a field day with it. Oddly, the plant was unknown in Germany when we visited there several years ago. The introduction from Japan to America was apparently made by veteran rock gardener Frank Cabot.

Several taller grasses have a reddish hue later in the growing season. *Panicum virgatum* 'Haense Hermes', to four feet, has the upper part of the leaf colored in deep red from August until frost; 'Rehbraun' is similar. These are attractive near Canadian burnet (*Sanguisorba canadensis*), which has pokers of white flowers borne on four-foot stems from August to October. *Cimicifuga americana*, bearing fragrant white bottlebrushes in August and September, and C. *simplex* 'White Pearl' (September-October) are candidates in the five- to six-foot range. If you want an open spray of white, try *Artemisia lactiflora*, usually four feet tall but taller in rich soil. *Boltonia asteroides* 'Snowbank' works well too, if a late-season white daisy is called for as a partner for these red-tipped grasses. You can round the planting out with *Artemisia* 'Silver Queen', two to three feet tall, preferably in a sunken bucket so it doesn't engage in territorial aggrandizement.

Purplish foliage is also useful in the same context. One of the most valuable of the many miscanthus grasses is *M. sinensis* 'Purpurascens', a four-footer that develops a pleasing tint in late summer that lasts for many weeks. It then becomes a chameleon, turning tawny orange in autumn and finally almost parchment-colored in winter, but still distinguishable from other miscanthus even in March. The milder the winter, the better the effect.

I regret that the beautiful purple-leaved fountain grass (*Pennisetum setaceum* 'Atrosanguineum') is not winter-hardy in the North. The foliage is deeply colored, and even the flower spikes are purplish. Plant height can vary from three to six feet, and this fountain grass needs plenty of sun if the leaves are to assume

Japanese blood grass (*Imperata cylindrica* 'Rubra') is here tied to the earth by a sedum relative from Japan, *Orostachys furusei*. The scene is in the Dick Meyer garden in Columbus, Ohio.

their brightest hue. A single plant in a big tub, even a whiskey barrel, surrounded by lamb's-ears, dusty-miller, or another silverling, makes a very fine display. It is ideal with a Victorian home in the background. In cold climates the hardiest fountain grass is *Pennisetum alopecuroides*, a delightful three-footer when in bloom in the fall, but the foliage isn't purple. The species varies greatly from seed, and a cultivar such as 'Hameln' (to two feet) will save disappointment.

HEDGING WITH THE SEDGES

There is even a brown-leaved grass, rather a sedge from New Zealand, *Carex buchananii*, which has become a design toy in collectors' gardens. Known as the leatherleaf sedge, it has narrow coppery brown foliage that is curled at the ends. It is more or less hardy to coastal New England, requiring sun and reasonably moist soil for best effect. I have lost it to winter on two or three occasions with no tears from my wife. A while ago I grew it in a cold frame and was planning to set it out in the garden one fine spring morning. The plant looked healthy enough, for a *Carex buchananii*. Mary Ann, peeking over my shoulder, gleefully remarked, "But it died two years ago! Didn't you notice?"

Several other *Carex* strike me as better garden plants than *C. buchananii*. The *Carex* nomenclature is Byzantine. *C. conica* 'Variegata' of gardens is a neat silver-variegated sedge, which some graminologists now call *C. morrowii* 'Variegata', a name used until recently for a handsome golden-variegated one-footer that is passingly hardy in New York. The latter was for a time also sold as *C. morrowii* 'Aureo-Variegata' and is now bearing a new moniker, *C. hachioensis* 'Evergold'. Got it? Nomenclature is an evolutionary sport.

The first plant, *C. conica* 'Variegata' of gardens, is roughly two hardiness zones hardier than the second, but a severe winter in coastal New England can maim it. Light shade seems ideal for this ten-inch-tall clump-former. Try it with Korean goatsbeard (*Aruncus aethusifolius*), which has lacy leaves, and the smallest of the hostas, *H. venusta*, for a pleasing textural contrast. 'Evergold' is a good companion in the shade for a small golden-leaved hosta such as 'Wogon'. *Carex stricta* 'Bowles' Golden' is an appropriate but slow-growing alternative to 'Evergold' in cold climates.

MOLINIA AND MISCANTHUS

Among other golden-variegated plants for our purpose is *Molinia caerulea* 'Variegata', a slow-growing but invaluable companion for toning down strong oranges and yellows. Protection from afternoon sun helps keep the foliage from discoloring, even in the North. Plants grow two feet in height (fleetingly taller in bloom) and endure light to medium shade and moist soil.

Zebra grass (*Miscanthus sinensis* 'Zebrinus') is better known, an old-timer growing to a billowy six feet, with horizontal yellow markings as the season progresses. Usually just one plant does the trick, giving respectable visual support to late summer rudbeckias that have a hint of burnt orange in their yellow flowers. Porcupine grass (*M. s.* 'Strictus') is similar in leaf pattern to zebra grass but with stiffer growth habit and brighter yellow markings.

All of the miscanthus are best in sun, but one seems to hold up better in light shade than others, *M. s.* 'Variegatus'. This has clean white vertical variegation and grows about six feet tall. It combines well with strong floral colors nearby, especially red, rose pink, or no-nonsense purple. Deep, moist soil gives most prolific results for miscanthus, and at least one species will romp in it. This is the giant of the genus, *M. floridulus*, which can attain twelve feet. It looks best along a pond but is a menace in the border. Like other tall grasses, its rustling in even a slight breeze gives a different dimension to the garden. Not all miscanthus are huge plants, however. A relatively new *M. sinensis* introduction to American gardens comes from the Japanese island of Yakushima, which is noted for the dwarf *Rhododendron yakusimanum*. This grass has grown only eighteen inches tall in our garden, though it is reported to top off at three to four feet in a milder climate. The selection is called 'Yaku Jima', and nice specimens can be seen at the National Arboretum in Washington, D.C.

Our most striking miscanthus? 'Silver Feather', without a doubt. Plants are vigorous, growing about eight feet tall and starting to flower a few weeks earlier in autumn than their kin, for whom good bloom is nip and tuck in a cool or overcast climate. The stout stems of 'Silver Feather' hold up well in winter, despite gales and heavy snows, which make quick work of some grasses, including *M. floridulus*. (You should cut the latter to the ground in the fall before its detritus is blown to your neighbor's garden.) In fall and winter the foliage of 'Silver Feather' undergoes a series of subtle changes, eventually becoming parchment-colored. Needle evergreens make a good backdrop, and the long-lasting red fruits of *Viburnum trilobum*, the highbush cranberry, provide the base for a winter garden even in harsh climates. In some respects the taller ornamental grasses can be a more important element in the cold-climate landscape than in a mild one, because of the length of winter and the snow cover on lower-growing plants. Placed on a rise, above eye level, they can be dramatic in the winter horizon. Their leaves also "speak" with the winter wind.

It is an exciting time for ornamental grasses, for lots of new ones are appearing in the trade. Many are attractive, but a sorting-out process will inevitably take place, because not all of them are equally adapted. Each year, it seems, we come on one or two beautiful kinds that we never knew existed. Among recent finds — whose seed heads are excellent for dried arrangements when the garden is on the downhill side toward winter — are *Spodiopogon sibiricus*, which grows to about four feet, and *Calamagrostis arundinacea* var. *brachytricha*, a five-footer from Korea. Both of these grasses are sun lovers, but the *Calamagrostis* tolerates light shade quite well.

IN THE SHADE

Are there grasses for primarily shaded areas? Indeed there are, though most are for sun. One of the most attractive shade dwellers is *Hakonechloa macra* 'Aureola', which is best pronounced without marbles in the mouth. It attains about a foot in height and has rich yellow-green foliage with irregular green lines.

Hakonechloa expands more slowly than most other grasses do, but it is worth the wait of two or three years before plants settle in. The intensity of the leaf color in a shady area is noticeable even across a fair-sized lawn, drawing the eye like a beacon. It makes an elegant small-scale ground cover with hostas of golden hue, or to emphasize the existence of green-leaved hostas of modest stature. It is also appropriate with hellebores, whose somber foliage occasionally needs light relief. Even in winter the dead foliage, which is buff-colored, has character.

A couple of low white-variegated grasses are good for shaded areas. One is *Holcus mollis* 'Albo-variegatus', which grows about eight inches tall and creeps its way into ground cover status in a relatively brief time. The foliage bears a high proportion of white to green, making *Holcus* a logical choice where you need an injection of light. If the leaves become tatty by midsummer, a good shearing restores attractiveness quickly, but be careful about site. Sun and overly dry soil force the plants to close down shop for the summer season, to reappear in fall or the next spring. *Holcus* makes a nice mate for European wild-ginger (*Asarum europaeum*), *Waldsteinia ternata*, or another neat dark green ground cover.

The variegated bulbous oat grass (*Arrhenatherum elatius* 'Variegatus') grows about a foot high and also has a good proportion of white to green on the foliage, which has more body than *Holcus*. It is also tolerant of a wider range of sites, growing well here in sun or shade. Growth is fairly rapid in our clay loam, but not to the nuisance point, which it could reach in sandy soils. You can quickly tell this grass from other variegated sorts by the bulbils at the base of the foliage. Plants look good with *Geranium macrorrhizum* 'Ingwersen's Variety', which has pale pink flowers on fifteen-inch stems in late spring, borne above solid foliage mounds. *Epimedium* is also enhanced by the presence of this *Arrhenatherum*. (Ribbon grass, known botanically as *Phalaris arundinacea* 'Picta', is another white-variegated grass, described on page 68.)

Every so often I am astonished to find on our land native treasures I have overlooked before. In clearing a lightly wooded area several years ago we came upon a healthy stand of northern sea oats (*Chasmanthium latifolium*, formerly placed in the genus *Uniola*). Twenty years back I perhaps would have whacked it down with a brush hog because it was a common, here-and-there, rather inconspicuous plant of the New England woods. In a group, however, it takes on character, with leaves the widest of any grass I have mentioned, a good inch across. Plants grow about three feet tall and mildly suggest a bamboo. The seed heads in late summer and autumn aren't showy like the ones of *Miscanthus* or

Calamagrostis, but they have a neat charm that works well in smaller dried arrangements. And the northern sea oats do take the shade. A gardener's perception of certain plants changes with time, and sometimes the supporting actors in the garden turn out to be the best performers, long after the delphiniums have croaked.

· 17 ·

The World of
Alliums

As the interest in perennials continues to grow, a number of lesser-known kinds are attracting attention. Among them are the alliums, or ornamental onions as they are somewhat inelegantly called. Many have nicely scented flowers, some are without fragrance, none are objectionable. You are not likely to notice the oniony scent of the foliage unless it is bruised.

The genus *Allium*, comprising some six hundred species, includes in fact the culinary onion and its relatives — chive, garlic, leek, shallot, top onion, Welsh onion, and a few others. To the alliumphile most of these are ornamental in their own right, the best example being kitchen chives (*A. schoenoprasum*), which have hopped the fence from the herb garden to the perennial border. As are a lot of alliums, chives are quite variable, and it is good to keep alert for cultivars with larger clusters of flowers borne well above the foliage or with more brightly colored blooms. One such recent introduction is 'Forescate'.

Distinguishing among the numerous alliums may seem to some gardeners like separating globs of Jell-O, but it isn't terribly complicated to sort out the common types. Apart from the culinary kinds, perhaps a hundred species of alliums are cultivated in America, and most of these in botanical gardens or specialist collections. Fortunately, although even botanists disagree over which larger grouping to place alliums in, the lily family or the amaryllis family, two principal distinctions within the genus are clear enough.

On the one hand, there are the SUDS, or summer-dormant species. Their leaves wither after flowering occurs in spring or early summer. Many in this group have distinct, often stout bulbs. They include *Allium giganteum*, stars-of-

Persia (*A. christophii* or *A. albopilosum*), *A. aflatunense,* and the burgundy-colored drumstick allium (*A. sphaerocephalum*), which is lovely in early summer mingled with Shasta daisy 'Little Miss Muffet' (and whose leaves may persist in a moist season). These sorts are available in autumn from bulb dealers. Many come originally from Turkestan or Central Asia, lands of dry summers, and the straplike or grassy foliage is discarded by nature as an economy measure to cope with drought, even though we may continue to water the section of the garden they are in with no apparent harm to the plants.

Often the umbels of pink or lavender-pink — or less often blue, yellow, or white — flowers in this group are quite showy, and the scapes are of height and substance, as in the four-foot-tall *Allium giganteum.* You must give a bit of thought to the placement of these bulbs in the flower border, so you will have no bare spots when their leaves shrivel. Most of the SUDS are best placed in midborder so other plants can fill the gap when the leaves disappear. One technique is to interplant them with hemerocallis, the foliage of which hides the evidence of withering allium foliage as the season progresses. With a few exceptions, these alliums are sun lovers, and they perform well in average garden soil. It is best to plant taller-growing sorts a foot or so apart, lower-growing ones about eight inches.

The other main group of alliums is the SUTS, or summer-thriving species. The leaves make active growth all summer long, and flowering is usually in late spring or summer. Bulbs are smaller, less pronounced, and frequently joined by rhizomes. These species are mainly from parts of the world with fair summer rainfall. As a result, their moisture requirements in the border are higher, though the SUTS are hardly sots by garden standards. Examples are kitchen chives, nodding onion (*A. cernuum*), *A. senescens,* garlic chives (*A. tuberosum*), and the fragrant allium (*A. ramosum*), whose grayish white flowers in late spring or early summer mingle so well with blue columbines.

Apart from a small group of alpines with special cultural requirements, the SUTS are by and large rugged garden plants, though because of their very toughness the gardener tends to stretch them beyond their limits by giving them poor or no soil preparation and ignoring their need for modest watering during drought. As a result, these durable Cinderellas are often tatty when they should be looking their best.

The person whose ardor for gardening disappears by the Fourth of July is likely to have a dim impression of SUTS (and a few SUDS) alliums for another reason. They self-sow, unless someone removes the seed heads that develop after flowering. This is the normal process of tidying that you should perform with almost any perennial, and it takes only a little time to do the task, but if you ignore it, a fair colony of seedlings will probably have sprouted by the next season. It is an oversight the conscientious gardener is likely to make only once.

The grooming process is easy. After the flowers wither, take a few minutes to cut the scapes at ground level with pruning shears or scissors, for the scapes themselves eventually turn brown and detract from the late-season appearance of an otherwise good planting. Put them in the garbage can, not on the compost heap, because even the keenest alliumphile doesn't relish the thought of alliumlings coming up all over the garden.

The essence of gardening, it seems to me, is getting the right partners together. It is particularly important with alliums, because the delicate beauty of some kinds allows them to be overshadowed by all too flamboyant mates.

BIG BOYS

Not all alliums are retiring sorts, especially *A. giganteum*, and it might be best to consider its uses first. This plant looks like a giant lollipop, with a four-inch-wide ball-like cluster of rosy lilac flowers on top of a four-foot scape. *A. giganteum* is a difficult plant to incorporate in flower borders, because it demands to be looked at. One technique is to plant a few bulbs toward the back of the border with other alliums of similar raspiness and intensity nearby: *A. rosenbachianum* and *A. aflatunense*, with *A. christophii* toward the front, all visually fastened to the earth with interplantings of white baby's-breath, of which *Gypsophila paniculata* 'Perfecta' would be a logical choice. Over the season the baby's-breath will hide the decaying foliage of these SUDS. This is the power-chained-by-lace approach!

From a design standpoint there is more than one way to skin an allium. *A. giganteum* can be quite presentable if you group a few in a border in front of a good planting of variegated miscanthus (*Miscanthus sinensis* 'Variegatus'), whose cooling green-and-cream leaves rise four or five feet from the ground with a gentle, graceful curve. Or place *A. giganteum* in front of needle evergreens, especially dark-colored ones such as yews of some size or even Norway spruces, just so you have a solid background that won't be overpowered. Even a gray-leaf shrub of some age, such as Russian-olive (*Elaeagnus angustifolia*), can provide a serviceable backdrop, its own foliage being brightest in color at the time *A. giganteum* is in flower, in late May or June. But *A. giganteum*'s a tough allium to crack.

Although stars-of-Persia (*A. christophii*) is much lower, usually eighteen to

An interplanting of drumstick allium (*A. sphaerocephalum*) and a tall Shasta daisy, *Chrysanthemum* × *superbum* 'Alaska', is at its peak in early summer.

twenty-four inches, it is a more striking allium than *A. giganteum*. On occasion the loose cluster of lilac-pink flowers is a foot across, and the spent inflorescence can be attractive far into summer, though the foliage disappears early on. We like to plant several bulbs behind a group of glistening white astilbe such as 'Bridal Veil', the loose steeples of the latter mingling among the stars. This is a pleasant enough way to end a spring border or start a summer one. Friends of ours who are taken with dried arrangements are so fond of stars-of-Persia they grow it in a cutting garden. Even then, it's not a bad idea in late April or May to scatter a little seed of the annual white sweet-alyssum in the row, for the flowers come quickly and complement this allium nicely.

OTHER SUDS

Allium oreophilum 'Zwanenburg', a selection made for its carmine-red flowers, attains a height of only six or eight inches when in flower in June. Low-growing SUDS demand a little thought as to placement, too, because if you plant them in the front of a border, the absence of their leaves will be especially noticeable by midsummer. Besides, the narrow straplike leaves of many alliums don't stand out if the border is adjacent to a lawn; allium and grass foliages are too similar. Gardeners usually prefer for frontal positions those low plants with blocky leaves (such as alchemillas, some geraniums, bergenias, and hostas) that say, "Okay, this is where the border starts." Call it definition, if you will.

A better spot for 'Zwanenburg' or its fellow runts in the SUDS group is to be planted in periwinkle (*Vinca minor*) in a sunny or half-sunny site. Periwinkle is evergreen, of course, and the allium leaves wither away without a whimper. The dark oval foliage of periwinkle serves as good foil for a wide range of bulbs, and a four- by seven-foot patch of this useful ground cover next to our terrace incorporates several kinds of daffodils and colchicums, the periwinkle obscuring the leafy evidence. The area receives a light scattering of 10-10-10 fertilizer in early spring, which seems adequate because the various bulbs keep returning year after year and the vinca continues to bear its good blue flowers in May at daffodil time. If you would like complementary bloom for *Allium oreophilum* 'Zwanenburg', interplant with blue- or white-flowered *Campanula carpatica*.

Campanula carpatica is also a good companion for the low-growing golden garlic (*A. moly*) in a lightly shaded edge-of-the-woods garden with soil that is neither rich nor moist. In the well-prepared soil of a border this strongly scented bulb can increase a little too freely, both underground and above. Another way of keeping golden garlic under appropriate stress is to grow it between stepping-stones or at the base of a wall. Plant a dozen of the inexpensive little bulbs in a six-inch-wide hole, then jump back. The turf of a meadow garden also keeps golden garlic relatively honest. This attractive bright yellow allium is not as invasive as some alliums, but it is not really a border plant either.

Another member of the SUDS group is *Allium caeruleum*, which bears true blue flowers on two- to three-foot scapes in June. The foliage is wispy and of little account except to the plant, so it is a good idea to spot these bulbs among white or pink astilbes for a jack-in-the-box effect. After mid-July you will no longer be conscious of the plant except perhaps for a none-too-prominent seed head. A good matchmaker might also put this selection to work with the clear yellow plates and grayish foliage of *Achillea* 'Moonshine' or with the chartreuse flowers of lady's-mantle (*Alchemilla mollis*).

A FEW SUTS

Summer-blooming alliums with foliage that stays green through the season are in many respects the most valuable border plants in the genus. Although some of the less memorable forms of *Allium senescens* have wishy-washy pink flowers, it is in general a useful species, growing from fifteen inches to two feet tall and flowering mainly in midsummer. The best use we have found for it is as an enhancer of other plants with similar but clearer tints, such as the purple cone-flower (*Echinacea purpurea*) and one of the bee balms, *Monarda* 'Croftway Pink'. Face down the monochromatic scheme with something white, say *Veronica* 'Icicle' or *Achillea* 'The Pearl', and you will have a pleasant, rather long-lasting scenario for the sweet sultry days of July.

Allium senescens is native from Europe to the Far East. It has a low-growing form from the Oriental end of its range that is useful for lavender-pink flowers in late August or September. This is *A. senescens* var. *glaucum*. The leafy new growth in spring is twisted horizontally, evoking the common name of cowlick chives. This habit becomes less pronounced as the season advances, but the gray-green leaves are distinctive enough to attract the eye through the season. Plants look their best at the top of a low stone wall. The leaves and flowers go well with natural granite or flagstone. Mix in some white sweet-alyssum or a good rock garden carpeting perennial with similar white flowers repeated through the season, such as *Hutchinsia alpina,* which benefits from a little afternoon shade. If a nearby spot has slightly deeper shade, as in our garden, a low-growing, late-flowering hosta such as silver-variegated 'Ginko Craig' may be an appropriate companion.

The nodding onion (*Allium cernuum*), which has a wide natural distribution in the United States, is variable too, but plants with abundant clear pink flowers in July and August are to be treasured. The elegant clusters resemble pink parasols, the bell-shaped flowers suspended like little jewels from arched pedicels. After the flowers are pollinated the pedicels straighten up. Our plants seem to thrive in sun or light shade, a condition that brings about fewer flowers but a longer bloom period. They are usually eighteen inches tall at flowering, but I have seen lower and taller ones in other gardens. A photographer friend of ours, after spending a summer taking pictures across the country for a wildflower book he was working on, declared that one of the finest natural sights he had seen was on a Midwest prairie where *Allium cernuum* cavorted in numbers with gay-feather (*Liatris*), softening the latter's rigid pinky purple spikes. In the garden you can emulate this nicely by putting a few plants of the nodding onion in front of *Liatris* 'Kobold', which is a tidier and more compact gay-feather than is customarily found in the wild.

Garlic chives (*Allium tuberosum*) have bolstered many a border in August. Although the common name strikes me as a misnomer, since the straplike leaves of our plants have not a garlicky but a strong oniony scent when bruised or chewed, there is no confusion about this broad-leaved chive's horticultural value. The clusters of white flowers, borne on two- or three-foot stalks depending on soil fertility and moisture, combine well with a variety of perennials, or for that matter, annuals. We use them to soften the brassiness of orange dwarf marigolds in the foreground, which are further toned down by variegated moor grass (*Molinea caerulea* 'Variegata'). But *A. tuberosum* works well with pink or rosy flowers too.

Allium carinatum var. *flavum*, with pale yellow flowers and usually gray foliage, is another good species, blooming in July and early August on two-foot scapes. Massing is important because of the delicacy of the flower clusters, and we usually set out nine or ten young plants in a group. They tone down stronger colors nicely, but can also be part of subtle color schemes. The flower bud is a study in small architecture, shaped like a parchment canoe with a long prow. The flower cluster resembles a miniature Roman candle in form, some flowers suspended, others erect. *Allium carinatum* var. *pulchellum* is much the same but in purple-pink and with green instead of gray foliage.

There are autumn blooming alliums too, including one form of the prairie onion (*A. stellatum*), which has clusters of pink flowers in September and October on scapes twelve to fifteen inches tall. This is a fitting companion for the late-flowered coralbells (*Heuchera villosa*), whose white flowers usually do not appear for us until August, but last a long time. Even later is *A. thunbergii* 'Ozawa's Variety' from Japan. This has eight-inch scapes of diminutive purplish pink bells that resemble heather, but bloom is so far along into autumn and plants so small that we usually transplant them to pots and put them on the back porch, as a change from the chrysanthemums that customarily dominate October. After bloom, which may last as long as six weeks because of the coolness of the season and the protection from rain that the porch affords, we put these plants in the cold frame for the winter or set them out in the garden, covering them in December with a mulch of pine needles or other coarse winter mulch. Like all of the other species mentioned in this chapter, *A. thunbergii* is winter-hardy at least as far north as Vermont.

· 18 ·

Yesterday's
Flowers

SOME TIME AGO I begged a slip of a peony from a friend who is also a mossback. This wasn't a fancy new hybrid. Instead, it was a rather dowdy purplish pink bloomer with average-size flowers and a faintly mysterious scent.

My grandmother wore dresses like that peony. Our friend doesn't know its name; nor do I, for it probably dates from the past century and has long since been discarded by nurseries, though a few of the old-timers are still around. The peony came from the cellar hole of a house that burned to the ground in the 1930s after a murder and a suicide. This adds spice: a plant is more interesting to grow if you know its history.

There is a small cemetery on a barely negotiable dirt road near our home in northern Connecticut. It has but a dozen graves, the most recent dating from 1870. A child's tombstone is almost completely embedded in a sugar maple tree that has a trunk three and a half feet in diameter. One epitaph reads "In heaven there is rest." On earth there was little, at least for a rural New Englander in the 1860s. The young men died far from home, going down at Antietam and dozens of lesser-known battlefields. As often as not, those who survived the Civil War did not want to come back to the hardscrabble existence of the Connecticut farm, where the major crop was rocks, which could not be turned to gold. They listened to Mr. Greeley and went west. Slowly the little cemeteries faded, and no longer does the American Legion post flags on them at Memorial Day.

But the plants, or some of them, go on. Don't they do well! Is it our imagination that a few grow lushly on the phosphorus released by old Eben? There is the creeping rose no one now living has a name for. Perhaps it never had a name, but was just passed over a fence, or purveyed by an itinerant nurseryman who bought slips from the imaginative plant promoter William Robert Prince of Flushing, New York, whose firm in its heyday was the best-known of all American nurseries.

The feral summer phlox (*Phlox paniculata*) goes on in the old cemeteries despite yearly battles with mildew and no recourse to Benomyl, the systemic fungicide that so easily controls it on the handsome Symons-Jeune sorts we grow in gardens today. Though its range extends north to New York, summer phlox in the wild is particularly associated with the South. The irony is lost on old Eben.

Other old cemeteries, but not ones of quite the vintage I have described, have *Achillea ptarmica* 'The Pearl', a double-flowered yarrow that originated in the great French nursery of Lemoine, the lilac breeder. Little buttonlike flowers, most notable in chrysanthemums, were popular late last century and in the early

Stan Beikmann

Hemerocallis flava, called *H. lilioasphodelus* by some botanists now, has a less confusing common name: lemon daylily. This sweetly scented daylily, one of the first of the season to bloom, here oversees an abandoned New England cemetery.

years of ours, so it is not surprising that 'The Pearl' had great appeal. Derived from a European weed, it was, if anything, adaptable, and little slips were easy to uproot and pass over the fence (or went under it on their own).

Occasionally my wife accuses me of being a grave robber, and to a degree that is true. One nineteenth-century cemetery I know has a solid patch of the sweetly scented lemon daylily (*Hemerocallis flava; H. lilioasphodelus* of some botanists), which blooms in late spring. An Irish cutting once happened to make its way to my pocket, probably by leprechaun. I do not normally scratch my pants climbing fences.

DAYLILIES

The lemon lily is a plant that some hemerocallis hobbyists have forgotten in their mania for bigger-flowered sorts and ones with recurved petals or freaky frills. Hardly a nursery sells the real article anymore, for it has been "superseded." As a taxonomist, and apart from any sentiment I have for particular plants, I think it is important to treat true species, ones that are known in the wild in some part of the world, with a measure of horticultural respect, even if their ruffles may not in all cases be fluffy enough for the Saturday morning hybridist. There are sound genetic reasons for this, since once a species disappears, the gene pool declines.

Fortunately, the lemon lily, though not nearly as common as its summer-blooming big sister, the tawny daylily (*H. fulva*), is in little danger of dying out from old gardens, and it is still passed along to new growers who appreciate that sort of thing. There are several old-time cultivars that were never named or whose names have been lost through the mists of time.

This small-leaved daylily, originally native from eastern Siberia to Japan but grown in America since colonial days, happens to be an excellent garden plant, with hardly a pest. Eventually its rhizomes make a dense stand that no weed can penetrate. I have seen a fifty-year-old clump growing near a common lilac (*Syringa vulgaris*), a shrub that with age develops a stubborn suckering habit. It was irresistible object vs. immovable force, and both were holding their own at the line of demarcation.

Early this summer I attended a country fair, and at a pottery exhibit my eye was taken not by the pottery but by an exquisitely beautiful brick-orange-and-red flower in a vase. After a moment I realized it was the tawny daylily (*H. fulva* 'Europa'), of which I see a thousand clumps each July — but not close up. It is an object of scorn among the horticultural community, and no enlightened garden club matron would admit to liking the color. True, I wouldn't want the plant in my own garden unless I had a steep and difficult bank to cover. Like some corporate executives, it is an expert at takeovers, though not necessarily at community relations.

The tawny daylily is in some respects the most remarkable perennial from Asia to reach American shores, and it came to us, as did most of the colonial arrivals, via England and Europe. The common sort happens to be a clone, one named 'Europa', and every plant is genetically identical. The plant does not set seed (though the pollen is viable), and it has spread through America by vegetative means. Floods, chipmunks, people, and goodness knows what else break off little pieces of rhizome, which take root almost anywhere. I have seen the tawny daylily in Maine, in roadside ditches around Roanoke, Virginia, even near the Okefenokee swamp in south Georgia. There are probably few states where it is not naturalized.

It is an amazingly difficult plant to put under. Once, when starting a new compost heap which eventually grew five feet tall, I threw a tawny daylily on the bottom. Two years later, when we finally depleted the heap, the plant resumed growth. I suspect that one clump of tawny daylilies at a crossroads near our home dates from the eighteenth century, because a stagecoach inn of that period was adjacent for a few years. (Lily-of-the-valley also grows nearby.) The local highway crew cuts it to the ground each July, as part of the official vandalism conducted by small New England towns against roadsides.

This clump is a particular delight for Mary Ann and me in late June, because we pick the flower buds when they are small and simmer them two or three minutes, as reasonable people do garden peas. The taste is a subtle cross of asparagus and snap beans, but don't tell anyone — Craig Claiborne may be listening. Several parts of the plant are palatable, and in China the daylily has been grown for kitchen use since ancient times. The friend who gave us the murder-suicide-arson peony shocked me once by saying that he ate the new shoots of the lemon daylily like asparagus. But then, he cooks horseradish leaves the way we do Swiss chard. Another friend, a hemerocallis specialist, came to dinner and we served daylily buds. Later he asked what new Oriental vegetable Mary Ann had provided. We told him, and his face became ashen.

'Kwanso' is a double-flowered version of the tawny daylily. It arrived in America much later, probably in the middle of the nineteenth century. Because of the doubling, the blossom looks like a tawny daylily that is out of focus. It is a vigorous grower and is still seen in many old gardens, even in East Hampton and the Bronx. 'Kwanso' starts to flower shortly after the tawny daylily but blooms longer. You still sometimes see an unstable sport of it with silver-variegated leaves.

ANTIQUE HERBS

Nineteen hundred and eighty was the bicentennial year, more or less, for our home, Hillside. Only ten families have lived here. Hillside was a dairy farm until the early years of this century, when it was purchased as a summer home by a Columbia University law professor who was interested in the classics. We can stand at a certain distance and angle from the house and see how each family added on to what the previous family had done. Some things were improvements, others weren't, and we can glimpse the personalities of some past owners. The gentleman from Columbia, for example, must have been a formal, orderly person, judging from several masonry walls and a marble terrace that were imposed on the old farm. Nature resents formality in the New England hills, and winter is slowly destroying the walls, which will topple onto the feverfew someday.

I expect the feverfew (*Chrysanthemum parthenium*) will survive. It has for many years, regardless of the disdain, tolerance, grudging admiration, or love respective families have bestowed on it. How we wish we could go back in time and speak for five minutes with each owner! My first question would be, "Okay, which one of you planted the feverfew?" Was it there when Mr. Lincoln was president? Even more remotely, does it perhaps antedate the French Revolution? Was it for medicine (a febrifuge) or ornament? Or did the law professor enjoy the idea of cultivating a plant that was held in esteem by the ancients, including Plutarch, who in the first century A.D. recounted a then old story that its properties had saved the life of a construction worker who had fallen during the building of the Parthenon?

In fact, the American settlers and their immediate successors did not have much time for ornamental plants, except perhaps in the South, where boxwood, in the view of some, became a curse on horticulture, though the enlightened Thomas Jefferson tried to keep the field of interest broad. In the cities people had flower gardens in front yards, it seems, but cottage gardens as in England never quite evolved.

Most of the plants, apart from vegetables (and not many of them, by today's standards), were herbs. People grew them for home remedies, to relieve the monotony of a restricted diet or to disguise gamy meats, and for fragrance when dried. The air in homes was stale, especially in winter, and people didn't bathe often.

Early herbs, practically all of them brought from the Old World, included artemisia, sage, lavender, mint, santolina, chives, and garden heliotrope (*Valeriana officinalis*, a roadside escape even now, and, less known, a catnip substitute); also orris root (*Iris florentina*), with its haunting gray-white flowers, and sweet cicely (*Myrrhis odorata*), a fernlike perennial with licorice-scented leaves. Sweet cicely came with Hillside and we continue to accommodate it (or it us).

All of these plants have a role in the garden today, and some of them are rather fine perennials despite an Achilles' heel or two. Do not expect studlike flowers, though a few of these old-timers can dominate the border when in bloom. Others, while attractive, move from garden to field faster than an aphid finds a modern hybrid tea rose. Early fugitives included coltsfoot (*Tussilago*), used in cough remedies; angelica (confections); tansy (*Tanacetum*, for Easter pudding); teasel (*Dipsacus*), used in combing wool; and lady's bedstraw (*Galium verum*), a dye plant. (This account does not concern itself with woody

Feverfew (*Chrysanthemum parthenium*), a long-blooming, free-seeding perennial, performs well in sun or shade. Widely planted in former times, it is still especially useful in informal parts of the garden.

plants, but readers may find it of interest that the first Old World tree to escape was probably the peach; it was even cultivated by the Indians.)

OTHERS FROM THE PAST

Not surprisingly, a large proportion of perennial flowers came from Europe. Among them were golden marguerite (*Anthemis tinctoria*), whose finely cut leaves and yellow flowers still grace many an early summer flowering border, and dropwort (*Filipendula vulgaris*, formerly *F. hexapetala*), with handsome dissected leaves but inconspicuous white flowers that no one would write home to Kew about, though a double-flowered sort, 'Flore Pleno', can be a refreshing sight in June.

Dame's rocket (*Hesperis matronalis*) was another, with sweetly scented magenta flowers like those of phlox. Late one May when we drove the width of New York State, it was the most common of all the flowers of the field. A white variant was one of Marie Antoinette's favorite flowers. In some areas ragged-robin (*Lychnis flos-cuculi*), a plant mentioned by Shakespeare, is as frequently encountered. A field of its misty pink flowers suggests a painting by a French Impressionist.

Additional perennials that came early from Europe were German iris (*Iris × germanica*), Maltese-cross (*Lychnis chalcedonica*, a plant of the Crusades), perennial cornflower (*Centaurea montana*), and gas plant (*Dictamnus albus*). Dianthus came and often left early because it was not at home in the wet, acid clay that passes for soil in many parts of New England. Two popular old-time annuals, mignonette (North Africa) and nasturtium (the Andes), came along somewhat later.

I shouldn't give the impression that earlier Americans grew only foreign plants (literally exotics). Butterfly weed (*Asclepias tuberosa*), red bee balm (*Monarda didyma*), wild blue indigo (*Baptisia australis*), stokesia, lupine, and delphinium were natives that gained acceptance. As the nineteenth century moved along, people grew cultivars of the indigens, two of the best known being golden-glow (*Rudbeckia laciniata* 'Hortensia') and Martha Washington plume (*Filipendula rubra* 'Venusta').

Do the antiques have a place in modern gardens? They probably don't for many people, especially those taken with the notion of being the first on the block to grow a new phlox, daylily, or iris. For others, the charm of simplicity, durability, and often fragrance is important. This is not to say that the old-timers are necessarily better garden plants (some obviously are not), but in many cases they will be around long after many thoroughbred cultivars of today have been forgotten. And there is a certain innate pleasure in growing — and enjoying — the same plants our forbears did.

THE BOUNDARIES OF TIME

How long is a garden good for? Not as long as we are accustomed to think. A friend of mine, a veteran gardener, gives the average sort about twenty-five years. His garden consists of carefully chosen dwarf conifers and low-maintenance perennials. It is approaching forty-five years, and each year he laments that it is harder to keep up. Branches fall, plants run their course, and people's energy wanes. Trees have a life span roughly the same as a human being's, though there are greater extremes at both ends — a several-thousand-year-old giant sequoia or bristlecone pine, and a senescent twenty-year-old Norway maple on a city street. Few major woody plant collections of the nineteenth century are left.

But what of abandoned gardens? In the normally wet parts of America, nature takes back very quickly what was taken from it. Recently I visited a Japanese-style garden that was abandoned to the woods in the mid-1940s. A large, rambling stone house had been nearby — a summer place, as the old wealth called it — but had been torn down because the absentee owners did not care to pay the taxes. I had heard rumors of the garden and its now ramshackle *torii* for years, but had discounted them because I do not believe in Shangri-La.

I wasn't sure whether I had found Shangri-La. The setting was indeed idyllic, on a high stone ledge from which in winter, I am told, you can see Long Island Sound sixty miles to the south, across the entire state of Connecticut. Regeneration on rocky ledges is slow because of thin soil and dryness, and the primary vegetation on this one consisted of various mosses and lichens, along with a stonecrop native to northern Japan, *Sedum ellacombianum*. Had this been a moss garden? Not far away were boulders arranged, one could sense, by humans. Had there been a Ryoanji stone garden? Was this our Stonehenge?

By an outbuilding foundation I found Siberian iris. Nearby was a rusted white pan, hanging without explanation from a tree branch. Beyond, where once had been lawn, romped huge coppices of shrubby St.-John's-wort (*Hypericum prolificum*). Did the owners ever see its smooth and glistening brown stems in winter, as pretty as any paperbark maple's? I thought not.

Close by were other reminders of another era: copper beech, peegee hydrangea, and mock orange. An American honey locust was dying, certainly not

helped by a half-nelson from Oriental bittersweet. An Asiatic magnolia, its time coming, stood by and sulked. Japanese barberry and angelica tree (*Aralia elata*) made the going rough. Not far away was one of the largest katsura trees (*Cercidiphyllum japonicum*) I've seen in the United States.

What is the future? In a generation these trees will all be dead, except perhaps the katsura. The barberry and bittersweet will persist, and that will be that. Our gardens do not last for long. But what memories they have for people who are not afraid to acknowledge the past.

Opposite: Golden-glow (*Rudbeckia laciniata* 'Hortensia'), a popular perennial of the nineteenth century, still graces many an old farmhouse, as in the Dämm family garden in New Hampshire, but it usually needs staking to look its best.

· 19 ·

Kitchen Herbs

ONE CANDLELIT EVENING a dozen years ago, my bride-to-be enticed me with my first pesto, that ethereal sauce combining fresh basil leaves and garlic. It was love at first bite, and I wondered where this delicious and versatile concoction, equally at home on top of spaghetti and in soup, had been all my life. Certainly not in the staid Italian restaurants of my youth. Admittedly, I had a protected childhood; the principal culinary work in our home was the 1943 edition of Irma Rombauer's *Joy of Cooking*, which didn't mention pesto at all and included just a couple of fleeting references to garlic. In those days, garlic wasn't often used west of the Hudson River, except in bad jokes. That was the era of creamed vegetables, chicken à la king, and chipped beef, not to mention casseroles. The only basil that was known to Main Street Americans had the last name of Rathbone.

Basil, garlic, tarragon, and a host of other herbs have come a long way since the 1940s, and the herb garden is no longer the preserve of slightly dotty, generally harmless old women whose closets smell of lavender sachets. Even *Joy of Cooking* has been liberated, and revised editions recognize pesto. Culinary herbs have come into the mainstream as our diets and tastes have changed. As a result, American cooking is much more imaginative than it used to be, and the sale of herb plants has boomed.

People always used to grow herbs together in one section of the garden, and herb gardening evolved somewhat separately from other kinds of gardening. Indeed, a special lore was associated with herbs, and there was comfort in having the traditional plants bound together in tidy rectangles of dwarf boxwood and lavender. Plant culture was frequently made easier, too, by the fact that many of the basic herbs have similar growth requirements.

A PICKLE AMONG DILLS

Even today, a good case can be made for keeping herbs intended for culinary use separate from plants grown exclusively for ornamental purposes — if the latter are going to need spraying. More than once I have inadvertently showered the feathery leaves of dill with a systemic fungicide meant for summer phlox, which gets mildew as readily as a dog gets fleas. (*Systemic*, gardeners should remember, refers to poison taken up *within* the plant.) Since I don't like dill, my wife accused me of absent-mindedness the first time, and of sabotage the second. I lamely replied that one can be absent-minded twice.

Ever since then, Mary Ann has grown dill only in the vegetable garden, where no systemic pesticides are used, and we reserve the ornamental bronze-leaved fennel (*Foeniculum vulgare* 'Atropurpureum') for spots in the perennial border where we desire a gossamer effect. The height of this anise-scented herb is about four feet. Plants are short-lived perennials, but usually self-sow, sometimes to the point of being pesty in mild climates. They consort well with the cherry-red, summer-flowering *Phlox paniculata* 'Starfire' or the white-flowered cultivars such as 'Mt. Fuji' or the September-blooming 'World Peace'. *F. vulgare* 'Atropurpureum' mingles nicely with taller sorts of silver-leaved perennials, too, including *Artemisia ludoviciana* and its kin, 'Silver Queen' and 'Silver King'. Fennel leaves have an anise taste that Mary Ann doesn't like, so no part of the plant ever reaches our kitchen table, spraying or no spraying.

In most gardens there are a few sound reasons for incorporating herbs where they will best fit in aesthetically, rather than isolating them in a single area. Most gardens today aren't large enough for specialized plantings. Also, although the carefully designed herb garden is a joy to see in May and June, it usually becomes unkempt by midsummer unless you crop many of the rank-growing sorts — and there are many — almost to the ground. Of course, until lush new growth appears, this kind of drastic pruning leaves gaping holes, which are all the more conspicuous if you have planted a number of wayward herbs together.

Some traditional herbs are first-rate ornamental plants, and it seems a shame to restrict them to a little corner of the garden instead of casting them into the mainstream, as is usually done in England. Once, when designing a perennial border for a client, I mentioned that I planned to work in some sage and lavender because of the buffering effect their cool gray or gray-green foliage has on other plants. I was taken aback by my client's reaction: "But they are herbs, and I want a *perennial* border." I was tempted to inquire whether she wanted a ghetto or a garden, but temperance prevailed, and I substituted gray-leaved artemisias. The fact that artemisias are considered herbs in the conventional sense, or indeed that most herbs are perennials, was lost on her, but I do hope she is enjoying her perennial border.

A KITCHEN BORDER

Mary Ann and I like to grow a wide range of plants and have no formal herb garden as such. Near our kitchen door, however, a small border does include a mixture of kitchen herbs and a few ornamental sorts that haven't been used much lately, such as lady's-mantle (*Alchemilla mollis*), which alchemists employed in the Middle Ages. This species grows a foot tall or more and tolerates dry shade better than most plants do. It has handsome, blocky, gray-green foliage with pronounced lobes, and water has a way of forming glistening, almost silvery beads on the leaves after a rain or a dewy night. The chartreuse flowers, which appear in June, are esteemed more by flower arrangers than by zinnia growers. However, they are quite pleasant when combined with *Gaillardia* and *Geranium* 'Johnson's Blue'. Should we forget to remove the inconspicuous clusters of spent *Alchemilla* blossoms (as is often the case during an indolent July), seedlings grow in awkward spots the next year. But it takes just a few minutes to remove the unwanted plants — if we are in a tidying mood. We can then move the excess plants to a nursery area, pot them, and eventually sell them.

Our kitchen border is convex, curving for a length of twenty-two feet to extend the line of a small back porch — one that is just large enough for two deck chairs, a grill, four cats or one Labrador retriever, and an inordinate number of potted plants. The border is six feet wide at its broadest point and is bounded by lawn on one side, and on the other by a fieldstone path so we can weed in the back of the border without stepping into it any more than necessary. (Most plants, including herbs, grow best in fairly loose earth that roots can penetrate readily, and they falter in soil that is compacted by human feet.) Between the fieldstone path and the house are several shrubs, near the base of which lady's-mantle consorts with scillas, a hellebore or two, and Oriental adonis, each planted for an early spring serenade. The border faces southeast, and most of it receives six hours of sun — just enough for the sun worshipers, which most herbs are — but the back part is shaded by the shrubs.

The shrubs are a mixed lot, including an uncommon spice bush from the Orient, *Lindera umbellata,* whose aromatic, narrow leaves turn brilliant tawny orange, then buff-colored, before falling in late winter; a Japanese holly that resembles the traditional herb garden accompaniment, English boxwood, which we avoided because its brittle branches break easily in heavy snows; and a hybrid yew, which we have kept sheared to three feet high and eight feet wide, and which protects some of our herbs from the hot afternoon sun.

Sweet cicely (*Myrrhis odorata*), a stout-growing herb with finely cut light green foliage like that of the lady fern, grows here and there among the shrubs, softening the somber green foliage of the yews and providing a lacy contrast to the holly. This plant is a charmer, with flat clusters of white flowers that appear in May and inch-long, anise-scented seeds that I find refreshing to chew on a warm June day. In fact, every part of the plant has an odor of anise. I occasionally add a few fresh chopped leaves to a salad as a welcome change of pace from tarragon (*Artemisia dracunculus*). (Tarragon, incidentally, is one of the least

The kitchen border at Hillside has a blend of culinary and ornamental herbs, perennials, and annuals. Roman wormwood (*Artemisia pontica*) and chives (*Allium schoenoprasum*) grow with *Delphinium tatsienense* and Shasta daisies.

attractive plants in the garden and should be placed where it is inconspicuous.) A sprig of sweet cicely in iced tea is unexpectedly pleasant, too.

These plants perform best in partial shade. To forestall the premature yellowing of foliage that is sweet cicely's weak point, and to encourage a flush of good foliage later in summer, we frequently cut stalks back sharply in late June. Plants grow three to four feet tall and are vigorous enough to emerge through pachysandra.

CURLY PARSLEY

One of the handsomest edging plants for a border is parsley (*Petroselinum crispum*), at least the curly-leaved kind that we have today. It is refined and goes well with practically everything in the garden, as it does in the kitchen. Parsley is a biennial; the slow and erratic germination of its seeds led to the old saying that parsley seeds go nine times to the devil and back before coming up, and he keeps some of them. Instead of growing parsley from seed, we buy young plants in spring and set them six inches apart in the front of a border. Sprigs are available for picking all summer, and in autumn we pot several plants to grow during the winter in the kitchen. Parsley does not transplant well, so we pot a couple more plants than we actually need. Once adapted to the house, they put up with subdued light and low temperatures, but they need to be watered more often than most plants. They usually stagger through to March unless the whiteflies get the best of them.

We sometimes let parsley overwinter in the garden. In spring, these second-year plants produce a flush of new foliage for a month or two, but then flower and die. To avoid gaps, you therefore do best to treat parsley as an annual.

In ancient times parsley was associated with death, and victors at funeral games in Greece were given wreaths made from it. Later the phrase "to be in the parsley" was used in reference to someone on the deathbed. The term "Welsh parsley" meant the gallows.

Parsley happens to be of Mediterranean origin, but it is not at home in the parched surroundings we associate with that region. Plants grow best in garden soil to which compost or peat moss has been added. The site need not be in full sun, and if the soil is not moisture-retentive, plants should receive light afternoon shade.

Bear in mind that parsley's foliage lends a fresh spring-green color to the garden until December, even in a very cold climate. You can produce a prolonged garden scene by grouping parsley with lamb's-ears (*Stachys byzantina*),

Lamium maculatum 'Beacon Silver', *Lamiastrum* 'Herman's Pride', *Pulmonaria* 'Mrs. Moon', *Salvia officinalis,* or *Lavandula angustifolia,* all of which have long-lasting silvery or gray-green leaves. Parsley also looks good with the reddish late-season foliage tints of coralbells (*Heuchera*), *Bergenia,* or *Epimedium* × *rubrum.* You can even eat it if it gets to be a bore, although most people are happy just toying with it on the plate.

MINTS

The mints are not very good garden plants because they spread so rapidly underground, but it is nice to have a patch or two near the kitchen door if friends drop in unexpectedly for dolmas or juleps. Peppermint and spearmint fend for themselves quite well on poor sites and are thoroughly at home in light shade. Ideally, you should plant them to one side, out of the garden, and keep them honest with the blade of a lawn mower. Running water nearby makes them really romp, but such a rare site should be reserved for watercress.

In the garden mints are thugs, and you should fully recognize them as such before they abuse the rights of fellow herbs with less invasive root systems. The solution, of course, is confinement — in a bucket sunk in the soil, with the rim slightly above ground level, for they will try hard to escape. Old plastic wash buckets work well. Brown buckets, which blend with the surroundings, are preferable to brightly colored ones. Poke a few holes in the bottom of the bucket with an ice pick to allow for drainage. Every two years you will have to take up the mint and set it back again in replenished soil, but this procedure is preferable to pulling the strands of its invading roots from choked plants nearby every year.

For kitchen use I am fondest of apple mint (*Mentha suaveolens,* formerly *M. rotundifolia*), whose rounded, inch-wide, hairy leaves are easy to pick and are excellent for iced tea. A variegated cultivar called pineapple mint (*M. suaveolens* 'Variegata') appeals to some; to others, its cream-and-green leaves suggest herbicide injury. Orange mint (*M.* × *piperita* var. *citrata*) is esteemed more highly by some menthologists.

For gardening beauty, perhaps the nod should go to the variegated ginger mint (*M.* × *gentilis* 'Variegata'), which has yellow-and-green leaves that bring a welcome brightness to a dark corner. This cultivar has extremely invasive roots and surely deserves solitary confinement. Variegated ginger mint grows about fifteen inches tall; the others range from two to three feet in height. If you would like a tiny prostrate sort between steppingstones, try growing Corsican mint (*Mentha requienii*). This species resembles mother-of-thyme but has a strong mentholated odor. In winter in northern regions it is short-lived, so keep one or two plants in a cold frame during the cold months.

Basil (*Ocimum basilicum*) has been associated with the Mediterranean region since ancient times. This annual herb is in fact native to the tropical parts of India, where it is considered sacred. (The name *basil* means kingly or royal.) The plant made its way to Greece via the earliest routes of trade, and Greeks and Romans thought of it in sinister terms. Keats' tale of Isabella, inspired by Boccaccio, recounts how she preserved her murdered lover's head in a pot of basil, watering the plant with her tears. I figure the skull must have been a slow-release fertilizer of sorts, providing phosphorus for the healthy growth of the basil.

Basil doesn't need a very rich soil. Pesto addicts usually choose to grow basil in the vegetable garden because of the prodigious amounts of foliage needed for their sauce. This choice may be just as well, for the common kitchen basil is a rather nondescript plant, and gardeners can drop the pretense of ornament altogether within the row system of the vegetable garden. It is more appropriate to save the space in the kitchen herb border for bush basil (*Ocimum basilicum* 'Minimum'), which is tidier, or better still for 'Dark Opal', a maroon-leaved seed strain of common or sweet basil that was developed some years ago at the University of Connecticut. Rue (*Ruta graveolens*), whose lacy but bitter gray foliage is seldom used in the kitchen anymore, makes a fine background for 'Dark Opal'. From a distance, the combination of their foliage gives a flowering effect all season long. However, rue's foliage can present a problem to the gardener, as noted many years ago by Dioscorides: "If anyone rubs his face with the hand that gathered it, it will immediately raise a violent inflammation." On a hot day, some gardeners indeed develop a bad rash from touching rue.

An annual, basil is grown yearly from seed. Although the seed is easy to germinate, seedlings are subject to rot if you overwater them, and many gardeners elect to buy young plants from garden centers after the danger of frost has passed. In the border basil performs best during hot summers. Common basil grows about eighteen inches in height; 'Dark Opal' is usually under fifteen inches tall, but rich soil encourages lankiness. Both enjoy full sun. Rue, a perennial, is apt to be short-lived in colder parts of New England, especially if winter drainage is poor. Young plants are usually available from garden centers in spring.

SAGE, BAY, AND ROSEMARY

Kitchen sage (*Salvia officinalis*) needs the same growing conditions as 'Dark Opal' basil and rue, and thus makes a good companion for these plants. The typical kind has gray-green leaves of respectable substance and is more versatile in the garden than in the kitchen (though a New England sausage maker or a British duck stuffer might disagree). This low-growing Mediterranean shrub is a straight man — not striking in its own right, but an excellent complement to plants with maroon foliage or with pink or lavender flowers. Kitchen sage is quite variable. To me, the most attractive cultivar is *S. officinalis* 'Purpurascens', whose new leaves are tinged with purple. It makes a sumptuous tub plant and goes well with companions that have subdued pink flowers. I am fondest of it with purple sweet-alyssum (*Lobularia* 'Royal Carpet').

Like many pungent herbs, sage was originally used for medicinal purposes.

Purple sage (*Salvia officinalis* 'Purpurascens') and lavender (*Lavandula angustifolia*) are equally good partners in the sunny herb garden and the ornamental border.

(The botanical name for the genus, *Salvia*, comes from the Latin *salveo*, meaning to be well.) It was associated with immortality, and was also believed to have teeth-cleaning and gum-strengthening properties. One old proverb queries, "How shall a man die who has sage in his garden?" Just as old Soviet Georgians today might attribute their longevity to yogurt, people of an earlier time put much stock in sage. Perhaps one day an imaginative health-food entrepreneur will market a sage-flavored yogurt for those who don't like to take chances.

Bay (*Laurus nobilis*) and rosemary (*Rosmarinus officinalis*) are two other very useful and attractive herbs from the Mediterranean. In colder areas you must treat them as house plants during winter months. South of Baltimore, they are reasonably hardy outdoors year round. I recall growing bay in New York City for several years as a die-back shrub; top growth was killed each winter, but a new surge came from the base in spring. In mild climates people often train bay into a single stem and clip the top into a formal globe. Rosemary thrives best in the dry, alkaline soils of the Southwest, where it sometimes makes a fine, loose, eight-foot-tall hedge. The branches take on considerable character with age, and plants lend themselves well to bonsai treatment, or at least to some pruning for special effect. Small leaves and good blue flowers add to a sense of refinement.

Bay, the true laurel of the ancients, was used to make wreaths for life's winners. Crowns of bay also conveniently covered up bald spots on the heads of Roman dignitaries. (Do not confuse bay with mountain laurel, *Kalmia latifolia*, an American shrub with vaguely similar but toxic foliage.) Bay has a summer home in the back of our herb garden. In May we plunge it, pot and all, into the ground. Then in October we move it indoors, prune back tops and roots slightly, and repot it. This is a vigorous shrub when it becomes established, and pruning with shears is necessary. The dense dark green foliage serves as an enhancing background for a number of low-growing herbs. Bay brings out the best in gray-leaved plants or plants with gold or white variegation, especially the silver-leaved thymes. The leaves are intensely aromatic, and just one or two are sufficient for flavoring a stew.

Rosemary means dew of the sea, an allusion to the plant's home on the shores of the Mediterranean. It is the herb of remembrance as well as love, death, and eternity. In the garden rosemary is accustomed to a hot, dry spot once it is established; in the home, it is easy to kill inadvertently, since most people tend to forget to water those plants with low water requirements. During summer we give it the same outdoor treatment as bay, but I also like to keep rosemary as a potted plant on the terrace. That way, it is easier to keep an eye on its somewhat wayward growth habit and make corrections with pruning shears. There is a prostrate form of rosemary that is quite seductive if allowed to drape over the side of a pot. The trimmings are of course classic accompaniments for pork and lamb. They make especially handsome whiskers for a suckling pig, too.

· PART III ·

*THE GARDENER
AT LARGE*

· 20 ·

Reflections on
Muck and Mysticism

SOME FIFTEEN YEARS AGO at an annual meeting of the American Horticultural Society in New Orleans, I had a chance meeting with L. C. Chadwick, who
had long served as head of the Department of Horticulture at Ohio State University. There was a tour of plantation gardens that day, and having lingered
longer than I should have over a dozen properly iced oysters at the Sazerac Bar,
I was a bit tardy getting on the bus at the Fairmont-Roosevelt Hotel. Only one
seat was left, and without noticing my new traveling companion, I sat down,
out of breath but quite happy with the world, as anyone is who has just partaken
of that number of God's finest bivalves.

I should have recognized my companion at once, for the evening before he
had been awarded the Liberty Hyde Bailey Medal, the highest honor conferred
by the American Horticultural Society. We introduced ourselves and had a
delightful conversation. Professor Chadwick had been an institution within an
institution at OSU, a Mr. Chips of horticulture revered by two generations of
students. I came to understand why. He was in an expansive mood that day,
and we discussed everything from house plants to well-known gardens to his
particular specialty, the genus *Taxus*. But mostly the talk was reflective, on
developments that had taken place in gardening over the years. His prime interest was, quite naturally, in horticulture as a science, as opposed to an art.

Professor Chadwick was proud of these changes, some of which he had helped
to bring about, but he was quick to admit that a great deal still had to be learned
about plants and gardening. So much horticulture is plain supposition, he remarked. One of his thoughts has stayed with me to this day. It was, essentially:

"All my life I have heard and read that if you remove the spent flowers of a lilac or some other shrub, there will be better bloom the next year. I *think* this is true, but in all of the literature issued by the various universities and botanic gardens, you will not find an instance of a *controlled* study where someone has actually proved it."

In my own years as an editor I have learned to be cautious too. A good friend of mine, Pamela Harper, reads garden books and articles more carefully than I do and becomes amused, annoyed, or exasperated (depending on the offense) at conflicting claims about gardening techniques, cultural recommendations, or even plant descriptions. She summed it up succinctly for me once when we became involved in a discussion about one of the more obscure points of "organic" gardening: "Gardening is muck and mysticism."

Wave Hill, on a bluff overlooking the Hudson River, always has something to offer the visitor. *Crocosmia* with orange flowers, Russian-sage (*Perovskia*), and pink clematis form a pleasing midsummer scene.

DIVIDE AND CONQUER

The first twenty years that I gardened I never divided a clump of monkshood (*Aconitum napellus*), a lovely blue-flowered perennial with glossy leaves incised like those of the common buttercup, to which it has a botanical family tie (Ranunculaceae) despite its helmet-shaped flowers. Somewhere along the path of my horticultural education I had read in several books that monkshood could not be divided, and my friends stoutly confirmed this, though none had ever tried to do it.

Eventually a fungal disorder laid to rest our nice little thicket of monkshood, and we went without for a few years. Then a kindly soul down the road called one late summer day and offered her solitary large clump; she had young children and feared they might sample the leaves or roots, which are deadly poisonous. You see, another species, wolfsbane (*A. vulparia*), was used to poison the bait for wolves in Europe during the Middle Ages, and its roots were fed to criminals, knaves, wives, or husbands, depending on the occasion. But in general wolfsbane was not regarded as a poison for the upper classes, though a competitor or two of the influential Borgia family — presumably high class — may have been done in this way. In any case, *Aconitum* has made its way into lore. Warlocks love it.

Mary Ann ventured to our friend's garden and carefully dug the clump, treating it as a shrub and getting a good amount of soil around the roots, for I had stressed to her the difficulty of transplanting monkshood. Upon her return home, she dropped the clump while unloading it from the car, and it shattered into a hundred little pieces, each with a bulbous root attached. Undaunted by my dire warnings about the uselessness of this effort, Mary Ann planted and cut back the foliage of each one, and they all happened to live. We have divided monkshood happily ever since. Indeed, several species of it.

How does such a story begin, about a plant being hard to divide? True, some perennials do not convalesce well after division or do not divide very easily. (I once spent half a morning with a pickax getting a dozen divisions from a clump of *Miscanthus* grass.) In the case of monkshood, I suspect the story started this way: Garden Writer A wrote that it was a shame to divide an established clump of monkshood, because it took a while for it to assume a stately grace. A few years later Garden Writer B came along, and finding Garden Writer A's prose turgid, said in the interest of brevity, "You should not divide monkshood." A few years later still, Garden Writer C, a careless copier, came along and said, "You can't divide monkshood." Alas, the ring of authority that comes with a simple, quick statement! Editors — and readers — love it.

Now let us alter the story a bit. If our friend had given the clump of monkshood to Mary Ann for division in early July — just as the hottest and driest part of summer descended on us — the result might have been quite different, especially if we had been lax about watering and mulching. We once, in fact, lost a few divisions this way, because our New England summers are seldom as cool as they are pictured to be, even by New Englanders. If we lived in North Carolina, the July division would probably have meant death for the plants.

WHY PLANTS FAIL

The corollary point, of course, is that we gardeners are very apt to promulgate horticultural laws based on a single instance. How often have you heard, "Astilbes just won't grow in my garden"? Or "Shasta daisies aren't hardy for me"? In the case of the astilbe, one wonders if the gardener made a sole attempt in a sunny, parched spot of the garden — hardly the ideal place for these woodland plants from the Orient, which require a moisture-retentive soil in summer. As for the Shasta daisies, poor drainage in winter might have caused their demise, and the plants could have prospered nicely in another, more elevated location in the same garden.

It can be more complicated than that, of course. My friend and fellow astilbe enthusiast David Beattie, who teaches horticulture at Pennsylvania State University, has told me of photoperiod studies on several groups of perennials that are very uneven when raised from seed. In the case of the Shasta daisy (*Chrysanthemum × superbum*), researchers at Purdue University separated seed-raised plants into four or five distinct genotypes, including one that would flower the first year, like an annual, and another that would not bloom until the second year. Studies with hybrid gaillardias and columbines, as well as chimney bellflowers (*Campanula pyramidalis*), Beattie said, suggest that a short life is genetically directed for some, a longer one for others.

However, many times we don't really know why a plant has died, and if it happens not to come up in spring, we almost automatically assume that it was not winter-hardy. Yes, sometimes cold is the prime factor. But apart from improperly drained soil in winter (which is perhaps the most frequent cause of death for both herbaceous and woody plants), fungal or insect problems, drought, too-late planting, rodents, or some particular cultural condition could have weakened the plant in the previous growing season, and winter merely provided the coup de grâce.

One spring day when I was lamenting the over-winter loss of an unusually attractive anemone, a fellow gardening zealot consoled me by saying, "Fred, you can't really say you have failed with a plant until you have killed it three times." Later in the year I reminded him of his sagacious words. He paused for a few seconds, then remarked, "I think I should have said 'five times'!" Of course, if you are trying to grow a banana in New Jersey and it doesn't make it through the winter, that might be the time for automatic assumptions.

TELLING IT AS IT IS

By the same token, one winter's success does not spell hardiness. Nor two. Nor three. One of my good friends, Erica, hates to have me visit her in gardening season, because she considers me a harbinger of doom. I am welcome for tea, or dinner, or even travelogues on long winter evenings, but not on a golden summer afternoon. You see, Erica is a fairly new gardener and is still in the flush of great enthusiasm, some of which I hope she will always keep. She tries everything, including ornamental plantains and hawkweeds.

Several years ago after a visit to Scotland and to gardens in England, Erica decided to plant an extensive number of heaths and heathers. Two mild winters have intervened, and these plants, laden with a thick cover of evergreen boughs in the cool months (when many of the heaths are most ornamental), seem to be in thriving condition. The longer-term performance record for heaths and heathers in noncoastal parts of America is not very auspicious, though, and I have on occasion pointed this out to Erica. She plans to have a garden party next summer, when the heathers are in full bloom, and not invite me. I will come another time to admire her hawkweeds.

Telling it as it is does not always endear you to gardeners, who live more by dreams and catalogue descriptions than normal people do. Gardeners *want* to believe, and that is fine — even beautiful — unless it pushes reality too far off into a dark corner, to be tripped over when it is time to put on the light. Every few years, for example, some gardening magazine in the country, with new editor and new writer, carries a piece on the Himalayan blue poppy, *Meconopsis betonicifolia*. This is a hauntingly beautiful flower but is not a very good garden plant in the United States, except in a few areas with cool summers, and then uncommonly.

The author of the article may have seen the blue poppy in a garden in England, where it performs tolerably well, or even in Alberta (which also has cool summers). Perhaps he or she even has grown it for a year or two on the coast of Maine or in the Pacific Northwest before it has croaked. The article is apt to end on a plaintive and familiar note: "This fine plant should be more widely available." It once was. In fact, one of America's large perennial nurseries promoted it with pretty catalogue pictures for years before the outcry about the blue poppy's short life span made the firm realize it was engaging in horticultural genocide.

DIFFICULT PLANTS

For many people the joy is in the growing, not in the end result of a garden. Some enjoy a challenge — taming the untamable plant, taking pride in raising difficult sorts to fine specimen stage. They regard "easy" plants as a bit vulgar, the sort grown by a neighbor with whom one doesn't get along. There is usually no harm in this, provided the grower doesn't kill too many lady's-slippers, trailing arbutus, and shortias in the process. These are not really garden plants.

True, the vast number of endangered plant species in this country are endangered because of habitat destruction. But some responsibility must be borne by the horticultural community, since these natives — and quite a few others — are usually dug from the wild, either by home gardeners or by wildflower dealers who then sell directly to the public or to nurseries. Fortunately, nurseries that actually propagate their own wildflowers are increasingly prevalent, partly as a result of efforts by the University of North Carolina Botanical Garden and the New England Wildflower Society in recent years. Many wildflowers are easy to grow, but if one is difficult in cultivation, we may help keep the species going in the wild if we ask ourselves why we really want to grow it. Ego may play a larger part than we care to admit.

"Difficult" plants fail for a variety of reasons. For example, they may be fussbudgets about location, the soil may have mycorrhiza associations, or the plants may have exacting soil pH requirements. I recall a story told me some time ago by a conservation-minded nurseryman, Andre Viette, who feels that the best way to conserve a plant is to grow it. He obtained *Shortia galacifolia,* a delightful and increasingly-rare-in-the-wild southern wildflower sometimes called Oconee-bells. The plants, which he obtained from North Carolina, arrived in soil with quite a low pH, 4.2 to 4.7. They had to be potted on, and to increase the acidity of the moderately acid soil he customarily used, Mr. Viette added a large amount of leaf mold, mostly red oak. Don't many garden books report that oak leaf mold has an acidic reaction? The shortias languished, and on a hunch he took a pH test and discovered that the new medium was close to neutral. He adjusted the pH downward, and the shortias began to thrive again, along with

Lynden B. Miller

The Conservatory Garden in New York's Central Park demonstrates that large cities can have fine gardens even today, despite significant social problems. June is a good time to check out the foxgloves (*Digitalis*), valerian (*Centranthus ruber*), and *Geranium* 'Johnson's Blue'.

partridgeberry (*Mitchella repens*), coltsfoot (*Galax urceolata*), and wintergreen (*Gaultheria procumbens*) — other distinctly acid-loving plants potted in the same mix. As an addendum, Mr. Viette pointed out that he had tested peat, too. Canadian peat was usually in the 5 to 6 range (German peat, usually lower), so adding this common material would not have solved the problem.

LIMELIGHT

Luckily, not many of our garden plants are as demanding about soil pH as shortia, or else we would be driving our land-grant universities wild with requests for pH tests of garden soil. (Many perform this function for a nominal fee.) In general, garden plants are tolerant of a fairly wide range of soil pH levels, although optimums are known for certain ones, especially vegetables. In high-rainfall areas soils are as a rule distinctly acidic, and the majority of plants perform satisfactorily with small or no additions of dolomitic limestone.

The matter of soil pH is usually overemphasized, unless you happen to live on a bog or on top of a lime pit. I do know from quite personal experience that generous use of limestone on moderately acid soil can do more harm than good to a lot of herbaceous perennials, especially the shade-tolerant sorts such as hostas, epimediums, and astilbes, as well as summer phlox (*P. paniculata*) and Japanese iris (*I. kaempferi*). (The wet-soil requirement for this iris is an old wives' tale.) Dianthus, gypsophila, and scabiosa are among the few that lime distinctly helps if soil acidity is low.

For years no one challenged the assumption that the optimum pH range for mineral soils was 6.5 to 6.8. This may be true for many of the traditional sun lovers, including vegetables, but the shade plants or woodlanders so common in today's gardens usually come from parts of the world with substantial rainfall and benefit from a lower pH. But what about the popular soilless mixes? Some experiments by Professor John C. Peterson of the Ohio State University show that 5.2 to 5.5 on the pH scale is best for such a medium. He observed that the availability of phosphorus, an element important for root growth and flowering, *increased* more than ten times as the pH was lowered from 6.5 to 5.2. For his studies, Professor Peterson used a commercial mix containing sphagnum peat, perlite, vermiculite, granite sand, and composted pine bark, and added major nutrients and trace elements.

BEETLEMANIA

We shouldn't be too quick to take our bags of limestone to the dump, though, particularly if Japanese beetles are around. At the Ohio Agricultural Research and Development Center in Wooster, some experiments have shown that beetle larvae decrease in number after ground limestone is spread on a lawn. In one test on a lawn whose soil had a very low pH, one hundred pounds of dolomitic limestone were applied to a thousand square feet of land. The result was little grub damage, whereas a surrounding area that was not treated was badly infested. The report also mentioned that if your lawn needs dethatching, you should do this aeration procedure before you apply lime, lest you break the lime "barrier." Since we had been greatly bothered by Japanese beetles in recent years, we decided to lime the lawn last autumn. (The most recent application had been five years earlier.) The happy result — probably not a coincidence — was a sharp decline in beetles this year.

The nadir of muck and mysticism was reached in our garden several years ago, and it had to do with Japanese beetles. One of the gardening magazines carried a piece on beetle control, which sounded very promising to Mary Ann. The author said that the beetles in her garden were not a problem anymore, and what's more, her remedy was "organic." The recipe involved grinding up Japanese beetles with a little soap and water and spraying this mixture on roses, hollyhocks, lythrum, and other plants they favor. Mary Ann dutifully did this, and after a few days there were still no results. If anything, the beetles proliferated. I asked her how she ground up the beetles. In the kitchen blender, she replied. It cured me of milk shakes for six months, and I lost five pounds. So muck and mysticism aren't all bad.

· 21 ·

Moving and Dividing
Perennials

"WHEN CAN I MOVE my peony?" Just about any time, provided there is enough soil around the roots and you are willing to give postoperative care. I once even got away with it on an 85° F day in May when I was renovating a flower border and had to lift all of its perennial contents. To my surprise, the peony bloomed beautifully several weeks later, as if it had never been moved. No wonder Grandmother was so fond of these plants!

Still, certain times of year are better for moving certain perennials than others. Peonies, for example, are among the few that are customarily planted in autumn; indeed, most mail-order nurseries will ship them only then. The common practice is to plant them so that the ruby-colored buds, which are visible at the base of the plant in autumn, are an inch below the surface of the soil. These are the magic capsules that hold next year's promises. Coralbells (*Heuchera*) and bearded iris, the latter of which should be cut back and divided after bloom in late spring, are other perennials that benefit from being reset slightly lower in the soil than their original depth. You should plant practically all others at the same depth they were before, so their crowns won't rot. A submerged delphinium just becomes mush.

When is the best time to move perennials? If they are container-grown plants just purchased from a garden center, you can set them out successfully in the garden almost any time in the growing season, though it is best to avoid the dog days of midsummer and the very frosty times of late autumn. Cut lightly through the outer roots if they are encircling the container ball, as you would for container-grown shrubs and trees.

The ideal planting day is overcast, calm, and cool — not so great for human beings, but awfully nice for the plants! If you have to plant on a bright day, late afternoon is a good time, and if the extended forecast is for sunny, breezy weather, you ought to place peach baskets or another loose protective cover over the newly installed plants for a few days. This practice is of real value in the re-establishment of plants, especially new divisions that you have moved around within the garden as they start active growth.

TIMING

The ideal planting time for fresh divisions of perennials varies according to climate. In the very coldest parts of the United States spring planting is safest, though late summer works well for many plants, too. Shallow-rooted kinds and late-season bloomers are often best divided in early spring. In the middle parts of the country, spring and early autumn are good. In areas with very mild

Viki Ferreniea

A June scene in Sydney Eddison's garden shows lamb's-ears (*Stachys byzantina*) coming into flower with a red peony.

winters, autumn or even winter is appropriate. Avoid spring planting if summers are normally bone dry.

Except in very mild areas, you will usually order the following perennials for spring delivery if you are dealing with a mail-order firm: yarrow (*Achillea*), Japanese anemone (*A. × hybrida*), plumbago or leadwort (*Ceratostigma*), dianthus, gaillardia, helenium, Christmas-rose (*Helleborus niger*), coralbells (*Heuchera*), hibiscus, kniphofia, rudbeckia, perennial sages (*Salvia*), and stokesia. Upon their arrival it helps to soak bare-rooted perennials in a pail of water in a shady spot for half an hour before planting. Some gardeners like to add a scant teaspoon of water-soluble fertilizer to the pail, to serve as a starter solution.

In recent years many gardeners in the normally colder parts of the country have found that lily bulbs ship better in spring than autumn. This is particularly true of tall summer-flowering hybrid sorts, which have a high mortality rate in part because their bulbs cannot safely be lifted by nurseries for shipping until well into the fall season. Since many lilies are selling for five or six dollars a bulb these days, it pays to be careful about planting times. Best stick with inexpensive tried-and-true sorts if you must plant in autumn: Mid-Century hybrids, including 'Enchantment', and regal lily (*Lilium regale*) and its hybrids. Madonna lily (*L. candidum*) is an exception to normal lily-planting seasons, for it should be planted in August or September in the North, and then just an inch deep, as opposed to six or eight inches for other sorts. The loss rate is high, but to some gardeners Madonna lilies have a strong appeal when in bloom in late spring. Extra lime in the soil is said to help.

Some perennials need to be divided every two or three years if they are to continue to grow well. These include many members of the daisy and mint families (Compositae, Labiatae). Telltale signs: if clumps take on the appearance of a traffic jam and become sparse in growth in the center due to self-strangulation, it is time to lift them with a spading fork or hefty trowel. Frequently you can break the lifted clumps apart easily with your fingers. Usually you do not even need to remove the soil around the roots. At other times, as with the woody roots of astilbe, you will have to use a sharp knife. Discard the inner section of the old plant, and make the divisions from the outer part. How many divisions depends on the number of plants desired, the season, and the nerve of the gardener. In the North, small divisions may be worth the risk in spring if you require a quick buildup of plants and flowers aren't essential the first year. Making small divisions in early autumn can be dangerous, however, because roots often don't have time to become anchored in the soil before winter. Heaving of new plants from the soil, from alternate freezing and thawing, is the main cause of death. Many a gardener, myself included, has lost tiny divisions made in consummate September greed.

The following perennials benefit from division every two or three years and can even be divided yearly if you like: asters, chrysanthemums, erigerons (some of which are literally autotoxic with age), heleniums, monardas, and physostegias. In cooler areas spring is the best time for this activity, when plants are two or three inches tall. Re-establishment is slower and more difficult if you wait until plants are seven or eight inches tall before dividing them. While plants are out of the soil, it is a good practice to work some compost or peat moss and a little superphosphate into the replanting area. Bee balm (*Monarda*) in particular exhausts soil nutrients and "moves" each year.

New divisions do not really need balanced commercial fertilizers such as 10-10-10 when they are set out, and fertilizers will be harmful if roots come in direct contact with them. However, a light application several weeks following division, once roots are re-established, is often helpful. On setting out the new divisions, gently firm the soil around plant roots, then give the plants a thorough, very slow watering. If the soil is bone dry, water the area a day ahead. If this isn't practical, water the hole immediately before planting, then again after. As a rule, you should mulch the area with a two-inch layer of some porous organic material (shredded leaves, buckwheat hulls, spent hops) to retain soil moisture and cut down on weeds. Keep mulch from direct contact with stems, to lower the chance of rotting. Follow-up care often determines success. If rains don't come, a good watering once or twice weekly for a month is advisable.

KNOWING WHEN AND WHEN NOT TO

It is usually better to make divisions out of large clumps than to transplant the parent in its entirety. Mature specimens, those more than several years old, often have trouble getting re-established, since they no longer have a vigorous fibrous root system. Most notably, the following should not be divided once they become senior citizens: wild indigo (*Baptisia*), gas plant (*Dictamnus*), euphorbia, baby's-breath (*Gypsophila*), Christmas-rose (*Helleborus niger*), perennial statice (*Limonium*), Oriental poppy (*Papaver orientale*), balloon flower (*Platycodon*), and yellow lupine (*Thermopsis*). Lenten-rose (*Helleborus orientalis*), unlike the Christmas-rose, is quite tolerant of division and the moving man. Even butterfly weed (*Asclepias tuberosa*), despite its carrotlike root, moves more easily than the gardener thinks it has any right to.

Some perennials can be relocated within the garden even when they are in bloom, provided they have a fair root ball and are carefully watered. Temporary wilting is not serious, but you should shade the plants for several days. Candidates for this treatment include astilbes, chrysanthemums, coralbells, low-growing asters and coreopsis, and geums. Such shifting about can be important if you have limited border space for display or if the local garden club descends on you with little notice.

A few perennials have stout, thonglike or woody root systems that lend themselves to division only with struggle. You may need a very sharp spade and an old pair of sharp pruning shears, as well as a good breakfast. Goatsbeard (*Aruncus dioicus*), black snakeroot (*Cimicifuga racemosa*), globe thistle (*Echinops*), and some filipendulas are in this category. No doubt you will mash or tear a few roots during the procedure. Cut them off cleanly before replanting. Such plants should usually be divided in very early spring before top growth appears, or in early autumn. Fortunately, plants in this group do not need frequent

One section of the garden of Elaine and Keith Zinn, designed by the author, features black snakeroot (*Cimicifuga racemosa*), *Monarda* 'Cambridge Scarlet', butterfly weed (*Asclepias tuberosa*), and, in the rear, *Lythrum* 'Morden's Pink'.

division, or gardeners would have to invest in a pickax. In fact, goatsbeard and black snakeroot may never need to be divided or moved.

Most ornamental grasses, especially the taller kinds, such as *Miscanthus*, *Calamagrostis*, and *Erianthus*, are best divided in spring. Wait until new growth is well under way, since the broken roots of these grasses are subject to rot in cool, wet weather. Many begin to decline after four years without division, and the longer you postpone the task, the more difficult it becomes. Ironically, the roots of some grasses become woody with age. Once we broke a shovel and a spade within five minutes on a *Miscanthus* 'Silver Feather' that we had left in the ground too long. The best procedure is to dig up the old clumps, shake a good portion of soil from the roots, and divide them with an old saw reserved for this use. Wear gloves, too.

AS EASY AS APPLE PIE

Hostas and daylilies can go without division for many years, sometimes indefinitely, depending on cultivars and growing conditions. It is a shame to break up a large clump that may be forty or fifty years old. Yet you want more plants! You can circumvent the dilemma by making divisions much like the slices of an apple pie, removing one, two, or even three slices with a spade and filling in the empty hole with compost. The task is most easily accomplished in early spring, before the leaves attain any size. A month after growth starts, no one but you will know that the pie was pillaged.

If you are interested simply in increasing the number of hostas or daylilies and not in preserving a venerable clump, you can lift and divide plants by running a spade through them once or twice. Another technique, if you want smaller, neater divisions, is to insert two spading forks back to back through a clump, gently pry divisions apart, and then redivide them into smaller units. You can make large divisions at virtually any time of year when the ground is not frozen, but small ones are best made in early spring or late summer. The same technique applies to Siberian and Japanese iris (*I. sibirica* and *I. kaempferi* of the trade). If plants are in full leaf at the time of division, it helps to cut them back halfway. Japanese iris are often slow to regenerate, so don't make tiny divisions unless you are the kind of person who enjoys watching paint dry.

It was once the custom to divide spring bloomers in late summer or autumn and autumn bloomers in spring. The second practice is still standard, because dividing a chrysanthemum or other shallow-rooted, late-flowering daisy in fall can lead to its early demise. I know a gardener who has even killed his precious cultivated goldenrods from England this way.

The problem with the first practice is that you lose the better part of the growing season if you wait until autumn to divide a spring bloomer. Except where summers are particularly warm and dry, it makes sense to divide doronicum, Jacob's-ladder (*Polemonium*), early phloxes, and pulmonaria right after bloom in April or May. That is, provided you have time and inclination to do these tasks then! Luckily, there are seasonal options for division, and most perennials are rather tolerant of our fits and starts if we just leave them alone during the hottest and coldest parts of the year.

A LITTLE CODDLING

What about winter protection? In the North, if you have set out potted perennials in the course of the year, a light winter cover of evergreen boughs or salt hay around Thanksgiving, mainly to keep an even soil temperature over winter, is a good idea, though it is superfluous for hostas, daylilies, sedums, and summer phlox. Many of these will even overwinter in containers above the ground, provided they have a little cover. In general, give the most cover to naturally shallow-rooted perennials — chrysanthemums, Shasta daisies, and leadwort in particular — and ones you know are of borderline hardiness. Newly divided plants should also receive a little protection the first winter, especially if planted in the fall. In all cases, remove the cover gradually, as the crocuses come into bloom in spring. Large-scale coddling is not in order for established perennials, though you can expect some losses in unusually cold, dry winters with no snow cover. Such is gardening.

· 22 ·

Plant Snobs

PLANT SNOBS come in all genetic combinations, and I have met more than my share. Recently at a party I encountered a most fair lass who, it turned out, gardened in the fashionable East Seventies of New York and in East Hampton, a summer resort for the young, rich, and beautiful. We didn't have much in common otherwise, so the conversation turned to plants. After discussing the French intensive method for growing shallots on a windowsill and the best organic ways to raise sorrel in chalky soils, we seemed to be getting along famously, and I even offered to refill her Perrier spritzer. We talked about perennials, because they are at the height of a resurgence of popularity in America.

Then, somehow, I made the mistake of mentioning my fondness for sweet-alyssum, an annual. A frown came to her face, as if she had seen someone walking barefoot in seaweed. Her head snapped back so quickly I feared a whiplash injury. Retracting her eyeballs, she peered thirty inches down her nose and declared, "But no *experienced* gardener plants annuals." I had blown my chance for a garden party weekend in East Hampton.

Landscape architects can rank with the best of snobs, too. Some don't even acknowledge that they are involved with plants; rather, they work with plant *materials*. A common conceit, undoubtedly promulgated by lazy design teachers, is to profess ignorance of plants by saying that it is the *form* that counts, not the plant. Therefore, one need not know many plants at all.

If one landscape architect meets another at a party, the conversation is apt to start with, "I'm using only fifty kinds of plants these days." The other will respond, "That many? I'm down to twenty-five. It contributes to a unified design, you know." If a third architect is present and is skilled in gamesmanship, he or she will interrupt and say, "I'm designing only Japanese stone gardens now — Ryoanji types." The other two will give this person an admiring glance and remember to add this information to their palettes.

My idea of purgatory is to sit next to a hemerocallis collector on a bus on the Long Island Expressway late on a Friday afternoon during a heat wave when the bus breaks down. I've got nothing against hemerocallis, or daylilies as we used to call them. In fact I am fond of them, but I don't want to hear about their infinite variety for three hours. After the first ten dozen kinds, what differences can there be?

THE COLLECTOR

A friend of mine collects hostas. (Note: our grandmothers used to know them as funkias or plantain lilies, but it is not possible to play one-upmanship using either name, especially funkia.) He knows two hundred cultivars by sight, but, incredibly, has twin sons he sometimes confuses at the dinner table. Being caught at a banquet with a gesneriad buff, especially a collector of dwarf sinningias, is bad for the digestion.

If you are bothered by the advanced myopia of the monogenus gardener, consider also the monogeneriphobes — people who can't stand particular kinds of plants. For years I have known the self-proclaimed president of the Anti-Salvia League of America, Inc. The wife of a well-known botanist, she is normally a very pleasant soul, but she sees red when she spots salvia. So scarlet with rage at the sage is she that when reminded of perennial blue salvias, she says, "Piffle! I would just as soon grow a canna."

There is the Catalpa Society too, founded several years ago during a meeting of the American Association of Botanical Gardens and Arboreta. Catalpas haven't had a bad press in seventy-five years; in fact, they have had no press at all. So to honor one of the real canines of the tree world, a small number of undedicated catalpologists banded together to form a group that is unique in America today. It has no dues, no meetings, not even an address. All that is necessary is to stick your tongue out at a catalpa from time to time.

The chief executive officer of the Catalpa Society is thought to be a respected plant breeder at a major eastern university, but he prefers to keep a low profile. A newsletter describing ways to pollard the dwarf umbrella catalpa is planned for 1995, and perhaps a checklist by the year 2000. Society members are searching for new catalpas, including cut-leaved forms.

Some plants are so esteemed by true horticultural snobs that they are unknown to most gardeners, and meant to be. In Switzerland a farmer's wealth used to be gauged by the size of his manure pile. In certain New York suburbs today a gardener's degree of sophistication is judged by the grandeur of his clump of *Kirengeshoma palmata*. This is an autumn-blooming perennial with nodding, rather inconspicuous yellow flowers. The foliage resembles a London plane leaf with fallen arches. *Kirengeshoma*, which of course has no common name, is almost a cult in Japan. It propagates very easily by pickax.

Strange things happen in the Japanese horticultural community, where there is even a group devoted to the culture of *Taraxacum* — the Dandelion Appreciation Society. Apart from the common sort on lawns, fifty or sixty species of dandelion exist in the world, some of them alpine and some that are hard to grow, which is a trait admired by good snobs everywhere. Also, to swell and confuse the ranks, a number of dandelions are apomictic (capable of producing viable seed without the pleasures of sex). Turf growers everywhere have long suspected this anyway. A friend of mine was hiking a trail in the Himalayas last year when his guide took him miles out of his way to see a rare plant: a dandelion.

There are regional plant conceits too. In the Deep South of the United States it is common to refer to "japonicas," in this case *Camellia japonica*, with the word *camellia* dropped. In New England, where camellias can't be grown out-of-doors except in a few coastal areas, "japonica" usually refers to the orange flowering quince (*Chaenomeles speciosa*). It helps to remember what part of the country you are in, but once in Delaware, a halfway point between North and South, a friend told me about her "japonicas"; confused, I looked around for an orange camellia.

The way to put a stop to such nonsense is to refer to one's "maximowiczianas." "Japonica" is a species name (the botanist would call it a specific epithet) for hundreds of plants. Fortunately, there are not nearly so many "maximowiczianas."

Rock gardeners are notorious. At a horticultural meeting you can usually spot them yards away. The men resemble the Duke of Windsor fifty years ago, even when they are short, fat, and bald. The women look like V. Sackville-West in riding pants. All speak in hushed, reverent tones of Sir Montague Scree, the latest visiting authority from Edinburgh or Kew, now on a speaking tour of the provinces. Typical openers: "I never used to grow a plant more than eight inches tall, but I found this a bit confining. Now my limit is twelve." "Would you believe that last week I met a gardener who had just seen a *Lewisia tweedyi* for the first time? Poor girl must have been brought up in a convent."

TREATMENT

How to cope with plant snobs? Be gentle but firm. Avoid social contact with them except in winter, unless they are indoor-plantaholics, in which case summer is a slightly safer time. Stronger methods are sometimes needed. If a landscape architect starts to talk about his palette, tell him you thought this phrase went out with Whistler's grandmother. If he persists, ask him why the average schoolchild knows more plants.

The *Kirengeshoma palmata* snob can be dispatched with ease. If he asks whether you grow it, yawn and tell him you had to eradicate the plant a few years ago because it became weedy. Or casually mention that these days you raise only *K. sachalinensis* (which he will never have heard of), because it is a much rarer plant and one that is a bit "iffy" in cultivation. Should he call your bluff, show him an undernourished London plane and diffidently say what good culture can do.

A satisfactory put-down for the hemerocallis snob when he asks how many cultivars you grow is to say you are interested only in the true species, the ones found in the wild, not the mongrels the plant hybridizers have created and given names like "Fluffy Ruffles." Since the average daylily snob has probably never seen more than one or two true hemerocallis species, you will be on safe ground. Should you be called, show him a narrow-leaved hosta, feign amazement, and tell him you can't understand why the daylily breeders have lost the grace of the wild species.

Occasionally you will have to resort to rougher techniques, but bear in mind that most plant snobs are benign sorts, no more, no less demented than the rest of us and in general worthy of society's sympathy. If in doubt, take one to lunch someday. But don't talk about plants.

· 23 ·

Deer, Deer,
Oh Dear

IT WAS a magic evening. We were seated at the table of our friends Jake and Sylvie. The silver shone in the candlelight, and there was a twinkle in the eye of our host, who had donned a tuxedo for the occasion. Sylvie was radiant in a blue satin dress, and her eyes went from husband to roast to wine as we quietly discussed which perennial came closest in flower color to the Châteauneuf-du-Pape 1980 we were sipping.

Pauses in the conversation, the sort that come from contentment rather than unease, were frequent. I chewed very slowly, moistened my lips with the good wine, and cut another savory morsel. The rare moment was occurring — all was right with the world, or at least the gardeners' world. This was the first time in my life I had ever really enjoyed eating venison, and I was pleasantly surprised, even delighted. There is nothing like retribution, which makes a better sauce than hunger does.

Two days before, in the fading light of a late autumn afternoon, Sylvie had entered the living room and from the corner of her eye had seen a deer chewing on an azalea by the terrace. This was hardly the first time. Deer had in fact made gardening a frustrating experience for our friends in recent years. She called to her husband, who was in the kitchen, and Jake ran upstairs for his rifle, which he quickly loaded. He threw open the terrace door, stared at the startled deer for a split second, and dropped it with one shot.

How seldom this occurs in the real world is known only by the beleaguered gardener; and most civilized souls who normally have qualms about destroying a beetle, even organically, can be goaded into the atavistic act if deer repeatedly maim the garden. We lifted our glasses in a final toast: "Veni, vidi, *boom*, venison!"

THE BAMBI BOOM

In the past fifteen years there has been a remarkable increase in the deer population in much of the East. The reasons for this are open to some conjecture. Gardeners in rural areas and even the suburbs of large cities can suggest a wealth of theories, which they are more than willing to discuss at every social gathering. Among the litany: shorter hunting seasons in some areas, a total ban in others; more housing construction, with fewer natural areas for deer to browse in; mild winters, which enable more deer to live over; natural cycles of species increase and decrease, with a current peak; more food available for deer. Take your pick, and add some theories, as you probably will.

It's always nice to have an outside devil on which to blame things, and a friend of mine who studies patterns in natural vegetation likes to fix the deer increase on the Arabs. His reasons are intriguing. For most of this century people have tended to abandon farms in the eastern United States, which has resulted in natural reversion to woodland. There is in fact more woodland in rural areas now than there was one hundred years ago. With the abandonment, trees have eventually grown to some size and density. Contrary to the popular impression, little thinning was done in most areas in the postwar period, though plenty of clearing for housing developments took place in the suburbs. Deer do not browse on mature trees, and mature woodland offers little food for them. This serves as a natural population check.

During the first Arab oil crisis, in the early 1970s, a great number of people bought chain saws to cut firewood to fuel their new wood stoves, which would save on the suddenly high price of heating oil. A lot of trees were felled in the eastern woodlands — the first real thinning many of these areas had received since their rebirth. More light could penetrate, and growth near the forest floor was stimulated; more seedling trees, lusher saplings, plenty of nonwoody plant growth appeared. Briefly, there was a sudden abundance of deer browse, and the population increased.

But nothing in nature is static, and nature is always in some state of imbalance. These days the trees are growing larger, and shade again falls on the forest floor, so there is less browse for the deer, who will decrease in number in the long run. Meanwhile, the impatient gardener, shaking his head over the soup kitchen he is forced to maintain for Bambi, mutters in the fashion of John Maynard Keynes, "But in the long run we will all be dead."

The nature of gardening is not to have it all one's own way. Even in periods of greatest success there are failures, and this is probably one reason that gardening has enduring attraction. If the gardener were to win them all, the subject would become boring, and he or she might be tempted to go on to basket weaving, golf, or some other foolish endeavor. Twenty-five years ago the principal problem in our garden was woodchucks. We curbed them by more frequent mowing and mowing larger areas. Twenty years ago rabbits were the spoiler, until we were adopted by cats. Ten years ago the garden was laid siege by Japanese beetles, who probably ran their own course, though I like to think that applications of dolomitic limestone to the lawn and garden befuddled their reproductive systems.

DETERRENTS

Now we have deer, and I am not so sure of the solution. As with the common cold, where there are many remedies, there is none. One year the garden writers herald ground-up hot peppers, or bars of soap strung around the garden. Another year they give miracle status to human hair, put in old stockings and hung from trees. Still another, they exhort us to spray plants with egg whites, preferably rotten ones. They also tell us of the benefits of radios blaring at night, preferably with hard rock, not Stravinsky. By now, too, most everyone has heard about the properties of lion dung. Perhaps each of these miracle cures has worked from time to time, for a time. However, deer are very adaptable animals and quickly become used to most of our quirky deterrents.

One type of deterrent seems fairly constant in its effect, and it is based on the observation that deer shun human scent. I can think of three ways to put this to work, none of which is entirely desirable. When I can get away with it, I stockpile my dirty T-shirts for a few days and put them out toward dusk, draping them on hostas, summer phlox, daylilies, and other plants that deer esteem. This is like a tear gas bomb but more local in effect. The shortcoming of this system is that a great variety of plants appeal to deer, especially when the herd is large. Even if I were to change shirts five times daily for a week and throw in undershorts too, the garden would still have unguarded flanks.

There are also limits to what my wife will tolerate. More than once Mary Ann has confiscated a mellowing hidden stockpile of mine for the laundry. I am one of the few people in our county who looks forward to a malfunction of the washing machine, but I have also learned not to mention this in front of her. Mary Ann is still a bit touchy about the morning she was giving a tour of our borders to an exceedingly proper garden club and belatedly noticed that I had forgotten to remove the evidence. One ripe T-shirt is worth a thousand words. And each one was directed at me.

Calls of nature, human nature, are also an effective deer deterrent for a few yards around, but they do not always come at convenient times. Large gardens pose particular problems, requiring the combined capacity of experienced Bavarian beer drinkers from several tables of the Hofbrauhaus in Munich. One August evening when the hosta-munching season was in full progress I mildly suggested that we hold an Oktoberfest, but Mary Ann let it be known, in another thousand words, that she preferred the deer.

Another, neater method of employing human scent has worked reasonably well in the two years we have tried it. This involves a very light broadcasting of Milorganite fertilizer (6-2-0) twice a season on groups of plants that are especially susceptible to deer browse. Milorganite is processed sewage sludge from the County of Milwaukee in Wisconsin. Although people detect no odor from it, deer, with their much keener noses, apparently pick up a human scent. I wear gloves when applying Milorganite and use the lowest possible effective dose, because prolonged use can lead to cadmium build-up in the soil. This can pose a problem, particularly in vegetable gardens, over the longer term, because the plants take up the cadmium and eventually pass it into the human body, where it accumulates in the kidneys. In addition, Milorganite is being investigated for a possible relationship with Lou Gehrig's disease. It is unlikely that our borders will ever be used for growing vegetables, but that is an option we would like to leave for future generations.

Commercial animal repellents are a possibility too, with one or more advantages but disadvantages as well. Most are based on Thiram. Some must be applied frequently, are costly, or easily clog a sprayer. One repellent, called Hinder, is effective in the earlier part of the growing season, but later, when growth slows, Ro-Pel seems to work better. Ro-Pel's active ingredients are benzyldiethyl ammonium saccharide and thymol. It tastes vile for hours when you inadvertently spill a little on the fingers, if you should be forgetful enough to move fingers to mouth. A quart, already diluted and ready for use in a sprayer bottle, runs about fourteen dollars and is guaranteed to make a Scot with a large garden blanch. Obviously, you cannot treat the whole garden.

Ro-Pel, which can last in effect for up to a year, strikes me as most practical to use on woody plants that are highly prone to deer browse. These include yew (*Taxus*), the evergreen *Euonymus fortunei*, rhododendron, azalea, arborvitae (*Thuja*), hemlock, pine, and other needle evergreens. It also seems to work well on the bark of sapling trees, which are especially subject to damage in rutting season, when the Don Juans of deerdom test their antlers on imaginary foes.

A singularly dark moment in the garden for me occurred one October morning in pre–Ro-Pel days, when I found an eight-foot specimen paperbark maple (*Acer griseum*) thoroughly maimed. The paperbark is a slow-growing tree in this climate, and I had nurtured it for years from a one-foot graft. This came to mind one recent evening as I threw a slipper at the television set. During the newscast a representative of the Bambi lobby in a suburban town suggested that the obvious solution to the excess in deer herds was to relocate them to state parks in less populated areas. Since we live in a less populated area next to a state park, I took this very personally; for a few days Mary Ann considered changing the name of our garden from Hillside to Apoplexy Acres.

In our experience Ro-Pel has not been as effective a deterrent with herbaceous perennials as with woody plants. Many perennials put on flushes of growth over a longer preiod, especially with the rejuvenation pruning and routine deadheading that gardeners give their borders. Still, there is a noticeable decrease in browsing in areas where this repellent has been applied. I can recall one notable lapse, when we applied Ro-Pel to about fifty lilies (*Lilium*) as they were in flower bud stage. The opening flowers expand very quickly, and the deer ate nearly all of them one night. The petals in tight bud had not been exposed to Ro-Pel.

OTHER WAYS OF COPING

Deer are real flower lovers. Frequently they will devour the flowers and buds of true lilies and daylilies and leave the remaining parts untouched. Vexar or another inconspicuous dark bird netting of the sort used to protect blueberry bushes works fairly well as a cover on lilies and daylilies when their buds form, but you must adjust the netting daily to keep expanding buds from being caught in it. Deer have no more desire to eat a lily bud through such a cover than we would want to eat a steak through a hairnet. Netting spread on the ground around borders has some deterrent effect too, for deer are timid around anything that hinders quick escape. Keep good mental notes, though — if you spread netting over lawn areas adjacent to borders, it can play havoc with the lawn mower.

Careful siting of favored deer-browse plants also helps. Deer tend to be shy of areas that are partially blocked by some barrier. For example, if an area between house and garage or house and fence is not very wide, it is apt to offer more protection from marauders than outreaches of the garden. If steep steps lead up to a garden location near a building, they also offer a measure of safety.

Open areas adjacent to houses may or may not be relatively safe, depending on the size of the herd, the time of year, and the habits of the human dwellers. Deer are likely to feed more on such sites in winter, especially if yews or euonymus are there, because browse is in short supply in the woods and fields. Weekend places are especially prone to damage, because there is no human scent for days.

Properties surrounded by woods are prime feeding spots, but ones with lots of fields around, which give deer other opportunities for browsing, frequently have a lower incidence. Also, other grazing animals in the vicinity, as on a farm, appear to have a deterrent effect. However, it is a game of odds, not guarantees.

Dogs have always struck me as being incompatible with gardens. The ones I like best are old, lame, laryngitic, and on other people's property, preferably at least a mile away. However, the gravity of the Bambi boom obliges even the most rabid Fidophobes among us to reassess the situation. Gardening, like politics, often requires the choice of lesser evils for the greater good. *L'odeur du chien* is an effective deterrent, though it is not to be taken for granted. I know a Labrador retriever who slept beside a vegetable garden one night while it was being raided. But assuming your dog is neither lazy nor klutzy, you still have the problem of how to keep it out of the borders, especially when it sights a rabbit. Some dogs are trainable, but you must spend a great deal of time with one if it is to become an aid in the garden. Even then, would you entrust the lilies to it? The answer may have to be an agonizing yes. At least today you can buy a special wire that you can sink along the perimeter of your property, with a remote control device that gives dogs a sonar message to stay back. No doubt this can be adapted to borders for those dogs who have flunked out of obedience school.

Apart from a rifle, the last resort for many gardeners is an electrified fence, which can be an expensive proposition on a large property, particularly a partly wooded one. You constantly have to keep vegetation away from the fence, for brush can short-circuit the system. We know of one long-established garden where the electricity failed for only six hours and the deer jumped the fence, which is to suggest that deer are always testing.

Vertical fences of a height to keep deer out are not only very pricey but often unsightly as well. The most cost-effective fence that works is not vertical but angled away at forty-five degrees from the area to be protected, with a height of five or six feet and wires strung horizontally about one foot apart. It is not entirely deerproof, but it cuts the incidence greatly. In one garden near us where the owners installed such a fence five years ago, the deer jump or crawl under it once or twice a season, usually when the owners are out of town. This type is called the Cary Arboretum deer fence. The arboretum, a station of the New York Botanical Garden in Millbrook, New York, developed the simple but novel idea some years ago, when deer were ravaging the plant collection and the cost of traditional fencing for a large area was considered prohibitive.

HOSTAS AND OTHER BONBONS

Deer have browsed on about 80 percent of the kinds of perennials grown here at Hillside over the years, though not in any given year. Much of the eating has been at random, taste sessions occurring, albeit infrequently, even with foxglove (*Digitalis*), which is toxic. I recall once seeing in a group of foxgloves a single plant with browse damage, with mangled foliage lying beside it on the ground. Gustav Mehlquist, professor emeritus of horticulture at the University of Connecticut, did some informal testing I would not have the courage to undertake, tasting (and expectorating) virtually all of the state's toxic plants. He told me that most taste perfectly horrible, which may be one reason that there are so few accidental fatal poisonings from the ingestion of parts from higher (flowering) plants. Regardless, I would have appreciated a chance to photograph the deer's face as the foxglove foliage departed from its mouth.

Hosta is the most consistently eaten perennial here, the only unmolested one of seventy or so kinds being the smallest grower, *H. venusta*, which a deer probably figures is not worth its time if a good *H. sieboldiana* is around. A few years ago one fawn regularly bedded down in a large grouping of *H.* 'Frances Williams' and had to be shooed away periodically like a neighbor's dog. She stopped every twenty feet, looking over her shoulder with a doleful expression to see whether I really meant it. I did — 'Frances Williams' is a ten-dollar hosta, and she could at least have had the consideration to sleep in the lancifolias, at four dollars a plant.

Hosta lancifolia is usually the first of the hostas to be browsed. It is our first hosta to send up its leaves in spring, almost a month before *H. sieboldiana* awakens; and since very few native plants are yet in growth at that time, the deer will seek out virtually every grouping we have. The plants recover in due course but have been ruined as ornamentals for weeks. Later the deer go on systematically to other hostas, and are able to detect a single specimen hosta from borders composed of many different perennials, which for the moment they ignore, at least until the summer phlox comes into bloom in July. Perhaps an enterprising breeder will splice the appropriate foxglove gene into hosta and phlox someday.

← 50' →

Polygonatum odoratum 'Variegatum' VARIEGATED SOLOMON'S-SEAL (3', white, May) interplanted with *Ajuga pyramidalis* (8", blue, May)	*Aconitum napellus* COMMON MONKSHOOD (4', blue, July-August)	*Actaea rubra* BANEBERRY (3', white, May; red fruits in June-August)	*Rodgersia pinnata* 'Superba' (3½', pink, June, foliage)	*Osmunda claytoniana* INTERRUPTED FERN (5') interplanted with Narcissus of choice

Astilbe 'Deutschland' (2', white, June-July)

Scilla siberica (6", blue, April)

Adiantum pedatum MAIDENHAIR FERN (2', ethereal foliage)	*Dicentra* 'Luxuriant' (15", deep pink, April-June; repeats later)	*Polystichum acrostichoides* CHRISTMAS FERN (2', evergreen)	*Alchemilla mollis* LADY'S-MANTLE (18", chartreuse, May-June)	*Astrantia major* MASTERWORT (2', white or pinkish, June-August)
Lamium maculatum 'WHITE NANCY' (8", white, May-June, silver foliage)	*Geranium macrorrhizum* 'Ingwersen's Variety' (12", pale pink, June)	*Astilbe* 'Sprite' (12", pink, August)	*Carex conica* 'Variegata' of gardens (9", for variegated foliage)	*Ajuga reptans* 'Silver Carpet' (8", blue, April-May)

7'

DEER-RESISTANT SHADE BORDER
(High Shade from Deciduous Trees)

It should be noted that browsing patterns vary from garden to garden and from one part of the country to another. Many factors can influence them, including the nature of the surrounding terrain, what desirable browse it holds, what food deer become accustomed to eating, memory imprints from year to year, herd size, and chance. I recall reading a report in a California journal about deer-resistant plants there and being fascinated that hostas were on the list. Of course a different species of deer was involved, with perhaps different tastes, but hostas do not play the same role in California landscaping they do in other parts of the United States. In mild climates gardeners have a far greater number of foliage plants to choose from, and hostas are but one of many choices. It is just conceivable that California deer will have a taste treat in store when one of them stumbles onto a hosta and bays to its confrères, "Hey, guys, try a bite of this stuff!"

Despite the variability in browsing, certain broad categories of perennials stand out here at Hillside and in my clients' gardens as being generally less attractive to deer. One of course includes plants with a toxic substance. Besides foxglove, there are monkshood (*Aconitum*), baneberry (*Actaea*), narcissus, colchicum, and rhubarb (*Rheum*).

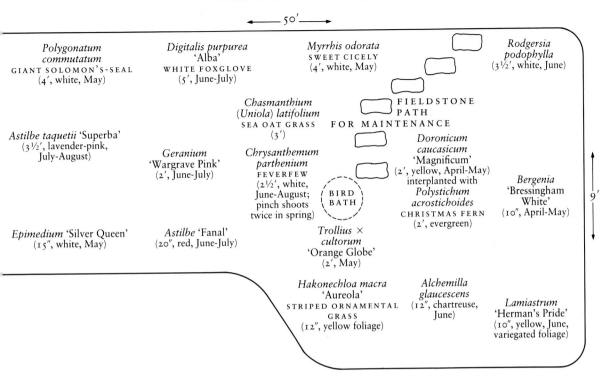

Boxwood appears resistant. However, deer often browse shrubs such as yews, rhododendrons, azaleas, and mountain-laurel (*Kalmia latifolia*), although these plants have varying degrees of toxicity. In the woods around here it is common now to encounter tall mountain-laurels with hourglass shapes, as my friend the student of vegetation has pointed out. In winter, the principal season in which these shrubs are browsed, the deer cannot reach the tops because of the plants' height nor the bottoms because they are usually under snow, so they concentrate their feeding in the midsection. Apparently no one has told them that mountain-laurel is toxic.

The thoughtful gardener must also feel uneasy about the longer-range effect of large deer herds on the native flora, especially since little concern about it has come from the conservation sources one might expect to be interested. I learned long ago that animals have a greater constituency than plants do, but it is still sad for me to walk in the woods and rarely see the native yew, *Taxus canadensis*, in haunts where it was once common in my lifetime.

PIECES OF RESISTANCE

Plants with dense woolly foliage or that are prickly often have a good degree of deer resistance. Among them are lamb's-ears (*Stachys byzantina*), silver sage (*Salvia argentea*), and many of the artemisias, as well as Scotch thistle (*Onopordum acanthium*) and globe thistle (*Echinops*). True, when herd build-up is substantial, we have noticed damage on each of these plants (and we have even heard of a yucca being browsed), but it is much less common than on hostas and summer phlox. Curiously, roses are often subject to browse, but much of the damage is restricted to loss of flowers and buds. That does not leave much, for a rosebush without flowers is like an ice cream cone without ice cream.

Deer frequently avoid plants with strongly aromatic foliage. Among plants on which we have noticed little or no damage are allium, yarrow (*Achillea*), catmint (*Nepeta mussinii*, N. × *faassenii*), thyme (*Thymus*), culinary sage (*Salvia officin-*

White epimedium (*Epimedium* × *youngianum* 'Niveum'), a dependable low-growing cultivar, is equally at home in a lightly shaded rock garden, in a woodland border, or as a ground cover. A deer resister, it blooms in spring.

alis), and many but not all kitchen herbs; *Geranium macrorrhizum* and certain other cranesbills; also sweet cicely (*Myrrhis odorata*), lamium, and feverfew (*Chrysanthemum parthenium*). However, we occasionally see the effects of browsing on autumn-flowering chrysanthemums and even wild-ginger (*Asarum*).

Ornamental grasses and ferns are usually spared, and when damage does occur it is less conspicuous than on other perennials, perhaps because of the plants' basic leafiness. We do not recall having the effect of any of our ornamental grasses spoiled by deer. When they have marred ferns, it is mostly because they have passed through good-sized stands or used them as mattresses. Actually, if numbers of deer are in the garden, damage to the crowns of plants from their hoofs may be worse than that from the nibbling.

Every general system, including this one, has a miscellaneous section. Some important browse-resistant perennials in it are epimedium, astilbe, lady's-mantle (*Alchemilla*), peony, waldsteinia, bergenia, *Campanula lactiflora,* doronicum, Siberian iris, and bearded iris. We have noticed browsing on astrantia, amsonia, trollius, and *Coreopsis* 'Moonbeam', but not very often.

Finally, in some genera the taller members are subject to browse but the smaller ones are usually overlooked. I have already given an example among hostas, but a better one is with sedums. Deer sometimes browse the tall border sedums, including *S. spectabile* and its cultivars, *S. telephium, S. aizoon, S. alboroseum,* and 'Autumn Joy', but they are less apt to damage the lower-growing sorts, such as *Sedum spurium, S. kamtschaticum, S. ellacombianum, S. ternatum, S. populifolium,* and *S.* 'Weihenstephaner Gold', as well as the common rock garden types. 'Ruby Glow' and 'Vera Jameson', sedums of intermediate size, are browsed here less often than the tall kinds but more than the low growers.

By the same token, low-growing phloxes, such as *P. subulata* and *P. stolonifera,* are not likely to be damaged as severely as *P. paniculata* and *P. maculata.* Deer here sometimes browse *Phlox divaricata* after its lavender flowers fade in late spring, but I consider this a benefit, because the plant's habit becomes more attractive when it is sheared then. Now, if we could only harness deer power. . . . This might not rival horse power, but it would be comforting if we could find some redeeming social utility in Bambi. Meanwhile, the advice given on a bumper sticker I saw the other day makes good sense: "Eat more venison!"

· 24 ·

Down with Leaves

THE LEAVES come tumbling down — red, brown, deep maroon, beige, yellow. . . . What to do with them all? A nongardening friend of ours who lives on a windy site has a simple solution: he cuts the lawn quite short in mid-October, and the leaves scuttle over it in the autumnal winds, settling around shrubs and stone walls at the edge. On Saturdays our friend can go for long walks in the woods. He is even able to read the Sunday *New York Times* on Sunday. Such are the perks of the nongardener.

Gardeners are different. For one thing, they are usually masochistic. Who else would turn over soil to plant peas on a soupy late March day when frost is still oozing out of the ground? Or wear nets on their heads in May as a black-fly deterrent, and hunch over delphinium seedings that will in any case rot before summer comes? Or, with ice clinging to shovel or pick, excavate holes in early December for the Asiatic lilies that just arrived from a mail-order nursery in a balmier land? True gardeners really need to have their heads examined.

Forget all you have read about gardening being a gentle art; it most decidedly is not, at least not at the time of year when trees start to undress and the gardener's sense of tidiness compels him or her to clean up. We live in New England, and our forerunners here were Puritans. Northern autumns, except for their Kodachrome beauty, were made for such hard-working people. We convince ourselves that the fallen leaves are nature's bounty for the garden of a future year. If spirits flag during cleanup, buzz words of the times, such as "recycle," "green manure," and "organic gold," can bolster them. Although there is some truth to the notion that fallen leaves are valuable, the fervor of the gardener's belief increases in relation to the soreness of his or her back.

Tools and machines decrease or increase — mostly increase — the gardener's sense of masochism. Masochism is of course related to sadism, which is a characteristic of many garden implement manufacturers. One of the most sadistic implements I can think of is a cheap rake. If you are a gardener, you know the sort very well, and your garage or barn may be half full of them from years past, as is ours. Usually one of the bamboo tines breaks during the first leaf-raking bout, and by the second round the flimsy wire coils start to uncoil. Round three brings a declaration of "no contest."

There may be a rationale to cheap rakes, though, because they enable the gardener to pause periodically and reflect on the benefits of leaf gathering. If a sense of comfort begins to settle in, the true gardener will postpone leaf raking for a windy day. A soggy day is also perfect for the died-in-the-wool gardener/masochist, for leaves should not be treated lightly. Fortunately for the gardener, autumn days are frequently both windy and soggy.

BLOWERS, SHREDDERS, AND SNARFERS

The true gardener loves to dabble with machines, all of which are intended to reduce labor. Goodness knows how many leaf blowers and shredders grace the garages of the North, rightfully gathering dust for forty-nine of the fifty-two weeks of the year. These machines inevitably fail to start when suddenly called upon one frigid autumn morn when you can no longer postpone the dirty deed. You belatedly learn that the worn-out blades come from a firm in Kansas that went out of business two years ago.

Leaf shredders merit a special word of praise; Lucifer must have had something to do with their creation. The gardener has a tacit understanding with these machines. The shredders agree to provide beautiful fluffy little bits of foliage that make low-cost mulch for next spring's flower borders, or magnificent weed-free compost by late summer; in return, the gardener agrees to a certain amount of labor. Fair enough? Shredders are in fact easy to operate if you have played fullback for the Los Angeles Rams. If you are in shape, shredder starting is a great sport. Then you get to do a lot of stooping to the ground, so the shredder's cute little hoppers, three feet or so high, can gobble up the leaves you feed them between stoops. It sure beats pushups! A few sticks and stones do wonders for discombobulating a shredder, and the noise can be heard in the next county.

Leaf blowers are special machines too. The masochist/gardener rates their effectiveness by their decibel level, not by their ability to move leaves. Ear plugs are frowned upon, of course. In some neighborhoods people hold a regular competition each Saturday during autumn to determine which brand of blower is the noisiest. The most admired model can outperform an old Harley-Davidson with muffler problems.

If a gardener owns a low-volume blower, he or she can compensate by operating it early in the day. A neighbor of ours has perfected the technique by commencing his activities occasionally at six o'clock on a Sunday morning. It is invariably after we have had a late night. He is the envy of early birds, namely blue jays.

Let us not forget the snarfer. This looks like a giant vacuum cleaner emerging from a big rectangular box mounted on wheels. It is hitched to the back of a sit-down rotary lawn mower. As you drive along, the mower roughly shreds the leaves and the snarfer sucks them into the box, which you then maneuver to a central depository. Before long you have humongous piles, either for eventual compost or for spreading as mulch in the borders the following spring. Some diehards even solicit their neighbor's cache of leaves.

Operating the snarfer is a bit like towing a whale that has a mind of its own, but on large properties it is easier on body and soul than blowing and shredding. You still need a blower for corners and cul-de-sacs. The noise of the snarfer pleases the Harley crowd too, and you always have the joy of finding storage space for the machine in an overstuffed barn.

THE END RESULT

In the end there is the compost heap. Whether you blow, shred, or snarf leaves, or just lug them all by burlap carrier, the compost heap is always on the most inconspicuous and inconvenient spot on your land — usually on the other side of a stone wall. Leaves have a distressing way of compacting over winter, much like boiled beef that shrinks in the cooking pot, and you must make a formidable pile if you want a solid return. To fulfill the masochistic urge, you can try to use the method described in gardening books — the compost sandwich. For every fifteen inches of leaves, add several inches of soil and a light scattering of dolomitic limestone; every couple of layers, add two or three handfuls of lawn fertilizer, whose high nitrogen content will hasten decomposition. The following summer you will spend one or two weekends (normally the hottest of the year) turning the heap.

Thank goodness Mary Ann and I do not live in California, where we would feel obliged to garden year-round. On to the Sunday *Times*!

Index

245